Social and Emotional Adjustment
and Family Relations
in Ethnic Minority Families

Social and Emotional Adjustment and Family Relations in Ethnic Minority Families

Edited by
Ronald D. Taylor
Margaret C. Wang
Temple University

LAWRENCE ERLBAUM ASSOCIATES, PUBLISHERS
1997   Mahwah, New Jersey

Lawrence Erlbaum Associates, Inc., Publishers
10 Industrial Avenue
Mahwah, New Jersey 07430

Cover design by Kathryn Houghtaling

Library of Congress Cataloging-in-Publication-Data

Social and emotional adjustment and family relations in
ethnic minority families / edited by Ronald D. Taylor,
Margaret C. Wang.
    p. cm.
    Includes bibliographic references and index.
    ISBN 0-8058-2155-4 (cloth : alk. paper). —ISBN
0-8058-2156-2 (pbk. : alk. paper)
    1. Minority youth—United States—Social condi-
tions. 2. Minority youth—United States—Family
relationships. 3. Minority youth—Education—United States. 4. Adolescent psychology—United States.
    I. Taylor, Ronald D., 1958– . II. Wang, Margaret
C.
    HQ796.S5627 1996
    305.23'5—dc20   96-22744
                                     CIP

Printed in the United States of America
10 9 8 7 6 5 4 3 2 1

Contents

Preface

Ethnic minority adolescents will make up more than 30% of the adolescent population in the United States by the end of this century. This pattern of growth is particularly prevalent in urban communities with high concentrations of families in economically disadvantaged circumstances, and where children and youth are faced with some of the most challenging social problems associated with the modern morbidities of our time. Nevertheless, there has been a pervasive lack of research on the development and learning of children and families from ethnic minority backgrounds. Furthermore, studies of minority children and families have largely focused on deficiencies and causes of maladjustment. Research on normative development of minority children is glaringly lacking, especially with regard to adolescent development.

There is a pressing need to develop a research base for preventive and intervention-oriented efforts that foster the resilience and educational success of adolescents from minority backgrounds who, for a variety of reasons, live in circumstances that place them at risk developmentally and educationally. It was within the context of attempting to take stock of what is known from research on development and adjustment of ethnic minority adolescents in communities with high concentrations of economically disadvantaged families that the National Center on Education in the Inner Cities hosted an invitational conference at the Temple University Center for Research in Human Development and Education.

The overall goal of the conference was to chart research and theoretical advances and to identify research priorities to further our understanding of the normative functioning of adolescents from varied ethnic minority backgrounds in multiple contexts and from multidisciplinary perspectives. The invited participants represented a broad range of disciplines and professional fields including developmental psychologists, economists, ment and education among adolescents from ethnic minority backgrounds, particularly those in circumstances that place them at risk.

The contributors to this volume were asked to draw from their research and respective disciplinary perspectives to specifically address the following questions: What are the mechanisms through which the economic prospects of families influence adolescents' psychosocial well-being? What impact do parent participation and experience in the labor market have on family functioning and adolescent adjustment? What is the impact of neighborhood/community on family functioning (including child-rearing practices) and adolescents' well-being? Are there parenting styles and practices that are unique to particular ethnic groups? Do differences in parenting styles among minority parents impact on competence development and school achievement of adolescents? With regard to reducing adolescents' risk of serious learning and social adjustment problems, what features of the contexts in which ethnic minority families function are amenable to intervention?

Social and Emotional Adjustment and Family Relations in Ethnic Minority Families, then, is the product of a multidisciplinary approach to analyzing both the state of the art and the state of practice of research on ethnic minority adolescents and their families. The book reflects the eclectic sources from which it was spawned, and is somewhat of a departure from much of the literature on ethnic minority children and families to date. In addition to emphasizing those factors associated with the negative social and academic functioning of children, (such as residence in areas with high rates of poverty and crime, single-parent households, perceptions of discrimination), the chapters included in this volume also address the mediating influences (authoritative parenting, strong kinship networks, positive peer groups) that impact on the development and school achievement of adolescents from a range of ethnic minority backgrounds. With chapters focusing on African-American, Latino, Asian-American, and Native-American students and their families, this volume is an attempt to summarize what we currently know about the complex social development experience of ethnic minority adolescents, and how this experience is shaped by the families with whom they live.

This book includes twelve chapters, organized under three sections: Part I, Economic Resources, Family Environment, and Adolescent Adjustment; Part II, Family and Peer Contexts and Adolescent Adjustment; and Part III, Neighborhood and Schooling Contexts and Adolescent Adjustment.

PART I: ECONOMIC RESOURCES, FAMILY ENVIRONMENT, AND ADOLESCENT ADJUSTMENT

This first section seeks to address linkages between families' economic resources and the nature of family functioning and adolescent adjustment.

It consists of four chapters, the first two of which deal exclusively with African-American children and families. In Chapter 2, Vonnie McLoyd examines processes linking African-American families' economic well-being to the social and emotional adjustment of their children. She presents direct and indirect evidence concerning the effects of poverty and low socioeconomic status on the socioemotional functioning of African-American children and adolescents, reviews processes that may mediate these effects, and identifies important gaps in current research. After describing the unique economic and social stressors facing poor African-American children and families, Ronald D. Taylor, in Chapter 3, calls attention to the manner in which these stressors affect parenting practices and adolescent functioning.

In Chapter 4, Constance A. Flanagan, Patreese Ingram, Erika M. Gallay, and Erin E. Gallay discuss adolescents' differing perceptions and rationalizations regarding the causes of poverty. These authors approach their topic within the framework of assessing adolescents' views of the "social contract" they hold with American society.

In the section's final chapter, Ardy Sixkiller Clarke argues that it is vital that educators disentangle behaviors of children linked to poverty and those linked to culture to accurately explain the impact of poverty and culture on the educational achievement of American Indian children.

PART II: FAMILY AND PEER CONTEXTS
AND ADOLESCENT ADJUSTMENT

Part II consists of four chapters, each addressing various aspects of family relations and parenting practices, as well as how the nature of the peer relations of ethnic minority children affects key areas of adjustment. In Chapter 6, Craig A. Mason, Ana Marie Cauce, and Nancy Gonzales present a study examining links between African-American parents' child-rearing practices and adolescents' peer relations to problem behaviors. The authors illustrate how the already difficult task of parenting adolescents is even more challenging in African-American families, and argue that researchers and policymakers have been overly critical when characterizing the so-called failures of African-American parents.

Ronald W. Henderson, in Chapter 7, surveys the role of parents' beliefs, values, and resources in the academic achievement of children of Mexican descent. He provides insight into a better understanding of the sociocultural, instructional, and motivational dynamics that influence learning outcomes in mathematics among students of Mexican descent, and discusses the need to develop instructional practices that are responsive to cultural, linguistic, and individual variations among this population of students.

In Chapter 8, Connie Chan explores the links between AIDS awareness of Asian-American adolescents—a group once considered to be at lower risk for HIV infection—and their level and type of sexual activity. In an interesting substudy, the attitudes and behaviors of youth of Cambodian descent are compared with those of youth from Chinese, Vietnamese, and South Asian backgrounds.

Melvin Wilson, Deanna Y. Cooke, and Edith G. Arrington, in Chapter 9, assert that the ecological reality for many African-American families is that they are both a part of and apart from the dominant American culture. Subsequently, attempting to strike a balance between their own backgrounds and the culture of the dominant society makes for a unique socialization experience. With this perspective in mind, the authors assess the nature of family and peer relations among African-American adolescents and its implications for school achievement.

PART III: NEIGHBORHOOD AND SCHOOLING CONTEXTS AND ADOLESCENT ADJUSTMENT

The three chapters that comprise the final section examine the manner in which contexts beyond the family environment impact adolescent adjustment. In Chapter 10, William L. Yancey and Salvatore J. Saporito explore the impact of racial and economic segregation on children's educational achievement in public schools in two large, urban areas. Their work makes a compelling argument that "freedom of choice" desegregation programs—an outgrowth of a 40-year-old mandate from the Brown decision—exacerbate the economic segregation of schools and have a deleterious effect on the academic achievement of ethnic minority and poor students.

Dena Phillips Swanson and Margaret Beale Spencer, in Chapter 11, investigate links between the African-American family environment, adolescents' perceptions of ecological contexts, and adolescents' school achievement and personality development. Much of the authors' discussion centers on processes by which African-American youth who perceive an inadequate fit between themselves and their ecological contexts sometimes exhibit negative coping responses.

In the book's final chapter, Leo C. Rigsby, Judith Stull, and Nancy Morse-Kelley discuss findings on the association of family, peer, and school factors with the school performance of European-American, African-American, Asian-American, and Latino adolescents. The authors first examine differences in the conceptual models explaining the school achievement of adolescents from different racial/ethnic and gender groups; they then address the question of whether the academic experiences of children in these groups differentially affect their schooling performances.

ACKNOWLEDGMENTS

We are grateful to many of our colleagues whose work in various capacities contributed to the development and timely production of this volume. We especially wish to express our deep appreciation to Jesse Shafer for his technical editing and organizational skills in making this publication a reality. Special thanks are also due to Don Gordon and Amanda Trayes for their invaluable editorial assistance. Finally, we would like to express our gratitude to Dr. Oliver Moles from the Office of Educational Research and Improvement (OERI) of the U.S. Department of Education for his continued support and guidance.

The publication of this volume was made possible by OERI through a grant to the National Center on Education in the Inner Cities at the Temple University Center for Research in Human Development and Education. It is important to note, however, that the opinions expressed herein do not necessarily reflect the positions of neither OERI nor Temple University, and no official endorsement should be inferred.

—Ronald D. Taylor
—Margaret C. Wang
Philadelphia, February 1996

List of Contributors

Edith G. Arrington University of Virginia, Charlottesville, VA

Ana Marie Cauce University of Washington, Seattle, WA

Connie Chan University of Massachusetts at Boston, Boston, MA

Ardy Sixkiller Clarke Montana State University, Bozeman, MT

Deanna Y. Cooke University of Virginia, Charlottesville, VA

Constance A. Flanagan Pennsylvania State University, University Park, PA

Erika M. Gallay University of Michigan, Ann Arbor, MI

Erin E. Gallay University of Michigan, Ann Arbor, MI

Nancy Gonzales Arizona State University, Tempe, AZ

Edmund Gordon 3 Cooper Morris Drive, Pomona, NY

Ronald W. Henderson University of California, Santa Cruz, CA

Patreese Ingram Pennsylvania State University, University Park, PA

Craig A. Mason University of Miami, Coral Gables, FL

Vonnie McLoyd University of Michigan, Ann Arbor, MI

Nancy Morse-Kelley 42-B Queen Catherine Court, Chester, MD

Leo C. Rigsby Temple University, Philadelphia, PA

Salvatore J. Saporito School District of Philadelphia, Philadelphia, PA

Margaret Beale Spencer University of Pennsylvania, Philadelphia, PA

Judith Stull Temple University, Philadelphia, PA

Dena Phillips Swanson University of Pennsylvania, Philadelphia, PA

Ronald D. Taylor Temple University, Philadelphia, PA

Margaret C. Wang Temple University, Philadelphia, PA

Melvin Wilson University of Virginia, Charlottesville, VA

William L. Yancey Temple University, Philadelphia, PA

1

Introduction:
The Resilience Phenomenon in Ethnic
Minority Adolescent Development

Edmund W. Gordon

In this very interesting collection of essays, the authors address issues related to the intersection between family relationships and several contexts for the social and emotional development of ethnic minority adolescents. These essays are organized in sections, under subtitles that reflect three contextual frames through which these issues may be examined. In Part I, the focus is on the relationship between economic factors and resources, on one hand, and family relations as environments for development, on the other. In Part II, the focus shifts to family and peer networks and relations as contexts for the emotional and social development of adolescents. The papers in Part III take neighborhood and school as contexts for, and determinants of, social and emotional adjustment in adolescence.

Like much of the extant work and current thought concerning development in ethnic minority children and adolescents, the authors of these papers have tended to highlight the more stressful and negative aspects of these several contexts. A few explicit and several implicit references are made to supportive and more positive contexts and manifestations of relationships that frame the developmental experiences of ethnic minority adolescents. These serve to remind us that many ethnic minority adolescents do overcome the odds against success and grow into healthy and wholesome adults. However, in large measure, *Social and Emotional Adjustment and Family Relations in Ethnic Minority Families* is a contribution to our understanding of the problematic circumstances under which a significant segment of the population exists. The essays serve to remind us that life for ethnic minority adolescents is difficult. The fact that some of these young people manage to overcome the negative and stressful aspects of their experiences and defy the implicit prediction of failure to thrive is truly remarkable.

Granted that development for many, but not all, ethnic minority adolescents is problematic, what is the character of the conditions that place them at risk of underdevelopment? In human social organization, when characteristics of some persons are at variance in significant ways from the modal characteristics of the social group that has achieved hegemony, we are likely to find little correspondence between the developmental supports provided by the social order and the developmental needs of the persons whose characteristics are different. This is a function of the operation of a principle of social economy whereby social orders design and allocate social resources in accord with the modal or otherwise valued characteristics of the hegemonic group. Thus, we have schools, public facilities, media, and so on that are designed and allocated to fit the needs of persons whose vision and hearing are intact rather than to serve the needs of persons with sensory impairments. Consequently, persons with impairments in these sensory modalities are at risk of developmental, educational, and social dysfunctionality, not necessarily because of the impairments, but because the society is not organized to adequately support the developmental needs of persons whose characteristics are at variance with those that are modal in the society. However, it is not only persons with mental, physical, or sensory disabilities who are placed at risk of educational, personal, and social underdevelopment. In our society, a wide variety of persons whose developmental or personal characteristics and conditions differ from those that are modal are placed at risk. Ethnic minority adolescents are a case in point.

Wholesome development and success in our society are highly correlated with access to several kinds of human resource capital. The distribution of human resource capital is extremely unequal in the United States and most of the world. Thus, an additional factor that places populations at risk of personal and social underdevelopment, even failure, is deprivation of essential complements of human resource capital. Miller (1994) and Gordon and Meroe (1991) have identified some of these categories of capital as follows:

- *Health capital.* Physical developmental integrity, health and nutritional condition, and so on.
- *Financial capital.* Income and wealth; family, community, and societal economic resources available for education.
- *Human capital.* Social competence, tacit knowledge, and other education-derived abilities as personal or family assets.
- *Social capital.* Social networks, relationships, social norms, cultural styles and values.
- *Polity capital.* Societal membership, social concern, public commitment, political and economic support.
- *Personal capital.* Disposition, attitudes, aspirations, efficacy, sense of power.
- *Institutional capital.* Quality of and access to educating and socializing institutions.
- *Pedagogical capital.* Supports for appropriate educational treatment in family, school, and community.

In the collection of essays that follows, the impact of some types of such capital deprivation is examined for its influence on patterns of family relations and, ultimately, on the social and emotional behavioral adaptations of ethnic minority adolescents.

A view of adaptation as an active exchange between the individual and his or her environment warrants a change in the terminology used to denote positive outcomes in the face of risk of failure. The term *resilience* refers to the ability to bounce back into shape—to recover strength or spirit. Although theoretical models of resilience have attempted to delineate some of the active manners in which individuals cope with experiential challenges, the term itself does not capture the relative amount of strength and determination that individuals must utilize in evaluating their circumstances and controlling their destinies. The term *defiance* captures better the process phenomena under study. In my work, *defiance of the prediction of failure* is used as a possibly more valid construct to refer to the resilience phenomenon sometimes noted in persons who overcome being placed at risk of failure by their conditions of life.

The perspective and resulting research that current definitions of resilience engender reflect the notion that events and experiences that are objectively assigned negative valence constitute experiential hazards, and that it is these hazards that place the developing person at risk of failure. But, the meaning of personal and ecological characteristics does not adhere simply to the characteristics themselves, but to the person's appraisal of the meaning and significance of those characteristics. Similarly, environmental factors are not intrinsically protective or stress-inducing but, rather, depend on the person's attributional representation of the environment and on his or her appraisal of personal abilities, dispositions, and resources to regulate and adapt to the environmental demands posed. Individuals actively construct personal realities or working models that serve as scripts for behavior.

Such positions as these are supported by data from prior studies by this writer, and indicate that the actions of resilient individuals are guided first by how they perceive and interpret their environments (Gordon & Braithwaite, 1985; Gordon & Song, 1994). These beliefs then form the basis for purposeful, planned actions undertaken to move away from or compensate for negative circumstances and move toward more adaptive end states. For example, poverty—a common risk factor noted in resilience research—was not perceived by many of the participants in our studies as an inevitable obstacle to success but, rather, as a challenge to be counteracted. In some instances, the condition was not perceived as such; for example, subjects reported that "we never thought of our family as poor." Additionally, it is not the case that social supports were immediately available to our subjects; instead, many actively searched out, established, and maintained favorable situations or good interpersonal relationships that helped them access other resources necessary for personal achievement. What seems to be missing from existing theoretical models of resilience is a concern with these existential processes that explain defiant behavior. Thus, it is that we seek to identify the "reality" and existential characteristics that are correlates of persons who defy the usual negative consequences of being placed at risk of developmental and educational failure—the resilient ones we call *defiers*.

We have then several perspectives with which to understand the social and emotional adaptive behaviors and the family relations which are a part of the context for ethnic minority adolescent development. There are the objective conditions posed by access to human capital resources. There are family, peer, and school relations that can complement, compensate for, support, or frustrate adaptation. Then there are attributional and existential expressions of both, which may account for the idiosyncratic and sometimes counterintuitive manifestations of adaptation in these adolescents. In the chapters that follow we find references to family, peers, and school as contexts that facilitate or preclude the development of such adaptations. This work reflects our considerable understanding of the influences of the objective conditions and relational contexts. They are the attributional and existential phenomena of which our knowledge remains limited, and that demand continuing research.

REFERENCES

Gordon, E. W., & Braithwaite, D. (1985). *Overcoming the odds*. Technical report submitted to the National Institute of Education, U.S. Dept. of Education. Washington, DC: U.S. Department of Education.

Gordon, E. W., & Meroe, A. S. (1991). Common destinies—continuing dilemmas. *Psychological Science*, 2(1), (23–30).

Gordon, E. W., & Song, L. D. (1994). Variations in the experience of resilience. In M. C. Wang & E. W. Gordon (Eds.), *Educational resilience in inner-city America: Challenges and prospects* (pp. 27–43). Hillsdale, NJ: Lawrence Erlbaum Associates.

Miller, L. S. (1994). *An American imperative*. New Haven, CT: Yale University Press.

I

Economic Resources, Family Environment, and Adolescent Adjustment

2

The Impact of Poverty and Low Socioeconomic Status on the Socioemotional Functioning of African-American Children and Adolescents: Mediating Effects

Vonnie C. McLoyd

Along with family income, the factors indicative of the economic well-being of children and families include poverty, parental employment, job (that is, promotion, demotion, stability), and socioeconomic status (SES). A bifurcation exists in the psychological and sociological literature that addresses these phenomena. One segment of the literature focuses on *economic decline* or *loss*, that is, unemployment, job loss, job demotion, and income loss as experienced by working- and middle-class individuals who characteristically are stably employed (e.g., Conger, Ge, Elder, Lorenz, & Simons, 1994; Flanagan & Eccles, 1993; McLoyd, 1989, 1990). The other segment focuses on *poverty* and *low SES* as ongoing, persistent conditions that are inextricably linked to employment-related factors such as unemployment, underemployment, low wages, and unstable work (e.g., Brody, Stoneman, Flor, McCrary, Hastings, & Congers, 1994). This chapter focuses on the latter segment of the literature. In particular, direct and indirect evidence concerning the effects of poverty and low SES on the socioemotional functioning of African-American children and adolescents is reviewed, processes that may mediate these effects are delineated, and important gaps in our knowledge that warrant redress are identified.

This chapter is divided into three major sections. Because it incorporates information about two related, but conceptually distinct indicators of economic disadvantage (i.e., poverty and low SES), it begins with a brief discussion of differences between these constructs. The second section summarizes existing research on the relation of poverty and low SES to children's socioemotional functioning, with special emphasis on African-American children. Also presented in this section is a discussion of proc-

esses through which poverty and low SES might influence children's socioemotional functioning. Three potential mediators are discussed: (a) discrete and chronic stressors, (b) experiences of inferiorization, and (c)
punitive, nonsupportive parenting. The discussion of mediational processes
is limited by its grouping of several diverse child outcomes under the general
rubric of "socioemotional functioning." Extant research is inadequate to
support extensive analyses of specific domains of socioemotional functioning. Mediating processes may be domain-specific; as such, documentation
of these processes can be pursued most productively in programs of research
focusing on specific categories of socioemotional functioning in children
(e.g., self-esteem, depressive symptomatology, self-efficacy, behavioral problems). The analysis of mediational processes also is limited by the fact that
it does not take account of individual child characteristics (e.g., age, gender,
temperament) that might influence mediational processes; again, this deficiency is due to the scarcity of relevant data. The final section of the chapter
summarizes major gaps in our knowledge about the impact of economic
disadvantage on African-American children's socioemotional functioning
and offers suggestions for future research.

It is critical to underscore that neither socioeconomic disadvantage nor
mediating variables can be seen as having inevitable, certain consequences
for child and adolescent functioning. Linkages exist among these variables
only in probabilistic terms determined by mutual influences operating
between children and their environments. As Baldwin, Baldwin, and Cole
(1990) pointed out, it is precisely this fact that makes it possible for economically disadvantaged children to have positive outcomes. Research on
resilience in children who experience economic hardship is in its infancy,
and very little of this work has focused specifically on African-American
children or other children of color (Clark, 1983). Nevertheless, research on
resilience is a critically important counterweight to inquiries into the adverse effects of economic disadvantage and the mechanisms responsible for
these effects.

DISTINGUISHING POVERTY AND
SOCIOECONOMIC STATUS

Poverty, in its official sense, refers to a condition in which the income of an
individual or family falls short of the amount needed for food, shelter, and
other necessities, as estimated by the U.S. government (Duncan, 1984). First
developed by the Social Security Administration in 1964 (then referred to
as the "Orshansky Index"), this standard has remained basically unchanged
for a generation. The U.S. government defines a person as living in poverty
if his or her cash income from all sources is less than three times the cost of
an adequate diet. Currently, there are well over 100 different "poverty
lines" reflecting a wide range of family types (as determined by family size,

sex and age of household head, number of children under 18, farm vs. nonfarm residence, and so forth). In the studies reviewed in this chapter, poverty is operationalized in various ways, including income-to-need ratios calculated on the basis of official poverty thresholds, family per capita income, eligibility for subsidies to the poor (e.g., free or reduced-cost lunch), or family income cutoffs corresponding to those used to determine eligibility for subsidies. Use of poverty thresholds, in general, is preferable to other operationalizations because it enhances comparability of findings, at least with respect to the influence of poverty on child outcomes.

The term *socioeconomic status* typically is used to signify individuals', families', or groups' rankings on a hierarchy according to their access to or control over some combination of valued commodities such as wealth, power, and social status (Mueller & Parcel, 1981). Although there is some dispute among social scientists about how SES should be defined or measured, there is considerable agreement that important components of SES include the occupation of the father, mother, or both, family income, education, prestige, power, and a certain style of life (House, 1981).

Poverty is not isomorphic with low SES. Unlike SES, poverty is based on an absolute standard or threshold and does not signify relative position. Its marker, cash income, is only one of several components or dimensions of SES and is clearly related to, but distinct from, occupational status, educational level, prestige, and power. In addition, poverty status is considerably more volatile than SES. During adulthood, income relative to need is more likely to shift markedly from one year to another than are SES indicators such as educational attainment and occupational status. For example, Duncan's (1984) examination of adjacent-year pairs of data from the national, longitudinal Panel Study of Income Dynamics for the period 1969–1978 indicated that one third to one half of those who were poor in one year were not poor the next. However, it should be noted that spells of poverty are far longer for African-American children and families than for their White counterparts (Duncan & Rodgers, 1988).

These distinctions between poverty and low SES are important because of their potential to affect children's socioemotional functioning differentially. Some evidence exists (e.g., Duncan, Brooks-Gunn, & Klebanov, 1994) that poverty and income status have effects on children's socioemotional functioning (i.e., externalizing symptoms) independent of SES indicators (e.g., parent education), although too few studies include both poverty status and SES indicators as predictors of children's socioemotional functioning to discern any pattern that might exist in the relative contributions of poverty versus various SES indicators. Notably more studies have assessed the effects of SES than poverty status on children's socioemotional functioning. We do not yet know how stability or instability in poverty and income status act synergistically with more stable indicators of SES to influence socioemotional functioning (Huston, McLoyd, & Garcia Coll, 1994).

It is also important to bear in mind that poverty and low SES rarely exist independently of one another. They often represent a conglomerate of conditions and events that amount to a pervasive rather than a bounded stressor. Belle (1984) and Pelton (1989) reported that a paucity of material resources and services is often conjoined to a plethora of undesirable events (e.g., eviction, physical illness, criminal assault) and ongoing conditions (e.g., inadequate housing, poor health care, dangerous neighborhoods, environmental toxins). Indeed, neither poverty as measured by official criteria nor low SES can be assumed to be identical to, or even particularly good proxies for, material hardship. Mayer and Jencks (1988) found, for example, that income-to-needs ratios explained less than a quarter of the variance in householders' reports of material hardship (e.g., spending less for food than the "thrifty" food budget published by the U.S. Department of Agriculture, unmet medical and dental needs, housing problems). Traditional measures of poverty and SES, then, may underestimate the direct and indirect effects of material hardship on children's socioemotional functioning.

The terms used in discussing the issues raised in this chapter vary as a function of whether the analyses cited center around constructs of poverty or of low SES. In the following discussion of specific findings from different areas of research, the terms used are those that most closely approximate the construct employed by given researchers. However, in the broader discussion of conceptual issues, poverty and low SES are used interchangeably, unless distinction between the two constructs seems critical.

POVERTY AND SOCIOECONOMIC STATUS AS PREDICTORS OF CHILD AND ADOLESCENT SOCIOEMOTIONAL FUNCTIONING

Main Effects of Socioeconomic Disadvantage

Current Poverty Status and Socioemotional Functioning

Most, though not all, of the studies reviewed in this section typify what Bronfenbrenner (1986) termed the *social address* model of analysis and rely on what Blumer (1956) designated *variable analyses*, that is, bivariate and multivariate analyses of the relation of sociodemographic variables, such as income and social class, to individual outcomes. Analyses of this kind are limited to comparison of outcomes for children living in contrasting environments as defined by socioeconomic background or physical characteristics, with no explicit consideration of intervening structures or processes through which these environments affect the course of development.

Numerous studies of children and adolescents in both health care and non–health care settings, the vast majority of which focus on SES status rather than poverty status, have reported an association between socioeconomic disadvantage and socioemotional problems. Most samples are White, although a substantial number of studies employ either solely African-American children and adolescents or ethnically diverse samples that include African-American children and adolescents. Prevalence estimates of mental health problems, although less precise than those for physical health problems (as a result of varying methods of assessment and thresholds used in making diagnoses), suggest that a significant proportion of children under 18 experience emotional and behavioral problems (Butler, Starfield, & Stenmark, 1984). Based on a review of diagnostic data from seven primary care facilities, Starfield et al. (1980) concluded that at least 5%, and as many as 15%, of children seen in 1 year had one or more socioemotional problems. In a similar study undertaken by Jacobson, Goldberg, Burns, Hoeper, Hanking, and Hewitt (1980), between 3% and 10% of children seen in four health care settings during a 1-year period were diagnosed as having mental health problems. Comparable prevalence estimates have been reported in other studies conducted in pediatric practice settings (Goldberg, Regier, McInerny, Pless, & Roghmann, 1979). In all of these studies, low SES was associated with a higher prevalence of emotional and behavioral problems.

Numerous investigations of nonreferred children in home and school settings have also reported a negative relation between SES and the presence of behavioral/emotional problems. Lower SES during early and middle childhood has been found to be associated with lower adaptive functioning; diminished self-confidence and self-esteem; strained peer relations; increased presence of severe temper tantrums; and higher levels of overall symptomatology, social maladaptation (e.g., shyness, aggressiveness, immaturity, learning problems), and psychological distress (e.g., feelings of sadness, tension, and nervousness; for a review of these studies, see McLoyd, Ceballo, & Mangelsdorf, in press).

Low SES and economic hardship during adolescence have been linked to diminished adaptive functioning with respect to relationships, school, and work; delinquent behavior; a less positive self-image; and increased vulnerability to depression (for a review of these studies, see McLoyd, 1990; McLoyd et al., in press). In addition, researchers have identified a host of negative behavioral and cognitive symptoms accompanying adolescent depression. Gibbs (1986), for example, found that low-income adolescent females with high depression scores, compared to their counterparts with low depression scores, were more susceptible to somatic symptoms and problems with memory, concentration, or studying; had poorer self-images; and experienced a greater occurrence of obsessive ideas, compulsive habits, and phobias. Depressive symptomatology also is associated with delinquency, though whether this link is causal remains unclear (Chiles, Miller, & Cox, 1980; Gibbs, 1981).

The basic relation between SES and children's socioemotional functioning appears to be modified by age of child and domain of functioning. A few epidemiological studies of very young children (3 years or younger) have found no significant relation between SES and socioemotional functioning (Earls, 1980; Richman, Stevenson, & Graham, 1975). It appears that social class differences in rates of behavioral/emotional problems (behavioral problems in particular) gradually increase during the pre- and early school years (Stevenson, Richman, & Graham, 1985). Epidemiological research based on parent, teacher and self-reports of behavioral/emotional problems also suggests that SES differences are more prevalent for externalizing problems than for internalizing problems (Achenbach, Bird, Canino, Phares, Gould, & Rubio-Stipec, 1990; Achenbach, Verhulst, Edelbrock, Baron, & Akkerhuis, 1987).

A few community surveys of child mental health have been conducted in the African-American population and a number of small-scale studies of behavioral/emotional problems in African-American children have been done in school settings (Gibbs, 1986, 1989; Gillum, Gomez-Marin, & Prineas, 1984; Gould, Wunsch-Hitzig, & Dohrenwend, 1981; Kaplan, Landa, Weinhold, & Shenker, 1984; Schoenbach, Kaplan, Wagner, Grimson, & Miller, 1983). Some of these investigations report higher rates of behavioral/emotional problems (e.g., depressive symptoms, somatization, sleep disturbance, conduct disorders) among African-American children than in the general population. However, few directly assess race differences and some that do find only negligible race effects when SES is controlled (Achenbach & Edelbrock, 1981).

Duration of Poverty and Socioemotional Functioning

Most studies of the relation between socioeconomic disadvantage and children's socioemotional functioning have relied on static conceptualizations of the former variable. In recent years, conceptions of poverty, in particular, have grown more complex, largely due to Duncan's (1984) research underscoring the volatility and dynamics of poverty and Wilson's (1987) analysis of historical changes in the spatial concentration of poverty in inner-city neighborhoods wrought by structural changes in the economy. Poverty increasingly is seen as a multidimensional phenomenon that differs in chronicity, ecological context, and subjective meaning, among other factors.

Two recent child-focused investigations reflect this growing conceptual sophistication. Both assessed the influence of duration of poverty on externalizing and internalizing symptoms in preadolescent children. McLeod and Shanahan (1993), in an investigation of 4- to 8-year-old children in the National Longitudinal Survey of Youth (NLSY), found that the length of time children spent in poverty, but not current poverty, had a significant and positive effect on the presence of internalizing symptoms (e.g., anxiety, sadness, depression, dependency) as reported by mothers.

In contrast, current poverty, but not duration of poverty, was significantly and positively related to the presence of externalizing symptoms (e.g., disobedience, difficulty getting along with others, impulsivity). Duncan et al. (1994) used longitudinal data from the Infant Health and Development Program, a 4-year, 8-site developmental study of approximately 900 low-birthweight, premature children. An analysis of maternal reports of children's socioemotional functioning at age 5 revealed that children who were occasionally poor (poor less than 4 years) and children who were persistently poor (poor all 4 years) had significantly more internalizing problems than never-poor children. Similar effects were reported for externalizing behavioral problems, although the effect of occasional poverty only approached statistical significance. For both internalizing and externalizing symptoms, persistent poverty had a much stronger effect than occasional poverty. Timing of poverty during the 4-year-period (early and late, early but not late, and late but not early) was unrelated to children's symptoms.

The investigations by Duncan et al. (1994) and McLeod and Shanahan (1993) are consistent in their reports of the relation between duration of poverty and internalizing symptoms, but conflicting with respect to the relation between duration of poverty and externalizing symptoms. The reasons for the disparity are unclear, but it is plausible that it stems from the fact that Duncan et al. did not distinguish current poverty from duration of poverty. These two studies significantly extend prior research and focus attention on the need for improvements in the specification of the economic determinants of children's socioemotional well-being.

Potential Mediators of Socioeconomic Disadvantage

Only recently have significant numbers of researchers begun to move beyond variable analysis to formulate and test models of how and why socioeconomic disadvantage affects children's mental health. House (1981) argued persuasively that tracing the processes through which social structures, positions, or systems affect the individual involves three theoretical tasks. First, we must understand the multiple aspects, dimensions, and components of the social structure, position, or system in question and, ultimately, develop conceptual frameworks that specify which of these are most relevant to understanding, in our case, observed SES or poverty–status differences in children's mental health. Importantly, this approach eschews traditional measures of SES that aggregate education, income, and occupation (Mueller & Parcel, 1981). It essentially calls for dissecting or disaggregating SES into its constituent parts; hence, education, income, and so forth would be considered distinct dimensions of SES or stratification. Furthermore, it argues for careful analyses of the complex nature of occupation or education, taking into account the various aspects or components of each.

Second, on the grounds that social structures, positions, or systems influence individuals through their effects on social interactional patterns, stimuli, and events that individuals experience in their daily lives, House (1981) maintained that we must understand the proximate social stimuli and interpersonal interactions associated with socioeconomic disadvantage that impinge directly on the individual. Finally, we need to understand when, how, and to what extent these proximate experiences affect behavior or mental health, a task that requires documenting the psychological processes through which interactions and stimuli are perceived, processed, and accommodated.

Detailed discussion of each of these tasks as they relate to poverty and low SES is beyond the scope of this chapter. As a starting point, however, the second task is examined in some detail. Three proximal variables are discussed as potential mediators of the link between socioeconomic disadvantage (that is, poverty and low SES) and children's socioemotional functioning: (a) discrete and chronic stressors, (b) experiences of inferiorization, and (c) nonsupportive and punitive parenting behavior. The discussion of the first two is based largely on indirect empirical evidence and ethnographic research, whereas the discussion of parenting behavior has the benefit of recent empirical investigations that directly assess its role in linking socioeconomic disadvantage to children's socioemotional functioning. Figure 2.1 presents a hypothetical model summarizing these mediating processes.

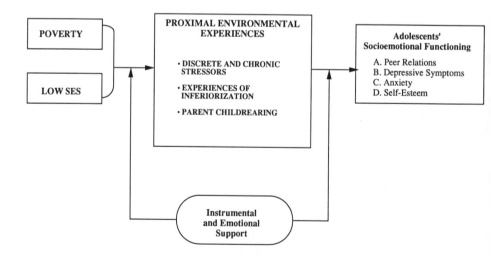

FIG. 2.1. Hypothetical model of how poverty and low SES influence socioemotional functioning in African-American Adolescents.

Discrete and Chronic Stressors

Poverty and low SES may adversely affect children's socioemotional functioning by increasing the presence of negative life events and chronic conditions. An overabundance of these events and conditions may place demands on children that exceed their coping resources (Sterling, Cowen, Weissberg, Lotyczewski, & Boike, 1985). If the corpus of events at issue includes positive (e.g, outstanding personal achievement) as well as negative connotations (e.g., death of a parent), socioeconomic or poverty status does not appear to be closely linked to the frequency of life events (life change) experienced by children or the degree of psychological readjustment required by these events (Coddington, 1972). However, the preponderance of research clearly indicates that children from poor and lower socioeconomic backgrounds, regardless of race, experience a significantly greater number of negative or undesirable life events (Gad & Johnson, 1980; Harper & Collins, 1975; Pryor-Brown, Cowen, Hightower, & Lotyczewski, 1986). Undesirability of life events, whether conceived in pure terms or in terms of balance between desirable and undesirable events, is a consistent predictor of socioemotional maladjustment. Its consistency and, in some cases, power as a predictor of maladjustment exceeds that of life change per se (Gersten, Langner, Eisenberg, & Orzek, 1974; McLoyd & Wilson, 1990; Sandler & Block, 1979).

Specific (e.g., death of a family member) and multiple negative life events largely, if not exclusively, outside the child's control are linked to a host of physical and mental health problems. In Gersten et al.'s (1974) epidemiological study of an ethnically diverse sample, the number of recent undesirable events experienced by children was positively and significantly correlated with maternal ratings of the child's adjustment (e.g., isolation, self-destructive tendencies). Similarly, a recent study of a large sample of African-American, predominantly low-income adolescent females seeking medical care indicated that adolescents who experienced a greater number of negative events displayed substantially higher rates of psychiatric disorders and symptoms such as depression, conduct disorder, and somatic complaints (Pryor-Brown, Powell, & Earls, 1989). Studies of young children report congruent findings. Sterling et al.'s (1985) investigation of first to fourth graders, for example, found that negative life events were associated with the presence of more serious school adjustment problems. These associations were strongest for children who had experienced multiple negative life events, a finding in keeping with other evidence that the adverse effects of clusters of negative life events are multiplicative, rather than simply additive (Rutter, 1979).

Adversity that is chronic, rather than discrete, may also exact a toll on children's mental health. Shaw and Emery (1988), for example, found that low-income school-age children exposed to a greater number of chronic family stressors (i.e., parental conflict, maternal depression, overcrowding, and lower family income) showed more internalizing and externalizing problems, lower levels of perceived social self-worth, and clinically elevated child behavior problems. For poor and lower SES children, chronic stressors often include their physical living environments. The pernicious living conditions with which many poor individuals routinely contend, such as lack of heat, inadequate plumbing, peeling lead-based paint, lack of laundry facilities, inoperable elevators, and insect and rodent infestation, in addition to threatening tenants' physical health, can chip away at their self-esteem, dignity, and sense of hope (Jordan, 1987a, 1987b; Klerman, 1991; Kotlowitz, 1991). In the words of one poor resident of a subsidized apartment building, "A rotten place to live leads to a rotten life. You feel less of a human being. You feel nobody cares. Eventually, you don't care" (Jordan, 1987a).

Sparked by the surge of murder, violence, and gang- and drug-related activities in poor inner-city neighborhoods during the 1980s, scholars have recently turned their attention to the psychological effects of neighborhood quality (Coulton & Pandey, 1992; Jencks & Mayer, 1990). Persistently poor African-American children are increasingly living in dangerous, crime-infested neighborhoods, aptly termed *war zones* (Dubrow & Garbarino, 1989). For example, a survey of youth in the south side of Chicago indicated that more than 25% had witnessed a homicide by the time they were 17 years old (Bell, cited in Garbarino, Kostelny, & Dubrow, 1991). Numerous poignant and tragic case studies published recently in the popular press liken the effects of this type of exposure to the posttraumatic stress symptoms that plague combat veterans. Although some therapists report signs of resilience, they also note that few children growing up in this maelstrom of violence and crime escape unscathed. They are prone to fear, anxiety, depression, irritability, apathy, poor concentration, and memory lapses. Some respond with aggression, while others withdraw and become inhibited. Many regress to early childhood behaviors and experience somatic ailments that appear to have no organic cause (Garbarino, Dubrow, Kostelny, & Pardo, 1992; Kotlowitz, 1991; Timnick, 1989; Zinsmeister, 1990).

Fitzpatrick and Boldizar's (1993) recent empirical study of the consequences of exposure to violence among 221 low-income African-American youth between the ages of 7 and 18 confirms observations from qualitative work. Reports of posttraumatic stress symptoms were moderately high in this sample, with 27% meeting all three of the diagnostic criteria considered. Males were more likely than females to be victims of and witnesses to violent acts. Being victimized and witnessing violence were significantly related to the reporting of stress symptoms, which were more pronounced among victimized females and victimized youth who had no male adult living with them in the household.

Focus on the level of danger that characterizes neighborhoods has been accompanied by attention to neighborhood economic conditions more generally (e.g., mean or median family income, mean education of parents, occupational mix, percentage of families with female heads, percentage of families on welfare) as determinants of educational and economic outcomes such as high school graduation, performance on tests of aptitude and achievement tests, teenage motherhood, and labor market success (for a review of these studies, see Jencks & Mayer, 1990). Only a few studies of this genre focus on children's socioemotional functioning. Duncan et al. (1994) found that neighborhood economic conditions, although less powerful than family-income differences, were significant predictors of behavior problems. In comparison to having moderate-income neighbors, having low-income neighbors predicted more externalizing problems in 4- and 5-year-olds. Connell, Spencer, and Aber's (1994) recent investigation of influences on the educational outcomes of three groups of African-American youth indicated that across all three samples, adolescents' experiences of perceived family support, sense of control over school performance, feelings of self-worth, emotional relationships with their mothers, and family economic resources guided their engagement and performance in school far more than neighborhood economic conditions. These conditions included high concentrations of family and individual poverty, female heads of household, and African-American residents; low concentrations of high-SES residents; and high levels of joblessness. These findings are consistent with Jencks and Mayer's conclusion that when family and individual characteristics are controlled, neighborhood economic status and other neighborhood characteristics often have mixed or weak effects.

Coulton and Pandey (1992) suggested, however, that existing research may underestimate neighborhood effects due to inadequate measurement of important characteristics of the environment and use of proxies that are less than optimal. In any case, existing studies that report neighborhood effects on socioemotional functioning and educational and economic outcomes leave open a host of questions regarding what processes are involved. Lack of attention to mediating influences and focus on "global or contextual ecological characteristics of places, to the relative neglect of social interaction within spatial domains" is a recurring limitation of these investigations (Tienda, 1991, p. 248). Hypotheses abound about the processes that mediate neighborhood effects (e.g., contagion, collective socialization, social comparison, institution-based practices), but these explanations have yet to be rigorously tested (Jencks & Mayer, 1990). Tienda argued cogently that such tests will require, at the very least, conceptual frameworks that specify which transmission mechanisms are more pertinent to specific behavioral outcomes and valid empirical measures of the transmission mechanisms themselves. They also will demand that researchers move beyond spatial characteristics of neighborhoods (e.g., physical proximity) to an examination of human interactional patterns within spatial domains. The scope of future investigation in this area should be expanded to include diverse indicators of children's socioemotional functioning and measures of neighborhood characteristics whose selection for examination rests on sound theoretical or conceptual grounds.

Experiences of Inferiorization

Poverty and low SES may adversely affect children's socioemotional functioning by increasing their exposure to demeaning, humiliating, and otherwise negative treatment precipitated by the stigmas of economic hardship. Economically impoverished individuals contend with stigmatizing living conditions and circumstances that publicly "mark" or symbolize their membership in the category of poor or economically deprived individuals (e.g., using food stamps, living in public housing, living in a "bad" neighborhood; Goodban, 1985; MacLeod, 1987; Marshall, 1982). These stigmas serve as cues for maltreatment at the interpersonal level largely because of widespread negative attitudes toward the poor and a strong bias in American society toward person-blame explanations of poverty (Feather, 1974; Leahy, 1990; Pelton, 1989).

By the time poor children enter early adolescence, if not earlier, they have more than an inchoate understanding of the negative social meaning of poverty and low SES. This understanding derives from their interpersonal experiences and often prompts efforts to mask their membership in a stigmatized group. Consider the observations of a father whose family was receiving food stamps: "When my kids go with me to the grocery store shopping, and we go through the checkout line, my kids usually take off. They told me they are embarrassed when I use our food stamps. They don't want to be seen with me" (Wiltfang & Scarbecz, 1990, p. 176).

MacLeod (1987) found that adolescent males living in a predominantly White, low-income housing development in a working-class neighborhood were acutely aware of the stigmas and disadvantages of living in public housing. One of them said "Out here, there's not the opportunity to make money. That's how you get into stealing and all that. . . . To get a job, first of all, this is a handicap, out here. If you say you're from the projects or anywhere in this area, that can hurt you. Right off the bat: reputation" (p. 5).

Self-esteem is the category of mental health functioning that would appear to be most obviously affected by the stigma of poverty and low SES. Numerous studies have investigated the relation between SES and self-esteem. On the basis of their review of these studies, Rosenberg and Pearlin (1978) concluded that the relation is strong for adults, relatively weak for adolescents, and virtually nonexistent for children. Their interpretation of this pattern of findings is that the psychological meaning of social class and the social experiences attendant to social class depend on the individual's developmental status. In particular, they argue that adults are more exposed to social inequality than children, pointing out that the world of work calls attention to a social stratification system and the worker's place in it, whereas the major extrafamilial context for children's socialization and development—school—tends to be socioeconomically homogeneous. Children typically attend schools where the average SES level is similar to their own. They also note that social class is generally viewed as achieved for adults and ascribed for children and adolescents and, consequently, adults, more so than children and adolescents, are evaluated and tend to evaluate themselves along class lines.

Wiltfang and Scarbecz (1990) argued that Rosenberg and Pearlin's (1978) conclusions are premature because studies have underestimated the effects of social class on adolescents' self-esteem as a result of relying on traditional measures of parental social class (e.g., father's education and occupation) that do not tap the dimensions of social class most likely to affect adolescents' self-esteem. Their assessment of social class in a study of 12-to 19-year-olds included traditional as well as nontraditional indicators. The latter included whether the family was receiving public welfare, whether the father was employed or unemployed, the adolescent's description of the neighborhood (whether it was described as luxurious, comfortable, average, run-down, a slum), and whether the adolescent perceived that lots of men in the neighborhood did not have work. These nontraditional indicators of social class were thought to better reflect the "hidden injuries" of social class (Sennett & Cobb, 1972), to have greater psychological relevance, and to carry more stigma for adolescents than parental education and occupation, especially in American society "where people measure one another by what they have or do, or by where they live" (Wiltfang & Scarbecz, 1990, p. 175). Consistent with their predictions, nontraditional measures of social class were much stronger predictors of adolescent self-esteem than were traditional measures.

Wiltfang and Scarbecz's (1990) study is important for its attempt to dissect the social class matrix into components that are more psychologically meaningful and more proximal to children's experiences than parental education and occupation. In keeping with House's (1981) suggestions, the next step in this line of work would be documentation of the immediate experiences and interpersonal interactions that stem from adolescents' stigmatized status and function to link nontraditional measures of social class and adolescents' self-esteem.

Even if children do not understand fully the social meaning and stigmas associated with poverty and low SES, they can be adversely affected socioemotionally by the maltreatment that stigmas evoke. A stunning example of this process is provided by Rist's (1970) longitudinal, observational study of a group of African-American children during their kindergarten, first- and second-grade years. Children's SES background was a powerful determinant of how they were treated by their teacher and classmates. Low-SES children were inferiorized by a process that was swift, deliberate, and unrelenting. Prior to the beginning of the school year, the school social worker provided to the teacher a list of all children in the kindergarten class who lived in homes receiving public welfare funds. This information apparently proved pivotal in the teachers' permanent seating assignments, made on the eighth day of kindergarten classes. Children's placement at one of three tables in the classroom was highly correlated with objective SES indicators (e.g., welfare status, family income, parental education and employment status) and with behavioral and physical markers of low SES such as dress, physical appearance, and adeptness at code-switching between standard English and Black English. No objective information directly relevant to the children's academic potential was used in the determination of seating assignments.

The physical organization of the kindergarten classroom according to children's SES and correspondingly, according to the teacher's expectations about the children's future academic success or failure, became the basis for the differential treatment of the children for the remainder of the year. In general, poor children were rejected, penalized, and marginalized by the teacher and by their more economically advantaged classmates for not having middle-class experiences. They were denied privileges granted to nonpoor children, received less of the teacher's attention and, in general, were not given equal opportunity to learn and participate in classroom activities (even to the point of being seated in positions that did not allow them to see exercises and assignments written on the blackboard). Emulating the teacher's behavior, nonpoor children adopted a condescending, authoritarian stance toward poor children, ordering them around and ridiculing and belittling their behavior, clothes, and appearance. Poor children responded to this treatment with withdrawal, both physical and psychological, and verbal and physical in-group hostility, calling each other, but not economically advantaged children, "dummy," "stupid," and other insulting epithets.

Rist's (1970) investigation suggests that as early as 5 years of age, children have begun to learn the acceptability of negative attitudes and behavior toward those who are poor. Moreover, in the case of poor children themselves, they have begun to show signs of low self-esteem as a consequence of internalizing these negative attitudes. As shown in another study allied with Rist's project, by the time children in the bottom academic track reached fifth grade (virtually all of whom were from lower SES backgrounds), internalization of negative attitudes about their academic and intellectual abilities had taken firm hold. As one of them said, "By the time we get to sixth grade, boy, we be dumb" (Gouldner, 1978, p. 62).

Class- and culture-based stigmatization in the classroom is also salient in the recollections of a group of poor, inner-city, African-American male dropouts studied by Glasgow (1981). These young men believed that "mainstream" education, in actuality, is intended to demoralize African Americans and to assure that they have bleak economic futures. They pointed to myriad ways in which instructors "put down" or stigmatized African-American culture (e.g., African-American dance, music, dress, speech patterns), core aspects of their definition of self, of poor people, and of their community at large. Understandably, these young men reacted to these explicit and implicit messages of cultural inferiority with resentment, defensiveness, and feelings of alienation. Reflecting on these inferiorizing experiences, one young man said, "I don't need the man [the White teacher] to tell me directly that my way of life is uncivilized, but I know what he's putting down; I ain't nobody's fool" (p. 58).

Brantlinger's (1991) investigation of high- and low-SES adolescents' reports of problems and punishment in school revealed processes reminiscent of those recounted by Glasgow (1981) and Rist (1970). Epithets from high-SES students referring to low-SES students (e.g., "scum") understandably evoked intensely negative reactions from the latter (all of whom lived in government-subsidized housing projects) and were often the precipitant of fights between schoolmates differing in SES. Poor students, compared to their more affluent schoolmates, reported a greater number of penalties, more severe, stigmatizing punishment, and more stringent consequences for similar infractions. The self-reported penalties experienced by low-SES students more often involved *public* humiliation (e.g., being yelled at in front of the class), ostracism (e.g., being made to stand in the hall for long periods of time), and rejection. Low-SES students were much less likely than high-SES students to believe that discipline meted out by school personnel was fair and much more likely to believe that teachers did not like them because of prejudice against either their social class or the groups with which they affiliated.

Whether teachers are given to social class and racial biases in their treatment and perception of children depends to a significant degree on teachers' own social class origins. Alexander, Entwisle, and Thompson (1987) found that low-SES and African-American first graders experienced their greatest difficulties in the classrooms of teachers with high-SES social origins (as measured by fathers' occupation when growing up). Teachers with high-SES origins evaluated low-SES and African-American children as less mature (e.g., fights too much, unable to concentrate, timid) than high-SES and White children, had lower performance expectations for them, and evaluated the classroom and school climate more negatively. These differences were markedly more pronounced than corresponding differences observed for teachers with low-SES origins. Not surprisingly, high levels of perceived maturity and high performance expectations were predictive of high grades and performance on standardized achievement tests at the end of the school year. Moreover, whereas significant race differences were found in the year-end achievements (especially for grades) of children in classrooms taught by high-SES teachers, the performance of children in classrooms taught by low-SES teachers was unrelated to race.

In addition to engendering negative self-appraisal, the stigmatizing process described in these investigations may foment aggression, disruptive behavior, anxiety, and depression, and encourage students to drop out of school. Given the large amount of time children spend in school, it is likely that cumulative exposure to inferiorizing experiences in the school setting is a major factor underlying the increase with age in SES differences in behavior problems (Stevenson et al., 1985). Indeed, in view of evidence that SES differences in behavior problems emerge and become more pronounced as children enter and progress through school, it is difficult to envision that such exposure plays no causal role in the overrepresentation of internalizing, and especially externalizing problems in poor and low-SES children. Longitudinal research that directly tests this hypothesis is essential.

Just as schools have the potential to engender socioemotional problems in economically disadvantaged children by increasing their exposure to inferiorizing experiences, there is some suggestion that they can also mitigate the effects of economic disadvantage. Schools distinguished by appropriately high standards, generous use of praise, the setting of exemplary models of behavior by teachers, and a tendency to give students positions of trust and responsibility appear to foster positive socioemotional functioning in poor children (Rutter, cited in Werner, 1984).

Nonsupportive and Punitive Parenting Behavior

Poor and low-SES children appear to be at increased risk of socioemotional problems partly because of their increased exposure to nonsupportive and punitive parenting (McLoyd, 1990). In a direct test of this hypothesized mediation process in a sample of African-American, Hispanic, and non-Hispanic White families with 4- to 8-year-old children, McLeod and Shanahan (1993) found that mothers' weak emotional responsiveness to their children's needs and frequent use of physical punishment explained the effect of current poverty on children's mental health (i.e., internalizing and externalizing symptoms), but not the effect of persistent poverty. Length of time spent in poverty neither increased the frequency of physical punishment nor decreased mothers' emotional responsiveness, perhaps indicating that family interactions stabilize as the duration of poverty increases and the family adapts to economic deprivation.

Considerable indirect evidence also suggests that punitive, nonsupportive parenting may contribute to the higher levels of socioemotional problems experienced by low-SES children compared to their more affluent counterparts. A number of studies of African-American and racially diverse samples drawn primarily from urban areas report that mothers who are poor or from low-SES backgrounds, compared to their economically advantaged counterparts, are more likely to use power-assertive techniques in disciplinary encounters and are generally less supportive of their children. They value obedience more, are less likely to use reasoning, and more likely to use physical punishment as a means of disciplining and controlling the child. Low SES parents also are more likely to issue commands without explanation, less likely to consult the child about his or her wishes, and less likely to reward the child verbally for behavior in desirable ways. In addition, poverty has been associated with diminished expression of affection and less responsiveness to the socioemotional needs explicitly expressed by the child (for a review of these studies, see McLoyd, 1990).

Although it is indisputable that only a small proportion of poor parents are even alleged to abuse their children, strong evidence exists that child abuse occurs more frequently in poor families than in more affluent families (e.g., see Daniel, Hampton, & Newberger, 1983; Garbarino, 1976). Indeed, poverty is the single most prevalent characteristic of abusive parents (Pelton, 1989). Several types of data contradict the claim that the relation between poverty and abuse is spurious because of greater public scrutiny of the poor and resulting bias in detection and reporting. First, although greater public awareness and new reporting laws resulted in a significant increase in official reporting in recent years, the socioeconomic pattern of these reports has not changed (Pelton, 1989). Second, child abuse is related to degrees of poverty even within the lower class, which admittedly is more open to public scrutiny; abusive parents tend to be the poorest of the poor (Wolock & Horowitz, 1979). Third, the most severe injuries occur within the poorest families, even among the reported cases (Pelton, 1989).

Several of the childrearing behaviors that are more prevalent among impoverished parents are predictive of a number of socioemotional problems in children. For example, as noted previously, punitive discipline by parents is associated with increased rates of delinquency, drug use, and socioemotional distress (e.g., depressive symptoms, moodiness, hypersensitivity, feelings of inadequacy) among adolescents, and more quarrelsome, negativistic, and explosive behavior among younger children (Elder, 1979; Elder, Nguyen, & Caspi, 1985; Lempers, Clark-Lempers, & Simons, 1989; McLoyd, Jayaratne, Ceballo, & Borquez, 1994). A recent investigation by Dodge, Pettit, and Bates (1994) indicated that harsh parenting during the preschool years predicted externalizing behavior problems in children as many as 4 years later.

Harsh discipline and low levels of positive responsiveness to children also have been found to be key mediators of the link between maternal depression and child maladjustment (Downey & Coyne, 1990). Furthermore, ample evidence exists that children whose parents are nonsupportive have lower self-esteem and more psychological disorders, exhibit more antisocial aggression and behavioral problems, and are more likely to show arrested ego development (for a review of these studies, see McLoyd, 1990). Indeed, recent evidence suggests that across all social classes, adolescents with nonsupportive parents report more psychological distress and engage in more delinquent activities in comparison to adolescents whose parents are warm, firm, and democratic (Steinberg, Mounts, Lamborn, & Dornbusch, 1991). Finally, children who have been neglected or physically abused, compared to children with no history of neglect or abuse, exhibit more anger, aggression, frustration, and noncompliance in problem-solving situations (Egeland & Sroufe, 1981) and behave more aggressively toward their peers and caregivers (George & Main, 1979).

Contributors to Punitive Parenting. A comprehensive model of punitive, nonsupportive parenting as a mediator of the link between socioeconomic disadvantage and children's socioemotional functioning must delineate the proximal antecedents of this style of parenting. We focus here on negative life events, undesirable ongoing conditions, and psychological distress, all of which are more prevalent among individuals who are poor than those who are not (Kessler & Neighbors, 1986; Liem & Liem, 1978). Gersten, Langner, Eisenberg, and Simcha-Fagan (1977) found that the occurrence of undesirable life events correlated positively with affectively distant, restrictive, and punitive parenting. Similarly, Weinraub and Wolf (1983) reported that mothers who experienced more stressful life events were less nurturant toward their children and, in the case of single mothers, were less at ease, less spontaneous, and less responsive to their children's communications. Even ephemeral, relatively minor "hassles" produce detectable, negative changes in maternal behavior. Patterson's (1988) observations of mother–child dyads over the course of several days indicated that day-to-day fluctuations in the mothers' tendencies to initiate and continue aversive exchanges with children were systematically related to the daily frequency of complications or crises the mothers experienced.

Chronic, undesirable conditions such as neighborhood crime may also condition the quality of parenting behavior, although firm conclusions about this issue are precluded by the scarcity of existing data. Research indicates that mothers who perceive their neighborhoods as dangerous and crime-infested, compared to those who perceive their neighborhoods as safer, report more conflict with their children (White, Kasl, Zahner, & Will, 1987) and are more likely to use physical punishment as a child management technique (Kriesberg, 1970). These relations may be mediated partly by mothers' mental health. Perceived neighborhood danger and crime, highly correlated with actual crime statistics (Kriesberg, 1970; Lewis & Maxfield, 1980), have been found to predict poor mental health among minority women (Kasl & Harburg, 1975; White et al., 1987). Mothers residing in dangerous neighborhoods probably are more likely to adopt punitive parenting strategies to ensure their children's safety and to discourage disobedience of rules (a logical goal when one considers the potentially grave consequences that may result from a failure to follow established safety rules). From the parent's perspective, achieving these goals may require the use of more severe child management techniques (Dubrow & Garbarino, 1989). Much more systematic study is needed of the links between neighborhood characteristics and parenting practices and the factors mediating these links.

A great deal of research has confirmed that differences in the psychological well-being of adults of varying SES are at least partly due to an overrepresentation in lower-class life of a broad range of frustration-producing life events and chronic conditions outside personal control. In view of the prevalence of such stressors and their resultant psychological distress, it is not surprising that low SES is associated with less positive and more punitive parenting behavior. Indeed, several studies focusing on specific stressors such as unemployment, job loss, and income loss, as well as studies that are not stress-specific in focus, directly tie parental mental health (e.g., depressive symptoms, anxiety) to parental punitiveness, inconsistency, and unresponsiveness. For example, research has shown that psychological distress in parents encourages the use of disciplinary strategies that are more aversive and coercive and require less effort (for example, physical punishment, commanding without explanation, reliance on authority) rather than more effort (e.g., reasoning, explaining, negotiating). Psychological distress also inhibits positive behaviors (e.g., hugs, praise, supportive statements) and responsiveness to children's dependency needs (for a review of these studies, see McLoyd, 1990).

Inhibitors of Punitive Parenting. In addition to understanding its antecedents, it is equally important to delineate the factors that moderate or lessen punitive, harsh parenting behavior. A burgeoning body of research based on African-American, White, and racially diverse samples indicates that social support not only improves parents' dispositions but, in turn, lessens their tendency toward insensitivity and coercive discipline. Both poor and more affluent mothers receiving higher levels of *emotional support* (i.e., companionship, expressions of affection, availability of a confidant) report being less likely to nag, scold, ridicule, or threaten their children and are observed to interact in a more nurturant, sensitive fashion with their children. They report feeling less overwhelmed by their parenting situation, more gratified by the maternal role, and more satisfied with their children (Crnic & Greenberg, 1987; Zur-Szpiro & Longfellow, 1982), factors that may both instigate and result from more positive parenting behavior. *Parenting support* (e.g., assistance with child care) also has salutary effects on parenting behavior. Crockenberg's (1987) observational study of impoverished adolescent mothers indicated that maternal sensitivity and accessibility to the infant, as well as promptness in responding to the infant's cries, increased with an increase in the number of family members who helped with various household and child-care chores. This is consistent with reports from poor mothers that they are warmer and less rejecting of their preschool children when given an opportunity to break continuous interactions with them for more than 2 hours (Colletta, 1979).

Because psychological distress among mothers is a risk factor for difficulties in children's socioemotional functioning, factors that protect against maternal distress may bolster the probability of children's adaptive resilience. Extant research supports this proposition. For example, availability of child care support to the primary caregiver has been found to distinguish stress-resilient from stress-affected children (Cowen, Wyman, Work, & Parker, 1990). Likewise, a recent study of rural, two-parent African-American families representing a wide income range indicated that adolescents whose mothers received more caregiver support from their spouses had more self-control (e.g., considering consequences of actions before acting, planning before acting, task persistence), which, in turn, predicted better academic outcomes and fewer externalizing and internalizing problems (Brody et al., 1994). Increased parenting or emotional support and the resultant increase in nurturant parenting behavior may explain why emotional adjustment in poor African-American children living in mother/grandmother families is almost as high as that of children living in mother/father families, and significantly higher than that of children living alone with their mothers (Kellam, Ensminger, & Turner, 1977).

Implications for Intervention and Prevention

The first steps toward both preventing and alleviating socioemotional problems in poor children and children from low-SES backgrounds are awareness of children's socioemotional functioning, appreciation of their present life concerns, and sensitivity to the environmental and life circumstances that pose threats to their socioemotional well-being. Toward this end, comprehensive family-centered child development programs in poor communities could, with parental consent, regularly assess children's physical, mental, and emotional development for the purpose of keeping well children well, preventing inchoate difficulties from becoming more serious, and facilitating intervention for distressed children (Lurie, 1974).

It is increasingly clear from a small but expanding body of research that childhood resilience is not an innate characteristic, but depends on a combination of child attributes, socialization experiences both within and outside the family, and interactions between these components (Cowen et al., 1990; Rutter, 1990). This means that intervention and prevention strategies that focus exclusively on the child, whether directed toward modification of intrapsychic or behavioral processes, are likely to be severely limited in their effectiveness. Psychiatric interventions for children who are victims of, or witnesses to, violence, for example, may prove effective in the short run, but impotent over time if violence is a mainstay of children's environments (Eth & Pynoos, 1985). Intervention and prevention strategies should seek to both decrease poor children's exposure to acute and chronic stressors and increase the number of protective factors, such as the availability of mentors and social support (Werner, 1984). These outcomes cannot be achieved without impacting the multiple contexts (e.g., classrooms, schools, neighborhoods) within which development occurs. For example, intervention and prevention strategies should include systematic efforts to disrupt negative treatment of poor children by teachers and peers. Ultimately, it is these contexts and conditions that must be altered in the interests of promoting optimal functioning in both parents and children. In short, in the words of Schorr (1989), it is urgent that we not only help individual parents and children beat the odds imposed by poverty and low SES, but work toward *changing* the odds as well.

As social and economic stress are often the root causes of maternal depression, psychological distress, and negative parenting, alleviating such stresses is likely to go a long way toward alleviating mental health problems in mothers, enhancing parenting, and contributing to positive socioemotional functioning in children (Belle, 1984; Rutter, 1985). Mental health professionals need to deepen their appreciation of the strong links among these factors and orient their therapeutic efforts accordingly. Needless to say, blaming poor mothers for their economic and psychological plights will exacerbate their psychological problems, heighten mistrust and apprehension, and undercut the professional's role as facilitator and helper. Because the typical middle-class therapist or mental health worker has never experienced the stressors that poor women routinely confront, this level of understanding cannot be achieved without concerted efforts to bridge the chasms between these professionals and the poor—chasms engendered by cultural, class, and gender differences. Visits to clients' neighborhoods and homes can help clinicians appreciate clients' ongoing struggles to survive and raise children in the midst of daunting environmental realities. Interventions that focus on intrapsychic flaws and parent education, while ignoring the environmental difficulties that undermine psychological and maternal functioning, are likely to be of limited usefulness and, indeed, may engender more, rather than less, passivity, guilt, and depression (Belle, 1984; Halpern, 1991; McLoyd, 1995).

Emotional support for poor women and children, then, needs to be complemented by advocacy activities that help families resolve concrete, environmental problems, and pressure bureaucracies and social agents to be more responsive to the needs of children and families. Belle (1984, p. 147) thoughtfully argued that clinicians who cannot undertake such efforts "should ally themselves with other service providers in a close working relationship so that all of a client's pressing and interlocking problems can receive attention as part of an overall treatment plan." The importance of a comprehensive, rather than fragmented, piecemeal approach is underscored by Schorr's (1989) research, indicating that intervention programs that are successful in changing outcomes for high-risk children, typically offer a broad spectrum of services. The prevailing wisdom of these programs is that social and emotional support and immediate, concrete help are usually necessary before a family can make use of interventions with long-range goals.

Mutual help groups for both children and parents can serve useful therapeutic purposes by bringing together individuals with similar experiences, providing support, and bolstering self-esteem by providing the opportunity to be helpful to others. Mental health workers can play an important role by helping to initiate and sustain such groups (Belle, 1984). Attention should also be devoted to devising creative strategies to strengthen culturally indigenous structures and patterns of relations among African Americans (e.g., strong kinship bonds, flexible family roles) that have long served to buffer parents and children from the deleterious effects of poverty and socioeconomic disadvantage.

Although instrumental and emotional support from informal and professional sources can help address the problems of poor parents and children, it is crucial to acknowledge the limits of what such support can accomplish. Many of the causes of difficult life conditions confronting poor families, and of poverty itself (e.g., racism in labor markets and lending institutions, low wages paid by traditionally "female" jobs, unavailability of affordable, high-quality child care, unjust housing policies), are impervious to family- and individual-level interventions (Halpern, 1990). As Halpern (1991) pointed out, there has been an overreliance in America on services to address problems created by poverty "due to an unwillingness to acknowledge that many of our most serious problems are a result of chosen social and economic arrangements and a reluctance to use the political process to alter arrangements even when it is acknowledged that they are harmful" (p. 344).

SUMMARY AND FUTURE DIRECTIONS

Ample evidence exists of greater socioemotional difficulties in African-American and White children who are poor or from lower SES backgrounds, compared to nonpoor and higher SES children. SES differences appear to emerge and increase during the preschool and early school years and are more pronounced for externalizing symptoms than for internalizing symptoms. In addition, recent investigations indicate that the presence of internalizing symptoms increases as the duration of poverty increases. No conclusive evidence is available about whether, among children, race and ethnicity are related to socioemotional functioning, independent of SES, or whether SES interacts with race and ethnicity. More methodologically rigorous studies have reported only negligible race effects on children's socioemotional functioning (e.g., Achenbach & Edelbrock, 1981), but additional, large-scale epidemiological research is needed to draw firm conclusions.

Research emphasis has shifted recently from descriptions of effects of socioeconomic disadvantage to analyses of processes by which such effects come about. The principal focus of most of the latter investigations has been family processes. Several recent studies have documented the role of harsh, punitive parenting, low maternal responsiveness, and parent–child conflict in linking economic hardship and socioemotional problems in children. This pathway has been documented in research with African Americans as well as Whites, and a direct test of race/ethnicity differences in the relations among poverty, parenting behavior, and children's mental health has revealed no race/ethnicity effects (African Americans and His-panics vs. non-Hispanic Whites; McLeod & Shanahan, 1993). We do not know, however, whether mediating processes are conditioned by duration of poverty. In addition, inadequate attention has been given to extrafamilial, but proximal, factors as potential mediators of the effects of poverty and low SES. Children's interactions with teachers, as well as day-care workers, peers, and extended family members are obvious areas for investigation of mediating pathways.

Neighborhood effects on children's development are an emergent focus in child development research. Advances in our understanding of these effects and the processes by which they emerge will depend on our ability to grapple successfully with a host of conceptual and methodological problems (Jencks & Mayer, 1990; Tienda, 1991). Race and ethnicity may be important considerations in developing mediational models focused on ecological factors. Residence in a neighborhood marked by widespread mental health problems, inadequate mental health services, restricted social resources, and high levels of crime and violence, for example, might be crucial considerations in an analysis of the processes by which poverty affects socioemotional functioning in poor, urban, African-American children (who are very likely to live in high-poverty neighborhoods where such conditions are more common).

Attention also needs to be focused on the extent to which mediating processes are conditioned or moderated by characteristics of the individual child such as age, gender, and temperament. Those involving interpersonal experiences outside the family (e.g., peer-mediated experiences of inferiorization), for example, are unlikely as explanations for socioemotional problems in very young poor children. Likewise, the extent to which parent socialization processes mediate the influences of poverty and low SES on children's mental health may depend, in part, on the child's temperament. Several studies suggest that temperamentally easy children are less likely than children with difficult temperaments to be the target of parental criticism and harshness (Elder et al., 1985; Rutter, 1979). When parents are depressed and irritable, they are more likely to direct abusive behavior toward children with adverse temperamental characteristics. Studies of child abuse also have identified children's temperament as a factor that appears to elicit maltreatment (Belsky, 1980). These critical considerations represent fertile and promising areas of study because of the potential of building on extant quantitative and qualitative research.

The linkages between the effects of poverty and low SES on physical health and their effects on socioemotional well-being need to be examined more systematically. Socioeconomic disadvantage is associated with increased exposure to environmental toxins, overcrowding, inadequate housing and homelessness, and myriad other conditions that threaten physical health (Klerman, 1991). Poor physical health could engender socioemotional problems in children by disrupting friendships, destabilizing school attendance, and adversely affecting academic performance.

REFERENCES

Achenbach, T., Bird, H., Canino, G., Phares, V., Gould, M., & Rubio-Stipec, M. (1990). Epidemiological comparisons of Puerto Rican and U.S. mainland children: Parent, teacher and self-reports. *Journal of the American Academy of Child and Adolescent Psychiatry, 29*(1), 84–93.

Achenbach, T., & Edelbrock, C. (1981). Behavioral problems and competencies reported by parents of normal and disturbed children aged four through sixteen. *Monographs of the Society for Research in Child Development, 46*(1, Serial No. 188).

Achenbach, T., Verhulst, F., Edelbrock, C., Baron, G. D., & Akkerhuis, G. (1987). Epidemiological comparisons of American and Dutch children: II. Behavioral/emotional problems reported by teachers for ages 6 to 11. *Journal of the American Academy of Child and Adolescent Psychiatry, 26*(3), 326–332.

Alexander, K., Entwisle, D., & Thompson, M. (1987). School performance, status relations, and the structure of sentiment: Bringing the teacher back in. *American Sociological Review, 52*(5), 665–682.

Baldwin, A. L., Baldwin, C., & Cole, R. E. (1990). Stress resistant families and stress resistant children. In J. Rolf, A. S. Masten, D. Cicchetti, K. Nuechterlein, & S. Weintraub (Eds.), *Risk and protective factors in the development of psychopathology* (pp. 257–280). Cambridge, England: Cambridge University Press.

Belle, D. (1984). Inequality and mental health: Low-income and minority women. In L. Walker (Ed.), *Women and mental health policy* (pp. 135–150). Beverly Hills, CA: Sage.

Belsky, J. (1980). Child maltreatment: An ecological integration. *American Psychologist, 35*(4), 320–335.

Blumer, H. (1956). Sociological analysis and the variable. *American Sociological Review, 22,* 683–690.

Brantlinger, E. (1991). Social class distinctions in adolescents' reports of problems and punishment in school. *Behavioral Disorders, 17*(1), 36–46.

Brody, G., Stoneman, Z., Flor, D., McCrary, C., Hastings, L., & Conyers, O. (1994). Financial resources, parent psychological functioning, parent co-caregiving, and early adolescent competence in rural two-parent African-American families. *Child Development, 65*(2), 590–605.

Bronfenbrenner, U. (1986). Ecology of the family as a context for human development: Research perspectives. *Developmental Psychology, 22*(6), 723–742.

Butler, J. A., Starfield, B., & Stenmark, S. (1984). Child health policy. In H. Stevenson & A. Siegel (Eds.), *Child development research and social policy* (pp. 110–188). Chicago: University of Chicago Press.

Chiles, J., Miller, M., & Cox, G. (1980). Depression in an adolescent delinquent population. *Archives of General Psychiatry, 37*(10), 1179–1184.

Clark, R. (1983). *Family life and school achievement: Why poor black children succeed or fail.* Chicago: University of Chicago Press.

Coddington, R. D. (1972). The significance of life events as etiological factors in the diseases of children, II: A study of a normal population. *Journal of Psychosomatic Research, 16,* 205–213.

Colletta, N. (1979). Support systems after divorce: Incidence and impact. *Journal of Marriage and the Family, 41,* 837–846.

Conger, R., Ge, X., Elder, G., Lorenz, F., & Simons, R. (1994). Economic stress, coercive family process and developmental problems of adolescents. *Child Development, 65*(2), 541–561.

Connell, J., Spencer, M., & Aber, J. L. (1994). Educational risk and resilience in African-American youth: Context, self, action, and outcomes in school. *Child Development, 65*(2), 493–506.

Coulton, C., & Pandey, S. (1992). Geographic concentrations of poverty and risk to children in urban neighborhoods. *American Behavioral Scientist, 35*(3), 238–257.

Cowen, E. L., Wyman, P. A., Work, W. C., & Parker, G. R. (1990). The Rochester child resilience project: Overview and summary of first year findings. *Development and Psychopathology, 2*(2), 193–212.

Crnic, K., & Greenberg, M. (1987). Maternal stress, social support, and coping: Influences on early mother-child relationship. In C. Boukydis (Ed.), *Research on support for parents and infants in the postnatal period* (pp. 25–40). Norwood, NJ: Ablex.

Crockenberg, S. (1987). Support for adolescent mothers during the postnatal period: Theory and research. In C. Boukydis (Ed.), *Research on support for parents and infants in the postnatal period* (pp. 3–24). Norwood, NJ: Ablex.

Daniel, J., Hampton, R., & Newberger, E. (1983). Child abuse and accidents in black families: A controlled comparative study. *American Journal of Orthopsychiatry, 53*(4), 645–653.

Dodge, K., Pettit, G., & Bates, J. (1994). Socialization mediators of the relation between socioeconomic status and child conduct problems. *Child Development, 65*(2), 649–665.

Downey, G., & Coyne, J. (1990). Children of depressed parents: An integrative review. *Psychological Bulletin, 108*(1), 50–76.

Dubrow, N. F., & Garbarino, J. (1989). Living in the war zone: Mothers and young children in a public housing development. *Child Welfare, 68*(1), 3–20.

Duncan, G. (1984). *Years of poverty, years of plenty.* Ann Arbor, MI: University of Michigan Institute for Social Research.

Duncan, G., Brooks-Gunn, J., & Klebanov, P. (1994). Economic deprivation and early-childhood development. *Child Development, 65*(2), 296–318.

Duncan, G., & Rodgers, W. (1988). Longitudinal aspects of childhood poverty. *Journal of Marriage and the Family, 50,* 1007–1021.

Earls, F. (1980). Prevalence of behavior problems in 3-year-old children: A cross national replication. *Archives of General Psychiatry, 37*(10), 1153–1157.

Egeland, B., & Sroufe, A. (1981). Developmental sequelae of maltreatment in infancy. In R. Rizley & D. Cicchetti (Eds.), *New Directions for Child Development: Vol. 11. Developmental perspectives on child maltreatment* (pp. 77–92). San Francisco: Jossey-Bass.

Elder, G. (1979). Historical change in life patterns and personality. In P. Baltes & O. Brim (Eds.), *Life span development and behavior* (pp. 117–159). New York: Academic Press.

Elder, G., Nguyen, T., & Caspi, A. (1985). Linking family hardship to children's lives. *Child Development, 56*(2), 361–375.

Eth, S., & Pynoos, R. S. (1985). Psychiatric interventions with children traumatized by violence. In D. H. Schetky & E. P. Benedek (Eds.), *Emerging issues in child psychiatry and the law* (pp. 285–309). New York: Brunner/Mazel.

Feather, N. (1974). Explanations of poverty in Australian and American samples. *Australian Journal of Psychology, 26*(3), 199–216.

Fitzpatrick, K., & Boldizar, J. (1993). The prevalence and consequences of exposure to violence among African-American youth. *Journal of American Academy of Child and Adolescent Psychiatry, 32*(2), 424–430.

Flanagan, C., & Eccles, J. (1993). Changes in parents' work status and adolescents' adjustment at school. *Child Development, 64*(1), 246–257.

Gad, M., & Johnson, J. (1980). Correlates of adolescent life stresses related to race, SES, and levels of perceived social support. *Journal of Clinical Child Psychology, 9*(1), 13–16.

Garbarino, J. (1976). A preliminary study of some ecological correlates of child abuse: The impact of socioeconomic stress on mothers. *Child Development, 47*(1), 178–185.

Garbarino, J., Dubrow, N., Kostelny, K., & Pardo, C. (1992). *Children in danger: Coping with the consequences of community violence.* San Francisco: Jossey-Bass.

Garbarino, J., Kostelny, K., & Dubrow, N. (1991). What children can tell us about living in danger. *American Psychologist, 46*(4), 376–383.

George, C., & Main, M. (1979). Social interactions of young abused children: Approach, avoidance, and aggression. *Child Development, 50*(2), 306–318.

Gersten, J., Langner, T., Eisenberg, J., & Orzek, L. (1974). Child behavior and life events: Undesirable change or change per se? In B. S. Dohrenwend & B. P. Dohrenwend (Eds.), *Stressful life events: Their nature and effects* (pp. 159–170). New York: Wiley.

Gersten, J., Langner, T., Eisenberg, J., & Simcha-Fagan, O. (1977). An evaluation of the etiological role of stressful life-change events in psychological disorders. *Journal of Health and Social Behavior, 18*(3), 228–244.

Gibbs, J. T. (1981). Depression and suicidal behavior among delinquent females. *Journal of Youth and Adolescence, 10*(2), 159–167.

Gibbs, J. T. (1986). Assessment of depression in urban adolescent females: Implications for early intervention strategies. *American Journal of Social Psychiatry, 6*(1), 50–56.

Gibbs, J. T. (1989). Black American adolescents. In J. Gibbs, L. Huang, & Associates (Eds.), *Children of color: Psychological interventions with minority youth* (pp. 148–178). San Francisco: Jossey-Bass.

Gillum, R., Gomez-Marin, O., & Prineas, R. (1984). Racial differences in personality, behavior, and family environment in Minneapolis school children. *Journal of the National Medical Association, 76*(11), 1097–1105.

Glasgow, D. (1981). *The Black underclass: Poverty, unemployment and entrapment of ghetto youth.* San Francisco: Jossey-Bass.

Goldberg, I. D., Regier, D. A., McInerny, T. K., Pless, I. B., & Roghmann, K. J. (1979). The role of the pediatrician in the delivery of mental health services to children. *Pediatrics, 63,* 898–909.

Goodban, N. (1985). The psychological impact of being on welfare. *Social Service Review, 59,* 403–422.

Gould, M., Wunsch-Hitzig, R., & Dohrenwend, B. (1981). Estimating the prevalence of childhood psychopathology. *Journal of the American Academy of Child Psychiatry, 20,* 462–476.

Gouldner, H. (1978). *Teachers' pets, troublemakers, and nobodies: Black children in elementary school.* Westport, CT: Greenwood.

Halpern, R. (1990). Parent support and education programs. *Children and Youth Services Review, 12,* 285–308.

Halpern, R. (1991). Supportive services for families in poverty: Dilemmas of reform. *Social Service Review, 65,* 343–364.

Harper, J., & Collins, J. (1975). A differential survey of the problems of privileged and underprivileged adolescents. *Journal of Youth and Adolescence, 4,* 349–358.

House, J. (1981). Social structure and personality. In M. Rosenberg & R. Turner (Eds.), *Social psychology: Sociological perspectives.* New York: Basic Books.

Huston, A., McLoyd, V. C., & Garcia Coll, C. (1994). Children and poverty: Issues in contemporary research. *Child Development, 64,* 275–282.

Jacobson, A. M., Goldberg, I. D., Burns, B. J., Hoeper, E. W., Hankin, J. R., & Hewitt, K. (1980). Diagnosed mental disorder in children and use of health services in four organized health care settings. *American Journal of Psychiatry, 137*(2), 559–565.

Jencks, C., & Mayer, S. (1990). The social consequences of growing up in a poor neighborhood. In L. Lynn & M. McGeary (Eds.), *Inner-city poverty in the United States* (pp. 111–186). Washington, DC: National Academy Press.

Jordan, M. (1987a, March 29). Lack of housing changes the course of people's lives. *The Washington Post,* p. A16.

Jordan, M. (1987b, March 29). Renovations come and residents go: Poor left with few options. *The Washington Post,* pp. A1, A16–17.

Kaplan, S., Landa, B., Weinhold, C., & Shenker, I. (1984). Adverse health behaviors and depressive symptomatology in adolescents. *Journal of the American Academy of Child Psychiatry, 23*(5), 595–601.

Kasl, S. V., & Harburg, E. (1975). Mental health and the urban environment: Some doubts and second thoughts. *Journal of Health and Social Behavior, 16*(3), 268–282.

Kellam, S., Ensminger, M. E., & Turner, R. (1977). Family structure and the mental health of children. *Archives of General Psychiatry, 34*(9), 1012–1022.

Kessler, R., & Neighbors, H. (1986). A new perspective on the relationships among race, social class, and psychological distress. *Journal of Health and Social Behavior, 27*(2), 107–115.

Klerman, L. (1991). The health of poor children: Problems and programs. In A. Huston (Ed.), *Children in poverty: Child development and public policy* (pp. 136–157). Cambridge, England: Cambridge University Press.

Kotlowitz, A. (1991). *There are no children here.* New York: Doubleday.

Kriesberg, L. (1970). *Mothers in poverty: A study of fatherless families.* Chicago: Aldine.

Leahy, R. L. (1990). The development of concepts of economic and social inequality. In V. C. McLoyd & C. Flanagan (Eds.), *New directions for child development. Economic stress: Effects on family life and child development* (Vol. 46, pp. 107–120). San Francisco: Jossey-Bass.

Lempers, J., Clark-Lempers, D., & Simons, R. (1989). Economic hardship, parenting, and distress in adolescence. *Child Development, 60*(1), 25–49.

Lewis, D. A., & Maxfield, M. G. (1980). Fear in the neighborhoods: An investigation of the impact of crime. *Journal of Research in Crime and Delinquency, 17*, 160–189.

Liem, R., & Liem, J. (1978). Social class and mental illness reconsidered: The role of economic stress and social support. *Journal of Health and Social Behavior, 19*(2), 139–156.

Lurie, O. R. (1974). Parents' attitudes toward children's problems and toward use of mental health services: Socioeconomic differences. *American Journal of Orthopsychiatry, 44*(1), 109–120.

Marshall, N. (1982). The public welfare system: Regulation and dehumanization. In D. Belle (Ed.), *Lives in stress: Women and depression* (pp. 96–108). Beverly Hills, CA: Sage.

Mayer, S., & Jencks, C. (1988). Poverty and the distribution of material hardship. *Journal of Human Resources, 24*, 88–113.

McLeod, J. (1987). *Ain't no makin' it: Leveled aspirations in a low-income neighborhood.* Boulder, CO: Westview Press.

McLeod, J., & Shanahan, M. (1993). Poverty, parenting, and children's mental health. *American Sociological Review, 58*(3), 351–366.

McLoyd, V. C. (1989). Socialization and development in a changing economy. *American Psychologist, 44*(2), 293–302.

McLoyd, V. C. (1990). The impact of economic hardship on black families and children: Psychological distress, parenting, and socioemotional development. *Child Development, 61*(2), 311–346.

McLoyd, V. C. (1995). Poverty, parenting, and policy: Meeting the support needs of poor parents. In H. Fitzgerald, B. Lester, & B. Zuckerman (Eds.), *Children of poverty: Research, health, and policy issues* (pp. 269–303). New York: Garland.

McLoyd, V. C., Ceballo, R., & Mangelsdorf, S. (in press). The effects of poverty on children's socioemotional development. In J. Noshpitz (Ed.), *Handbook of child and adolescent psychiatry.* New York: Basic Books.

McLoyd, V. C., Jayaratne, T., Ceballo, R., & Borquez, J. (1994). Unemployment and work interruption among African-American single mothers: Effects on parenting and adolescent socioemotional functioning. *Child Development, 65*, 562–589.

McLoyd, V. C., & Wilson, L. (1990). Maternal behavior, social support, and economic conditions as predictors of psychological distress in children. In V. C. McLoyd & C. Flanagan (Eds.), *New directions for child development. Economic stress: Effects on family life and child development* (Vol. 46, pp. 49–69). San Francisco: Jossey-Bass.

Mueller, C., & Parcel, T. (1981). Measures of socioeconomic status: Alternatives and recommendations. *Child Development, 52*(1), 13–30.

Patterson, G. (1988). Stress: A change agent for family process. In N. Garmezy & M. Rutter (Eds.), *Stress, coping and development in children* (pp. 235–264). Baltimore: Johns Hopkins University Press.

Pelton, L. H. (1989). *For reasons of poverty: A critical analysis of the public child welfare system in the United States.* New York: Praeger.

Pryor-Brown, L., Cowen, E., Hightower, A., & Lotyczewski, B. (1986). Demographic differences among children in judging and experiencing specific stressful life events. *Journal of Special Education, 20*, 339–346.

Pryor-Brown, L., Powell, J., & Earls, F. (1989). Stressful life events and psychiatric symptoms in black adolescent females. *Journal of Adolescent Research, 4*(2), 140–151.

Richman, N., Stevenson, J., & Graham, P. (1975). Prevalence of behavior problems in three-year-old children: An epidemiological study in a London borough. *Journal of Child Psychology and Psychiatry, 16*(4), 277–287.

Rist, R. (1970). Student social class and teacher expectations: The self-fulfilling prophecy in ghetto education. *Harvard Educational Review, 40*(3), 411–451.

Rosenberg, M., & Pearlin, L. (1978). Social class and self-esteem among children and adults. *American Journal of Sociology, 84*(1), 53–77.

Rutter, M. (1979). Protective factors in children's responses to stress and disadvantage. In M. Kent & J. Rolf (Eds.), *Primary prevention of psychopathology* (pp. 49–74). Hanover, NH: University Press of New England.

Rutter, M. (1985). Resilience in the face of adversity: Protective factors and resistance to psychiatric disorder. *British Journal of Psychiatry, 147*, 598–611.

Rutter, M. (1990). Psychosocial resilience and protective mechanisms. In J. Rolf, A. S. Masten, D. Cicchetti, K. Nuechterlein, & S. Weintraub (Eds.), *Risk and protective factors in the development of psychopathology* (pp. 181–215). Cambridge, England: Cambridge University Press.

Sandler, I. N., & Block, M. (1979). Life stress and maladaptation of children. *American Journal of Community Psychology, 7*(4), 425–440.

Schoenbach, V., Kaplan, B., Wagner, E., Grimson, R., & Miller, F. (1983). Prevalence of self-reported depressive symptoms in young adolescents. *American Journal of Public Health, 73*, 1281–1287.

Schorr, L. (1989). *Within our reach: Breaking the cycle of disadvantage.* New York: Doubleday.

Sennett, R., & Cobb, J. (1972). *The hidden injuries of class.* New York: Vintage.

Shaw, D., & Emery, R. (1988). Chronic family adversity and school-age children's adjustment. *Journal of the American Academy of Child and Adolescent Psychiatry, 27*(2), 200–206.

Starfield, B., Gross, E., Wood, M., Pantell, R., Allen, C., Gordon, I. B., Moffat, P., Drachman, R., & Katz, H. (1980). Psychological and psychosomatic diagnosis in primary care of children. *Pediatrics, 66*, 159–167.

Steinberg, L., Mounts, N., Lamborn, S., & Dornbusch, S. (1991). Authoritative parenting and adolescent adjustment across varied ecological niches. *Journal of Research on Adolescence, 1*(1), 19–36.

Sterling, S., Cowen, E. L., Weissberg, R. P., Lotyczewski, B. S., & Boike, M. (1985). Recent stressful life events and young children's school adjustment. *American Journal of Community Psychology, 13*, 87–98.

Stevenson, J., Richman, N., & Graham, P. (1985). Behaviour problems and language abilities at three years and behavioural deviance at eight years. *Journal of Child Psychology and Psychiatry, 26*(2), 215–230.

Tienda, M. (1991). Poor people and poor places: Deciphering neighborhood effects on poverty outcomes. In J. Huber (Ed.), *Macro-micro linkages in sociology* (pp. 244–262). Newbury Park, CA: Sage.

Timnick, L. (1989, September 3). Children of violence. *Los Angeles Times Magazine*, 6–15.

Weinraub, M., & Wolf, B. (1983). Effects of stress and social supports on mother–child interactions in single- and two-parent families. *Child Development, 54*(5), 1297–1311.

Werner, E. (1984). Resilient children. *Young Children, 40*(1), 68–72.

White, M., Kasl, S. V., Zahner, G., & Will, J. C. (1987). Perceived crime in the neighborhood and mental health of women and children. *Environment and Behavior, 19*(5), 588–613.

Wilson, W. J. (1987). *The truly disadvantaged: The inner city, the underclass, and public policy.* Chicago: University of Chicago Press.

Wiltfang, G., & Scarbecz, M. (1990). Social class and adolescents' self-esteem: Another look. *Social Psychology Quarterly, 53*(2), 174–183.

Wolock, I., & Horowitz, B. (1979). Child maltreatment and material deprivation among AFDC recipient families. *Social Service Review, 53*, 175–194.

Zinsmeister, K. (1990, June). Growing up scared. *The Atlantic Monthly*, 49–66.

Zur-Szpiro, S., & Longfellow, C. (1982). Fathers' support to mothers and children. In D. Belle (Ed.), *Lives in stress: Women and depression* (pp. 145–153). Beverly Hills, CA: Sage.

3

The Effects of Economic and Social Stressors on Parenting and Adolescent Adjustment in African-American Families

Ronald D. Taylor

Stressful life experiences affect the lives of a substantial number of African-American children. In 1991, Census figures indicated that 51.2% of African-American children 6 years of age and under were poor (U.S. Bureau of the Census, 1992). For many of these children, poverty will be a persistent experience; research reveals that about 24% of children who are poor early in life will experience poverty when they are 10–14 years old (Duncan & Rodgers, 1988). Being poor exposes children and families to a variety of chronic stressors that have been shown to negatively influence the functioning of individuals. Chronic stressors experienced by poor African-American parents can undermine their parenting practices because poor parents are psychologically distressed (McLoyd, 1990). Children and adolescents exposed to less adequate parenting are at risk for a number of psychological and behavioral problems (Aber & Cicchetti, 1984; Egeland & Sroufe, 1981; McLoyd, Jayaratne, Ceballo, & Borquez, 1994). Research also indicates that poor families employ a variety of strategies and living arrangements designed to moderate the effects of poverty. These strategies may include the sharing or pooling of resources across extended families, the sharing of childrearing, or coresidence, among other possibilities (McLoyd, 1990).

This chapter first characterizes the nature of some of the chronic stressors experienced by poor African-American families, then discusses the impact of the stressors on adolescent functioning. Finally, the processes linking stressors to adolescent adjustment are addressed. The conceptual model underlying this chapter is shown in Fig. 3.1. In the model, stressors such as financial strain or neighborhood crime have an effect on adolescent socioemotional adjustment through their impact on parents' well-being and parenting practices. Parents living in the context of financial hardship and neighborhood problems may be more psychologically distressed, and,

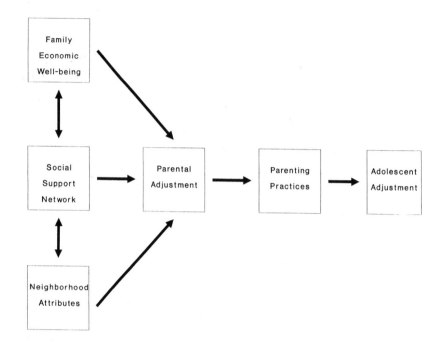

FIG. 3.1. Conceptual model of the linkage of stressors and social support
with adolescent adjustment.

hence, less able or inclined to engage in more adequate parenting. Diminished quality of parenting may have adverse effects on adolescents. Social support is expected to enhance adolescents' well-being through its positive effects on parental well-being and parenting behavior. Social support may also moderate the negative effects of stressors on parents and adolescents.

FAMILY ECONOMIC HARDSHIP

Of the 86% of African Americans living in metropolitan areas, most (56%) live in the inner city as opposed to suburban areas. Most poor African Americans live in urban areas (73%). But the poverty rate is even higher for African-American families living in nonmetropolitan areas (40%) than for those living in metropolitan areas (32%). Given the high rate of poverty among African-American families, it is not surprising that those cities with the highest percentage of African-American children also tend to be the cities with the highest percentage of poor children (Children's Defense Fund, 1992).

As mentioned earlier, 25% of African-American children who are poor early in life spend most of their childhood and adolescence in poverty. African-American children are more likely than White children to fall into poverty as a consequence of events that lead to a reduction in family income, such as divorce, work cutbacks, or family illness (Duncan, 1988). Poverty among African-American children is associated with their living arrangements, in that 12% of African-American married-couple families are poor, whereas 50% of African-American female-headed households, and 30% of African-American male-headed households are poor.

African-American families also face a higher level of job uncertainty than White families, caused by such factors as lower levels of education, less job seniority, and the movement of jobs from the central cities to suburban and outlying areas (McLoyd, 1990). It comes as no surprise that poor African-American families also live in neighborhoods lacking in social and financial resources. Indeed, Wilson (1987) documented the transformation of some urban neighborhoods from ones that included middle-class, working-class, and poor Blacks, to communities made up almost exclusively of poor African-American families. Economic shifts in urban areas have resulted not only in jobs leaving the city, but also in increasing educational requirements for the jobs that remain or move into the cities. There has also been a population migration away from central cities to suburban areas (Massey & Denton, 1991). This migration has decreased the tax base and the political influence of urban areas, leading to a decrease in social resources to address a rising number of urban problems.

Wilson (1987) noted that many urban neighborhoods are populated by poor African-American families who tend to also be young. The overall age of urban residents and the concentration of young people in certain neighborhoods is an important matter. Age is significantly related to crime, out-of-wedlock births, female-headed homes, and welfare dependency (Wilson, 1990). After a critical mass has been reached or surpassed, youngsters, particularly adolescents and young adults with a high number of problems, may tax the neighborhood's limited resources.

Economic Hardship and Adolescent Functioning

Findings from a number of investigations have shown that economic strain is associated with a variety of socioemotional problems in both childhood and adolescence. Indeed, poverty has been associated with problems in peer relations (Langner, Herson, Greene, Jameson, & Goff, 1970), depression (Gibbs, 1986), somatic symptoms (McLoyd, 1990), and conduct disorders, as well as social maladaptation and psychological disorders (Kellam, Ensminger, & Turner, 1977; Myers & King, 1983). Specific findings have shown that family income is associated with children's neurotic, psychotic, and sociopathic symptomatology. Across a number of investigations research has shown that family income is associated with the quality of adolescents' relations with their peers. Elder's research (Elder, 1974; Elder, Van Nguyen, & Caspi, 1985) on families experiencing the Great Depression revealed that mothers in families experiencing deprivation were likely to report that their adolescents had emotional problems. Further, Conger and his associates (Conger, Conger, Elder, Lorenz, Simons, & Whitbeck,1992) have shown that family income is linked to adolescent school performance and self-confidence.

Recent work has also examined the impact of parental employment on family functioning (Flanagan & Eccles, 1993). This work shows a positive association of unstable employment with disruptive behavior by adolescents and low rating of competence by teachers.

Neighborhood Effects on Adolescent Adjustment

There is a growing body of research examining the impact of living in stressful neighborhoods on adolescent functioning. A number of investigations have assessed the effects of living in neighborhoods characterized by high levels of unemployment and poverty on adolescent functioning. This research consistently shows that living in stressful neighborhoods is linked to adolescent problem behaviors. For example, Brooks-Gunn and associates (Brooks-Gunn, Duncan, Klebanov, & Sealand, 1993) and Hogan and Kitagawa (1985) showed that living in a neighborhood with a high proportion of poor families increases a youngster's likelihood of becoming pregnant. Crane (1991) showed that the dropout and pregnancy rates for teenagers increases dramatically as the proportion of high-status workers in neighborhoods declines. However, it is unclear which processes mediate the association of stressful circumstances in the neighborhood and adolescent functioning. Anderson (1991) suggested that adolescents' perceptions of their life chances and the nature and quality of youngsters' peer relations may explain the links between neighborhoods and adolescent outcomes. He maintains that to the extent that youngsters perceive that they have a constrained set of options and an accepting peer culture, teenage pregnancy is more likely.

In an ongoing study, Roberts and Taylor (1994b) have compared family functioning and adolescent adjustment in two types of urban neighborhoods. The first neighborhood is characterized by high levels of poverty and unemployment, declining community resources, and high crime linked to an active drug trade. The second neighborhood is middle class and characterized by clean streets, significantly lower crime, and availability of extensive resources. Both neighborhoods are predominantly African American. Parents and adolescents in both neighborhoods were interviewed concerning their perceptions of the neighborhood in terms of safety, physical condition, and access to important services (financial, medical, educational, civic). Parenting practices and styles were also assessed, as were adolescent and parental psychological well-being. Findings from the disadvantaged neighborhood show that the more that both parents and adolescents perceived the neighborhood as rundown and unsafe, the more adolescents reported lower self-esteem and higher psychological distress, including depression and anxiety.

In addition to examining the impact of economic resources and neighborhood factors and the links to family and adolescent functioning, it is also important to understand how stressful experiences linked to living in poverty or declining neighborhoods influence individuals' functioning. For example, poor families may face an unremitting series of stressful events, including frequent changes of residence, poor health, and marital discord, among others. These stressful life experiences may, indeed, mediate the relationship between economic resources, neighborhood quality, and adolescent functioning. Indeed, research has indicated that there is a link between individuals' financial well-being and the experience of stressful events (Dohrewend, 1970; Gad & Johnson, 1980). Further, stressful experiences have been linked to mental health problems, trouble with the law, and school adjustment problems (Masten, Nemann, & Andenas, 1994), as well as psychological distress (Taylor, Roberts, & Jacobson, 1995). Taylor et al. found that among poor families, stressful events in the areas of interpersonal relations (marital problems, family conflict) and family disruption (frequent moves, death in the family) are associated with adolescent psychological distress.

Recent research (Roberts & Taylor, 1994a) assessed the association between family stress, parenting practices, parental adjustment, and adolescent adjustment in families living below the poverty threshold. Findings revealed that mothers' health problems and marital problems are negatively associated with adolescents' sense of autonomy and self-reliance. These findings indicate the need to examine how stressful events that may be common experiences for disadvantaged adolescents and their families operate to undermine their coping capacities.

Social Support and Adolescent Adjustment

Discussing the association of social support with family stressors and adolescent adjustment is important because there is extensive discussion of the role of social support in moderating the effects of stressful experiences on minority families. However, research on the association of parents' social network with African-American adolescents' adjustment is scarce—despite the extensive literature arguing for the importance of kinship support as a culturally distinctive feature of family life (e.g., Aschennbrener, 1973; Billingsley, 1968; Hill, 1978; McAdoo, 1982). Empirical work has shown that adults and younger children benefit from the availability of an extended kin network (Dressler, 1985; Kellam, Adams, Brown, & Ensminger, 1982). For example, Dressler found that although economic strain is associated with increased support from kin, kin support is associated with lower levels of depression. Research has shown that African-American teenage mothers display more adequate parenting and better adjustment when assistance from kin is present (Colletta, 1981; Furstenberg & Crawford, 1978).

In research assessing the impact of kinship social and emotional support on adolescent psychological well-being, Taylor and colleagues (Taylor, Casten, & Flickinger, 1993; Taylor & Roberts, 1995) have found a positive link between support and several indices of adjustment. Specifically, in a number of investigations, a conceptual model was assessed that suggests that social support from kin enhances family functioning. Also, as families function more adequately, adolescents, in turn, are expected to be more well adjusted. To test the model, we first assessed a sample of working-class African-American adolescents for kinship social support, parents' parenting style, and adolescent adjustment. Findings revealed that for single-parent families, kinship support is positively associated with adolescents' self-reliance and negatively associated with problem behavior. Thus, in the context of support, adolescents report less dependency on others and less involvement in delinquent activities.

In a second investigation of the model, economically disadvantaged African-American mothers and their adolescents were interviewed. The families all had incomes below the poverty threshold, and the majority reported receiving some form of public assistance. The results revealed that the more support from kin that mothers received, the more the adolescents, in turn, displayed higher levels of self-reliance and fewer problem behaviors.

Summary

One half of African-American children are poor and many will remain poor for most of their childhood. African-American families who are poor and live in metropolitan areas increasingly tend to live in urban-area communities that have seen a rise in the concentration of poor, young residents and a decline in working- and middle-class families. The rising concentration of poor, young residents and the diminution of financial and social resources are linked to negative changes in the characteristics of the neighborhoods. Economic hardship, neighborhood problems, and stressful experiences all are associated with adjustment problems for adolescents, including mental health and school adjustment problems and problems in peer relations. Finally, social support may offset potential problems of poor adolescents by enhancing opportunities for beneficial experiences.

ECONOMIC HARDSHIP, PARENTAL WELL-BEING, AND PARENTING PRACTICES

In the conceptual model we have examined, it is proposed that stressors such as poverty or dangerous neighborhoods affect adolescents through their impact on parents. Thus, parents living in the context of these stressors are expected to exhibit less adequate parenting and poorer psychological adjustment. A substantial body of evidence suggests that economic hardship has a negative influence on individuals' psychological functioning and on the quality of family relationships (Conger, Ge, Elder, Lorenz, & Simons, 1994; Conger et al., 1992; Lempers, Clark-Lempers, & Simons, 1989; McLoyd, 1990; McLoyd, Jayaratne, Ceballo, & Borquez, 1994). Research has shown that economic hardship is associated with a variety of forms of psychological distress (Conger et al., 1994; Dressler, 1985; Liem & Liem, 1978; McLoyd et al., 1994; McLoyd & Wilson, 1990).

McLoyd (1990) has suggested that among the factors responsible for the elevated mental health problems in the poor are the large number of frustrating events and conditions that are beyond the individual's control. She argued that the poor are exposed to an "unremitting succession of negative life events" (e.g, criminal assault, illness) while living in the context of chronically stressful living circumstances (unsafe neighborhoods, poor housing). Indeed, a number of researchers have found a positive association between economic hardship and depression (Conger et al., 1994; Dressler, 1985; McLoyd et al., 1994). Conger et al. (1992) found that among families living in rural areas hard hit by the crisis in the agricultural economy, to the extent that parents perceived that they did not have resources to either pay their bills or meet their family's material needs, both mothers and fathers reported higher levels of depression. Research has also revealed a correlation between economic hardship and marital discord (Bishop, 1977; Furstenberg, 1976).

In addition to the association of economic disadvantage with parental emotional distress, job loss and unemployment (from which African Americans suffer disproportionately) have been linked to a variety of psychological and emotional problems, including: somatic complaints, neurosis, psychoticism, and suicide (see McLoyd, 1990 for a review). For example, McLoyd et al. (1994) found that unemployment was positively associated with depressive symptomatology in a sample of single African-American mothers. Others have also shown that job loss is associated with sadness and depression in African-American men and women (Brown & Gary, 1988; Thompson & Ensminger, 1989). Galambos and Silbereisen (1987) showed a link between income loss and pessimism about life.

Other research has focused on the effects of families' economic prospects on parents' child-rearing practices. This research shows that, like the effects of economic resources on parental functioning, the *lack* of economic resources has an adverse effect on parents' relations with their children. Economic hardship has been linked to diminished emotional support and harsh parenting (Conger, McCarty, Yang, Lahey, & Kropp, 1984; Dodge, Pettit, & Bates, 1994; McLoyd, 1988). For example, Conger et al. found that being on public assistance was negatively associated with the percentage of time mothers spent in positive interaction (supportive statements, praise, hugs, kisses) with their children, and positively associated with the amount of time spent in negative interaction (derogatory statements, expressions of dislike, threats, slaps).

Recent work suggests that there is, indeed, a link between parents' distress caused by economic difficulties and parents' child-rearing practices (Conger et al., 1984; Conger et al., 1992; Ge, Conger, Lorenz, & Simons, 1994). Specifically, it is proposed that stressors, such as financial problems, negatively affect parents' psychological distress, and parents' distress, in turn, is associated with less adequate parenting. Support for the model has shown that stressors including financial problems are associated with parents' depressed moods, which are positively linked to harsh, inconsistent parenting (Ge et al., 1994). The links between financial difficulties, parental distress, and less adequate parenting have been most clearly demonstrated with rural White families. Less work has been done with African-American families. McLoyd et al. (1994) found that among single African-American mothers, unemployment is associated with depression, which is associated with harsh parenting and negative perceptions of the maternal role. In research among rural African-American two-parent families, it has been shown that families with more resources report greater optimism and low depression. Higher optimism and low depression are associated with greater mutual support among parents and low conflict concerning care giving (Brody, Stoneman, Flor, McCrary, Hastings, & Conyer, 1994).

Neighborhoods and Parental Well-Being and Parenting Practices

There is a scarcity of research linking neighborhood or community context and parental adjustment and parenting practices. Rutter's research (Rutter, 1981; Rutter & Quinton, 1977) on the adjustment of children in inner-city London and on the Isle of Wight revealed that inner-city life is associated with adversities that affect children through the impact on family functioning. Rutter and Quinton found that a key difference between children in the two regions was the rate of depression among mothers. Ecological sources for the difference include high overcrowding in the home and higher unemployment in London than on the Isle of Wight.

It is important to note, however, that little of the work on neighborhood effects has directly examined the impact of important characteristics of a family's neighborhood (safety, availability of resources, integration vs. isolation) on parents' well-being and parenting practices. Furstenberg's (1993) work comes closest to assessing the direct links between parents' behavior and the quality of the community. This research has shown that families living in "cohesive" urban neighborhoods—that is, those with extensive social and financial resources, and with shared values and social trust among residents—tend to make use of a variety of agents in the community to facilitate youngsters' socialization. Parents in these neighborhoods look to other residents to report on their child or adolescent's behavior when away from their supervision, and also rely on resources within the community to expose their youngsters to opportunities for social and educational growth and stimulation.

In contrast are those families living in *anomic communities*, in which social and financial resources are impoverished and shared values and social trust are low. Families living in these neighborhoods, possibly perceiving the environment to be unsafe and the risk of exploitation high, tend to restrict their adolescents' contact with others in the community. Indeed, parents may use confinement as a strategy for ensuring their adolescents' safety and may look outside the neighborhood to develop their youngsters' social networks. It is expected that parents' well-being is enhanced in cohesive neighborhoods and that they are, thus, more likely to display better parenting practices.

Garbarino and Sherman (1980) have shown that the neighborhoods of families at high and low risk of child abuse differ in important ways. High-risk neighborhoods are less stable, suffer from greater physical deterioration, and have more crime and sources of nuisance (problem bars, vandalized buildings). These areas also have higher rates of social problems including alcoholism, mental health problems, poor nutrition, and a higher infant mortality rate.

Roberts and Taylor's (1994b) recent work examining parents' perceptions of their neighborhood and the relationship to their parenting practices complements the findings of Furstenberg and Garbarino and Sherman. Findings from families living in disadvantaged neighborhoods again show that the more mothers perceive their neighborhood to be physically deteriorated and unsafe, the more depressed they are, the less accepting they are, and the less they encourage mature behavior.

Social Support and Parental Well-Being and Parenting Practices

Families tend to seek support from relatives in times of need, and that support has important implications for family functioning. Research discussed earlier has shown a positive association between kinship support, economic difficulties, and adult functioning (e.g., Dressler, 1985). Dressler revealed that kin social support is associated with lower depression. Also, for men, those with social support are less depressed by stressful life events than those lacking support. Tietjen and Bradley (1982), meanwhile, found that mothers who had access to a stronger social support network during pregnancy report lower levels of stress, anxiety, and depression, and are more positive about their pregnancies. Similarly, McLoyd et al. (1994) revealed that among single, African-American mothers with adolescents, social support is negatively associated with maternal depression. Also, Taylor and Roberts (in press) found a positive association of social support with maternal self-esteem.

Social support has also been linked to parents' child-rearing behaviors. For instance, studies have shown that help from relatives is associated with more positive maternal attitudes (Colletta, 1983; Colletta & Lee, 1983) and more adequate parenting behaviors (Wandersman & Unger, 1983). In other research using both adolescents and parents as respondents, findings have shown that support from relatives is linked to parental attitudes and practices associated with adolescent adjustment. Specifically, across a number of studies (Taylor, 1994; Taylor et al., 1993; Taylor & Roberts, in press) it was revealed that in the context of kinship social support, African-American parents are more accepting, monitor adolescent behavior more firmly, and manage the home more effectively. For example, Taylor found that the more kinship support parents received, the more organized and structured is the home, and the more involved parents are in adolescents' schooling. Thus, in the context of social support, parents are more likely to structure the home environment around a clear schedule (e.g., provide regular meal, bed, and homework times) and are more likely to be involved in adolescents' schooling in ways that span from helping with homework to attending school functions. Taylor et al. (1993) also found that in single-parent families, kinship support is positively associated with authoritative parenting, a parenting style that consists of a high degree of acceptance, firm control and supervision, and encouragement of mature behavior.

In similar research, McLoyd et al. (1994) showed that the availability of social support is negatively associated with maternal punishment (scolding, yelling, hitting) and with mothers' negative perceptions of the maternal role. Hashima and Amato (1994), working with younger children, found that to the extent that low-income parents perceive available social support, they are less likely to exhibit punitive behaviors (yelling, slapping, spanking). Further, to the degree that parents have received help in the previous month, they are less likely to report unsupportive parental behavior (denying their children praise, or not hugging or cuddling). Work has also shown that for families, social isolation is positively associated with child abuse (Corse, Schmid, & Trickett, 1990; Garbarino, 1976; Garbarino & Sherman, 1980). For example, Garbarino and Sherman found that among families living in areas at high risk for child abuse, families have little available in the way of social networks, and make limited use of the constrained social resources present in their community.

Summary

Evidence suggests that financial problems have a negative impact on parents' emotional state and outlook on life. Parents experiencing financial difficulties and employment problems are more likely to report sadness, anxiety, and depression, and are more doubtful about the future. Research also suggests that parental depression and sadness related to financial matters spills over into their relations with their children—parental depression is associated with harsher punishment and dissatisfaction with the maternal role for mothers. Findings regarding the impact of neighborhoods on parents' well-being and parenting practices are scarce, but have shown that neighborhoods can be differentiated in terms of their financial and social resources; in short, parents in neighborhoods with abundant resources are in a better position to act on their children's behalf.

Further, neighborhood crime and physical deterioration are positively associated with parent depression and less adequate parenting. Finally, findings on the effects of social support have shown that in times of need, individuals receive assistance from support networks. Social support is positively linked to individuals' mental health and also buffers them from the effects of stressful experiences. The availability of social support is associated with more adequate parenting, whereas social isolation is associated with child abuse.

PARENTAL WELL-BEING AND PARENTING PRACTICES AND ADOLESCENT ADJUSTMENT

In our conceptual model, parenting practices and parents' psychological well-being are the variables that mediate the association of stressors with adolescent functioning. Thus, if our model is appropriate, we must be able to show that parents' child-rearing practices and parents' own adjustment are, indeed, linked to adolescent adjustment and competence.

A growing body of research has examined the linkage of parenting styles and practices with indices of adolescent adjustment. In the areas of parenting styles, the impact of authoritative parenting on measures of adjustment has been examined. Steinberg, Mounts, Lamborn, and Dornbusch (1991) assessed the effects of authoritative parenting on adolescents' grades, self-reliance, psychological distress, and delinquency. The findings revealed that African-American adolescents in working-class and middle-class homes are more likely to report feelings of self-reliance and independence, and are less likely to engage in delinquent activities, to the extent that their homes were authoritative. Similarly, Taylor et al. (1993) found that among female-headed, working-class, African-American families, authoritative parenting is also associated with self-reliance and lack of problem behavior. It has also been shown that among poor African-American families, parental acceptance and firm behavioral control (two components of authoritative parenting) are significantly linked to adolescent adjustment (Taylor & Roberts, in press).

It is important to note, however, that although authoritative parenting has been linked to adjustment among African-American adolescents, authoritativeness is not a prevalent style among African-American families. Indeed, in the work of Steinberg et al. (1991) just 12% of African-American families were authoritative. It has been suggested (Baldwin & Baldwin, 1989; Baumrind, 1972) that African-American parents may employ a more restrictive, authoritarian style of parenting aimed at protecting their children from the dangers of urban life. This more restrictive style is thought to enhance adolescents' adjustment. There are only limited findings to support the argument for the beneficial effects of authoritarian parenting. Baumrind found that authoritarian parenting is associated with independence and assertiveness for girls, but is not related to school achievement. Fletcher (1994) found that authoritarian parenting is associated with boys' school achievement.

Finally, other research relevant to the impact of parenting styles on adolescent adjustment has shown that maternal affection and communication of mothers' goals for children are associated with younger children's school success (Slaughter, 1977). Also, harsh punishment is positively associated with adolescent depression and cognitive distress—for example, difficulty making decisions and remembering things (McLoyd et al., 1994) and conduct problems (Dodge, Pettit, & Bates, 1994). Among White working and middle-class adolescents, inconsistent and punitive discipline is also associated with delinquency and drug use (Lempers, Clark-Lempers, & Simons, 1989). Brody et al. (1994) found that mutual caregiving support for mothers and fathers is linked to adolescents' self-regulation (concentration, patience, and planful behavior of tasks). Adolescents' self-regulation, in turn, is associated with higher academic performance, fewer conduct problems, and lower depression.

Additional parenting behaviors relevant to parenting style may be related to parents' racial socialization. Peters (1985) argued that African-American parents, in preparing their children for the likely experience of racism, actively seek to inoculate them by enhancing their racial self-perceptions and self-esteem. Bowman and Howard (1985) found that to the extent that parents socialize their youngsters to be aware of racism and racial barriers, the adolescents perform better in school.

Other research on parenting practices suggests that parents' family management practices may be linked to adolescent adjustment. For example, Clark (1983) in an ethnographic investigation of the factors that distinguish the homes of high- versus low-achieving, low-income African-American adolescents, found that parents of the former work to structure and monitor the adolescents' time and activities by establishing daily and weekly routines and schedules. These parents also actively monitor the adolescents' schooling through help with homework and attendance at school functions. In research on the impact of African-American family management practices on adolescent behavior, Taylor (1994) found that family organization and parental involvement in schooling are significantly linked to adolescent adjustment (self-reliance and problem behavior) and competence (grades in school).

These findings clearly indicate that many of the parenting behaviors that may be compromised by family stress (parental warmth, family organization, parental accessibility) are also behaviors and practices linked to adolescents' well-being.

Summary

Research suggests that authoritative parenting is positively associated with adjustment across ethnic groups, including African-American families. However, authoritativeness is not prevalent in African-American homes. Some research suggests that authoritarian parenting, which may result from the harsh conditions in which many African-American families live, is linked to some areas of adjustment. Research on other aspects of parenting style has revealed that warmth, communication of child-rearing goals, and communication about racism is positively associated with school performance. In comparison, harsh and inconsistent discipline is associated with a variety of adolescent problems, including depression and conduct disorder. Parenting practices aimed at creating order and structure in the home are positively linked to adolescent adjustment and school achievement.

CONCLUSIONS AND IMPLICATIONS

Stressors in a variety of forms (financial strain, neighborhood crime, social isolation) are negatively associated with adolescent adjustment because they have a negative influence on parental adjustment and parenting practices. Some evidence suggests that parents are emotionally distressed by stressors and, in turn, are less warm and more harsh and inconsistent in their relationship with their adolescent. Adolescents facing parents who are less warm, more severe, and less predictable are more likely to engage in problem behavior, to be more dependent, and to be more depressed.

It is important to note that, for the sake of clarity and simplicity, the factors related to stressful experiences (economic well-being, neighborhood quality, social support) were largely considered separately. However, it is clear that these factors are highly interconnected. Thus, families' economic resources will largely determine the kind of neighborhood in which they reside. Also, the qualities of a neighborhood or community are likely to influence families' economic well-being in a number of ways. Neighborhoods known to be dangerous are not likely to attract businesses or industries that might provide employment opportunities. In neighborhoods with poor-quality schools, parents may expend substantial financial resources sending their children to private or parochial schools. In addition, the quality of a neighborhood both affects and is affected by social support networks. In neighborhoods with strong support networks the functioning of parents and their children may be enhanced, thereby enhancing the community's general level of functioning. However, as Furstenberg (1990) showed, the qualities of a neighborhood (crime, shared trust) may determine whether support networks will be viable and sustaining. Clearly, to fully understand the manner in which stressors affect families requires complex, multi-factored models that consider the possibility of both unidirectional and bidirectional relations of the factors.

From a social policy standpoint, the work reviewed here suggests a number of imperatives. First, improving the financial well-being of disadvantaged African-American families is highly important. Locating jobs and educational services in communities that have seen the exodus of businesses and industries to largely unavailable sites, is critically important. Massey and Denton (1993) noted that improving the economic standing of poor African Americans must be combined with improving neighborhood environments by decreasing the concentration of serious problems. Further, there is currently a mismatch between the education and skills of many of the urban poor and jobs paying substantially more than minimum wage. The dilemma centers around increasing the wage rate of available jobs and/or increasing the skills of low-income, poor African Americans while improving the quality of neighborhoods.

Second, decreasing the social isolation and building the social networks of poor African-American families is also important. Research suggests that social support may have a positive impact on families and adolescents by enhancing their experiences and buffering the negative effects of stressors. Possible centers for building families' social networks include schools, churches, and community centers. Experimental programs in some urban areas have sought to support nearby neighborhoods by allowing important services (medical care, child care, adult education) to be administered on the school grounds. An important feature of a successful intervention in schools serving poor, African-American children and families has been the building of parent networks to work with the schools (Comer, 1988). Finally, as McLoyd (Chap. 2, this volume) notes, it is important that efforts at improving the conditions of the poor be comprehensive. Thus, interventions aimed at improving the conditions of poor families should address the financial state of a community, but should also consider the need for social resources and supportive networks while also examining ways of reducing neighborhood problems such as crime, high mortality rates, and poor health care.

In terms of the directions for future research, there are a number of areas requiring further work. First, more needs to be known about processes that link stressful experiences to parental and adolescent adjustment. Although stressors typically lead to distress, and distress to poorer functioning, this is not true for all individuals. For some, stressors have seemingly little impact on their psychological functioning (Masten, 1994). Work needs to be done to examine how factors such as age, gender, or temperament may influence parents' and adolescents' reactions to stressful experiences.

Second, more research is needed on the manner in which neighborhood characteristics affect family and adolescent adjustment. Much of the work on neighborhoods is still largely descriptive, documenting differences between families living in high-risk versus low-risk communities. Work should focus on identifying the key qualities of neighborhoods that influence family functioning. It may be that effects of neighborhoods on adjustment happen at the level of such factors as excessive crowding or noise, or the lack of convenient services. Or, the important factors may exist at the level of amount of criminal behavior and violence, or the lack of adequate health care. Indeed, it is likely that a combination of factors at several levels and their cumulative effects determine family and adolescent functioning.

Also, it is important to explore additional variables that may mediate the association of neighborhood factors with adjustment. Although psychological distress and, in particular, depression has been a key variable linked to stressful experiences, many others are possible and should be examined. Variables such as irritability, anger, fearfulness, helplessness, or anxiety are all possible reactions to neighborhood stressors that may affect children directly or through their impact on parents.

Finally, normative data on typical patterns of behavior in poor and nonpoor African-American families is needed. Interventions to improve the circumstances of the less fortunate require, for example, an understanding of normative patterns of parenting behavior and their outcomes for adolescents. The development of this kind of information requires that we eschew comparative approaches with preconceptions about appropriate patterns of behavior, in favor of research designed to examine the conditions and functioning of a single population.

REFERENCES

Aber, J. L., & Cicchetti, D. (1984). The socioemotional development of maltreated children: An empirical and theoretical analysis. In H. Fitzgerald, B. Lester, & M. Yogman (Eds.), *Theory and research in behavioral pediatrics* (pp. 147–205). New York: Plenum.

Anderson, E. (1991). Neighborhood effects on teenage pregnancy. In C. Jencks & P. Peterson (Eds.), *The urban underclass* (pp. 28–102). Washington, DC: Brookings Institution.

Aschenbrenner, J. (1973). Extended families among Black Americans. *Journal of Comparative Family Studies, 4,* 257–268.

Baldwin, K., & Baldwin, A. (1989, April). *The role of family interaction in the prediction of adolescent competence.* Paper presented at the biennial meeting of the Society for Research on Child Development, Kansas City, MO.

Baumrind, D. (1972). An exploratory study of socialization effects on Black children: Some Black–White comparisons. *Child Development, 43*(1), 261–267.

Billingsley, A. (1968). *Black families in White America.* Englewood Cliffs, NJ: Prentice-Hall.

Bishop, J. (1977). *Jobs, cash transfer, and marital instability: A review of the evidence.* Madison: University of Wisconsin Institute for Research on Poverty.

Bowman, P., & Howard, C. (1985). Race-related socialization, motivation, and academic achievement: A study of black youth in three-generation families. *Journal of the American Academy of Child Psychiatry, 24*, 134–141.

Brody, G. H., Stoneman, Z., Flor, D., McCrary, C., Hastings, L., & Conyer, O. (1994). Financial resources, parent psychological functioning, parent co-caregiving, and early adolescent competence in rural two-parent African-American families. *Child Development, 65*(2), 590–605.

Brooks-Gunn, J., Duncan, G. J., Klebanov, P. K., & Sealand, N. (1993). Do neighborhoods influence child and adolescent development. *American Journal of Sociology, 99*, 353–395.

Brown, D. R., & Gary, L. E. (1988). Unemployment and psychological distress among Black American women. *Sociological Focus, 21*, 209–221.

Children's Defense Fund. (1992). *The state of America's children*. Washington, DC: Author.

Clark, R. (1983). *Family life and school achievement: Why poor Black children succeed or fail*. Chicago: University of Wisconsin Press.

Colletta, N. (1981). Social support and the risk of maternal rejection by adolescent mothers. *Journal of Psychology, 109*(2), 191–197.

Colletta, N., & Lee, D. (1983). The impact of support for black adolescent mothers. *Journal of Family Issues, 4*, 127–143.

Comer, J. P. (1988). *Maggie's American dream: The life and times of an American family*. New York: New American Library.

Conger, R. D., Conger, K. J., Elder, G. H., Lorenz, F. O., Simons, R. L., & Whitbeck, L. B. (1992). A family process model of economic hardship and adjustment of early adolescent boys. *Child Development, 63*(3), 526–541.

Conger, R. D., Ge, X., Elder, G. H., Lorenz, F. O., & Simons, R. L. (1994). Economic stress, coercive family process, and developmental problems of adolescents. *Child Development, 65*(2), 541–561.

Conger, R. D., McCarty, J., Yang, R., Lahey, B., & Kropp, J. (1984). Perception of child, child-rearing values, and emotional distress as mediating links between environmental stressors and observed maternal behavior. *Child Development, 55*(6), 2234–2247.

Corse, S. J., Schmid, K., & Trickett, P. K. (1990). Social network characteristics of mothers in abusing and nonabusing families and their relationships to parenting beliefs. *Journal of Community Psychology, 18*, 44–59.

Crane, J. (1991). The epidemic theory of ghettos and neighborhood effects on dropping out and teenage childbearing. *American Journal of Sociology, 96*, 1226–1259.

Dodge, K. A., Pettit, G. S., & Bates, J. E. (1994). Socialization mediators of the relation between socioeconomic status and child conduct problems. *Child Development, 65*(2), 649–665.

Dohrewend, B. S. (1970). Social class and stressful events. In E. H. Hare & J. K. Wing (Eds.), *Psychiatric Epidemiology* (pp. 313–319). New York: Oxford University Press.

Dressler, W. (1985). Extended family relationships, social support, and mental health in a southern black community. *Journal of Health and Social Behavior, 26*(1), 39–48.

Duncan, G. (1988). *The economic environment of childhood*. Paper presented at a study group meeting on poverty and children, University of Kansas, Lawrence.

Duncan, G., & Rodgers, W. (1987). Single-parent families: Are their economic problems transitory or persistent? *Family Planning Perspectives, 19*, 171–178.

Egeland, B., & Sroufe, A. (1981). Developmental sequelae of maltreatment in infancy. In L. Rizley & D. Cicchetti (Eds.), *New directions for child development: Vol. 11. Developmental perspectives on child maltreatment* (pp.77–92). San Francisco: Jossey-Bass.

Elder, G. H., Jr. (1974). *Children of the Great Depression*. Chicago: University of Chicago Press.

Elder, G. H., Jr., Van Nguyen, T., & Caspi, A. (1985). Linking family hardship to children's lives. *Child Development, 56*(2), 361–375.

Flanagan, C. A., & Eccles, J. S. (1993). Changes in parents' work status and adolescent adjustment in school. *Child Development, 64*, 246–257.

Fletcher, A. C. (1994). *Parental and peer influences on the academic achievement of African-American adolescents*. Unpublished doctoral dissertation, Temple University, Philadelphia.

Furstenberg, F. F. (1976). *Unplanned parenthood: The social consequences of teenage child bearing*. New York: The Free Press.

Furstenberg, F. F. (1990, August). *How families manage risk and opportunity in dangerous neighborhoods*. Paper presented at the annual meeting of the American Sociological Association, Washington, DC.

Furstenberg, F. F. (1993). How families manage risk and opportunity in dangerous neighborhoods. In W. J. Wilson (Ed.), *Sociology and the public agenda* (pp. 46–52). Newbury Park, CA; Sage.

Furstenberg, F. F., Brooks-Gunn, J., & Morgan, S. P. (1987). *Adolescent mothers in later life*. Cambridge, England: Cambridge University Press.

Furstenberg, F. F., & Crawford, D. B. (1978). Family support: Helping teenagers to cope. *Family Planning Perspectives, 11*, 322–333.

Gad, M., & Johnson, J. (1980). Correlates of adolescent life stresses related to race, SES, and levels of perceived social support. *Journal of Clinical Child Psychology, 9*, 13–16.

Galambos, N., & Silbereisen, R. (1987). Income change, parental life outlook, and adolescent expectations for job success. *Journal of Marriage and the Family, 49*(1), 141–149.

Garbarino, J. (1976). A preliminary study of some ecological correlates of child abuse: The impact of socioeconomic stress on mothers. *Child Development, 47*(1), 178–185.

Garbarino, J., & Sherman, D. (1980). High-risk neighborhoods and high-risk families: The human ecology of child maltreatment. *Child Development, 51*(1) 188–198.

Ge, X., Conger, R. D., Lorenz, F., & Simons, R. D. (1994). Parents' stress and adolescent depressive symptoms: Mediating processes. *Journal of Health and Social Behavior, 35*, 28–44.

Gibbs, J. (1986). Assessment of depression in urban adolescent females: Implications for early intervention strategies. *American Journal of Social Psychiatry, 6*(1), 50–56.

Hashima, P. Y., & Amato, P. R. (1994). Poverty, social support, and parental behavior. *Child Development, 65*, 394–403.

Hogan, D. P., & Kitagawa, E. M. (1985). The impact of social status, family structure, and neighborhood on the fertility of Black adolescents. *American Journal of Sociology, 90*(4), 825–855.

Hill, R. (1978). *The strengths of black families*. New York: Emerson-Hall.

Kellam, S. G., Adams, R. G., Brown, C. H., & Ensminger, M. A. (1982). The long-term evolution of the family structure of teenage and older mothers. *Journal of Marriage and the Family, 44* (3), 539–554.

Kellam, S. G., Ensminger, M. A., & Turner, J. T. (1977). Family structure and the mental health of children. *Archives of General Psychiatry, 34*(9), 1012–1022.

Langner, T., Herson, J., Greene, E., Jameson, J., Goff, J. (1970). Children of the city: Affluence, poverty, and mental health. In V. Allen (Ed.), *Psychological factors in poverty* (pp. 185–209). Chicago: Markham.

Lempers, J., Clark-Lempers, D., & Simons, R. (1989). Economic hardship, parenting, and distress in adolescence. *Child Development, 60*(1), 25–49.

Liem, R., & Liem, J. (1978). Social class and mental illness reconsidered: The role of economic stress and social support. *Journal of Health and Social Behavior, 19*(2), 139

Massey, D. S., & Denton, N. A. (1993). *American apartheid: Segregation and the making of the underclass*. Cambridge, MA: Harvard University Press.

Masten, A. (1994). In M. C. Wang & E. W. Gordon (Eds.), *Educational resilience in inner-city America: Challenges and prospects* (pp. 3–26). Hillsdale, NJ: Lawrence Erlbaum Associates, Inc.

Masten, A. S., Neemann, J., & Andenas, S. (1994). Life events and adjustment in adolescents: The significance of event independence, desirability, and chronicity. *Journal of Research on Adolescence, 4*, 71–97.

McAdoo, H. P. (1982). Stress-absorbing systems in Black families. *Family Relations, 31*(4), 479–488.

McLoyd, V. C. (1988, June). *Determinants of the mental health of black and white children experiencing economic deprivation*. Paper presented at a study group meeting on poverty and children, University of Kansas, Lawrence.

McLoyd, V. C. (1990). The impact of economic hardship on Black families and children: Psychological distress, parenting, and socioemotional development. *Child Development, 61*(2), 311–346.

McLoyd, V. C., Jayaratne, T. E., Ceballo, R., & Borquez, J. (1994). Unemployment and work interruption among African-American single mothers: Effects on parenting and adolescent socioemotional functioning. *Child Development*, *65*, 562–589.

Myers, H. F., & King, L. (1983). Mental health issues in the development of the Black American child. In G. Powell, J. Yamamoto, A., Romero, & A. Morales (Eds.), *The psychosocial development of minority children* (pp. 275–306). New York: Brunner/Mazzel.

Peters, M. F. (1985). Racial socialization of young black children. In H. McAdoo & J. McAdoo (Eds.), *Black children: Social, educational, and parental environments*. Newbury Park, Ca: Sage.

Roberts, D., & Taylor, R. D. (1994a). Association of family stress, parenting and psychological adjustment among African-American adolescents and mothers. Unpublished raw data.

Roberts, D., & Taylor, R. D. (1994b). Neighborhood characteristics, parenting, psychological well-being and adolescent adjustment among African-American families. Unpublished raw data.

Rutter, M. (1981). The city and the child. *American Journal of Orthopsychiatry*, *51*(4), 610–625.

Rutter, M., & Quinton, D. (1977). Psychiatric disorder, ecological factors and concepts of causation. In H. McGurk (Ed.), *Ecological factors in human development* (pp. 173–187). Amsterdam: North-Holland.

Slaughter, D. T. (1977). Relation of early parent–teacher socialization influences to achievement orientation and self-esteem in middle childhood among low-income black children. In J. Glidewell (Ed.), *The social context of learning and development* (pp. 101–131). New York: Gardner Press.

Steinberg, L., Mounts, N. S., Lamborn, S. D., & Dornbusch, S. M. (1991). Authoritative parenting and adolescent adjustment across varied ecological niches. *Journal of Research on Adolescence*, *1*, 19–36.

Taylor, R. D. (1994). *Kinship support, family management, and adolescent adjustment and competence in African-American families*. Manuscript submitted for publication.

Taylor, R. D., Casten, R., & Flickinger, S. (1993). The influence of kinship social support on the parenting experiences and psychosocial adjustment of African-American adolescents. *Developmental Psychology*, *29*(2), 382–388.

Taylor, R. D. & Roberts, D. (1995). Kinship support and parental and adolescent well-being in economically disadvantaged African-American families. *Child Development*, *66*(6), 1585–1597.

Taylor, R. D., Roberts, D., & Jacobson, L. (1995). *Stressful life events, parenting, and adolescent adjustment among low-income, African-American families*. Manuscript submitted for publication.

Thompson, M. S., & Ensminger, M. E. (1989). Psychological well-being among mothers with school age children: Evolving family structures. *Social Forces*, *67*(3), 715–730.

Tietjen, A. M., & Bradley, C. F. (1985). Social support and maternal psychosocial adjustment during the transition to parenthood. *Canadian Journal of Behavioral Science*, *17*(2), 109–121.

U.S. Bureau of the Census. (1991). *The black population in the United States: March 1990 and 1989* (Current population reports, Series P-20, no. 448). Washington, DC: U.S. Government Printing Office.

Wandersman, L. P., & Unger, D. G. (April, 1983). *Interaction of infant difficulty and social support in adolescent mothers*. Paper presented at the biennial meeting of the Society for Research in Child Development, Detroit, Michigan.

Wilson, W. J. (1987). *The truly disadvantaged: The inner city, the underclass, and public policy*. Chicago: University of Chicago Press.

4

Why Are People Poor?
Social Conditions and Adolescents'
Interpretations of the Social Contract[1]

Constance A. Flanagan
Patreese Ingram
Erika M. Gallay
Erin E. Gallay

As the 1950s came to a close, a growing sense of national awareness regarding the plight of America's poor—fueled in large part by landmark publications such as Michael Harrington's *The Other America* (1962)—helped to motivate the federal War on Poverty. The objectives of the social programs in that "war" were not to equalize incomes or living standards, but to level the playing field and equalize opportunities so that people born into poverty had an even chance to compete with more privileged citizens. The trend of social policy in more recent years, however, stands in direct opposition to that of the 1960s. In the 1980s, regressive tax policies and cutbacks in social spending transferred money to the wealthy and increased income disparities in the population. According to the Congressional Budget Office, the incomes of the poorest 10% of American households declined by 8.6% during that decade, whereas those of the top 20% increased by 29.8% (Center for Budget and Policy Priorities, 1990).

The redirection of social policies, coupled with economic restructuring, were important factors that contributed to the widening of class divisions. In the 1970s and 1980s, deindustrialization increased levels of unemployment, especially in the rust-belt cities of the northeast and midwest. The impact of deindustrialization on African-American families was severe because the industrial sector offered one of the main routes for the group's social mobility. Not surprisingly, African-American communities experienced significant increases in unemployment and homelessness during the 1980s (Marable & Mullings, 1994). Today, urban poverty among African-American families is more concentrated than ever due to the combined effects of economic restructuring, cutbacks in social programs, and declining

[1]The research presented in this chapter was supported by a William T. Grant Faculty Scholars Award to Connie Flanagan.

investment in America's cities (Wilson, 1991).

Today's adolescents have grown up in the midst of these economic and political changes; they have no memory of the War on Poverty with which to compare contemporary social conditions. How, then, do they conceive of "the other America"?

This chapter represents an attempt to answer this question in light of differences in adolescents' perceptions of the social contract—that is, the bargain they believe exists between individuals and society. The principles of this contract are rooted in the everyday experiences of youth in poor versus those in more affluent communities in America. By virtue of their differential access to opportunities and social support, youth in these contrasting ecologies may develop divergent views of the social order. By focusing on the social isolation and lack of "safety nets" in poor, urban communities, the authors of this chapter posit that youth who hope to succeed under such conditions develop an intense awareness that self-reliance is essential to individual success.

This study builds on the pioneering work of William Julius Wilson, who contends that structural economic change and the redirection of social policy over the past 2 decades have caused poverty to be concentrated in America's inner cities and have cut off the minorities residing in those areas from social commerce with the rest of society (Wilson, 1991). Federal policies, such as decisions about highway construction and incentives for low-income housing and development outside of urban areas, have served to undermine the urban infrastructure. The exodus of White and middle-class African-American families has further quarantined inner cities, severing social ties that might link residents to the larger society, and fracturing any sense of collective efficacy in the community (Marable, 1992). The isolation of urban minorities from mainstream society is exacerbated by guardedness and mistrust among residents of poor communities. While these factors protect residents from crime, they also inhibit the formation of networks within the larger community.

Social isolation extends to the political process as well. Over and above the negative effects of family poverty on political efficacy, high levels of neighborhood poverty reduce the number of social connections (e.g. community organizations, church groups, or indirect ties to public officials) that enable residents to resolve the community's problems (Cohen & Dawson, 1993).

What do these conditions imply about the relationships between people and society? More specifically, what do children growing up in communities with vastly different ecologies conclude about the principles of the social contract that bind people with their society? The authors of this chapter argue that, more than other groups in society, minority youth from poor urban areas conclude that people are "on their own," and that they cannot count on social support from the community or a safety net from society to help them if they fail. Communities in the inner city lack the social capital that might link minority youth to opportunities, information, or social connections in mainstream society (Coleman, 1988; Wilson, 1987). In contrast, youth growing up in more affluent communities are accustomed to a broad system of social and community supports. Their neighborhoods have not declined in the wake of the economic and policy changes of recent years. As a result, youth from more affluent communities are likely to perceive poverty or homelessness from a distance—a social issue with little direct impact on their lives. These youth expect the system to work and, thus, may be more likely to interpret such social issues as failures of the system.

METHODS

Data were collected from 198 adolescents (7th–12th graders) drawn from schools in a northern metropolitan area. Sixty-two students were from the inner city, 67 from a blue-collar community bordering the city, and 69 from an affluent suburb 40 miles from the city. Like many industrial areas in the United States, this region experienced high levels of unemployment during the past 15 years. Consistent with national trends, industries in the region, by and large, had recovered by the end of the 1980s. That economic recovery, however, bypassed the poor (Danzinger & Gottschalk, 1993). The urban area in this study is one of five cities in the United States that has accounted for the growth in persistently poor communities in recent years (Wilson, 1991).

As the demographic comparisons in Table 4.1 show, there were significant ethnographic differences between families in the three communities.

TABLE 4.1

Demographic Characteristics of Youth in Three Communities

Characteristics	Inner City		Urban Ring		Wealthy Suburbs		F ratio/ or x^2
	N = 62		N = 67		N = 69		
	M	SD	M	SD	M	SD	
Paternal Education [1]	2.29	1.03[a]	2.74	1.42[a]	4.16	.88[b]	42.01*
Maternal Education [1]	2.28	1.15[a]	2.54	1.12[a]	3.82	.89[b]	34.46*
Number of Children in Household	2.70	1.50	2.95	1.65	2.67	1.42	.75
Race							
African American (%)	51.5		6.5		4.1		
Caucasian/White (%)	28.8		79.2		95.9		
Latino/Hispanic (%)	13.6		10.4		0		
Native American Indian (%)	6.1		3.9		0		88.42*
Family Structure							
Married (%)	38.5		59.7		78.4		
Single Parent (%)	41.5		23.4		12.2		
Remarried (%)	10.8		14.3		6.8		
Other relatives (grandparent, aunt; %)	9.2		2.6		2.7		27.57*

Note. [1]Scale: 1 = less than high school to 5 = PhD/professional. Groups with different superscripts differ significantly at $p < .05$ based on Scheffé tests p (*$p < .0001$).

More than half of those from the inner city were African-American, 14% were Latino, and 6% were Native American. Seventy-nine percent of those from the urban ring of the city and 96% from the suburb were Caucasian. Family structure also differed. Only half of the youth from the inner city lived in two-parent households, compared to 74% in the urban ring and 85% in the suburb. There were no differences in family size, as measured by the number of children living at home. The parents of the suburban youth were better educated than those in the two urban communities. However, there were no differences in parental education between families in the inner city and in the urban ring. This latter point is noteworthy in light of significant differences between median family incomes in the two communities revealed in the 1990 census (U.S. Bureau of the Census, 1992), which reported that the median family income was $16,500 for the inner city, $29,600 for the urban ring, and $70,800 for the suburb. Before continuing, it is important to note that, by sampling in schools, the study's inner-city sample was undoubtedly biased toward youth who were highly committed to school, a point that will be further examined later in the chapter.

PROCEDURE AND MEASURES

Participants were recruited from middle and high schools. Questionnaires were administered by research assistants during a 1-hour class period. The research was described as a study of adolescent opinions on issues in society and it was made clear in both verbal and written form that there were no right or wrong answers. The dependent measures were adapted from items developed by Leahy (1983). Students were asked how they would explain unemployment, homelessness, poverty, and affluence to a foreigner visiting the U.S. The students' open-ended responses were coded by trained scorers who were blind to the hypotheses of the study. The scorers had no knowledge of the ages, races, sexes, or school districts of the respondents. Students' explanations for poverty, unemployment, homelessness, and affluence were coded as distinct questions.

Categories and representative responses are listed in Table 4.2. Responses were assigned to categories based on whether the response reflected attributions to (a) personal/dispositional factors under the individual's control (e.g., people are unemployed because they do not try to find jobs; people who are poor did not work very hard in school); or (b) systemic/structural factors (e.g., people are unemployed because companies are moving many jobs to Mexico; homelessness exists in our country because the government does not provide enough low-income housing). A respondent's explanation could be coded in both categories but was only counted once within a category, that is, the response "when they were students, wealthy people were very motivated and studied hard" would be coded as one personal/dispositional reference, whereas the response, "companies are moving to Mexico and their employees, once they are laid

TABLE 4.2

Categories and Representative Statements for Personal/Dispositional
and Systemic/Structural Explanations

Category	Representative Statements
Personal/Dispositional Attributions (Attributing responsibility to the individual)	
Poverty	They did not save their money.
Unemployment	They did not care about school.
Homelessness	All of their money went to drugs.
	They do not try to find jobs.
Wealth	They worked hard to reach their goals.
	They managed their money wisely.
Systemic/Structural Attributions (Attributing responsibility to social institutions, forces, or conditions; i.e., factors individuals do not control)	
Poverty	There are not enough jobs.
Unemployment	They were born into a poor family.
Homelessness	There's not enough low-income housing.
	Their schools were not any good.
Wealth	They inherited it from their parents.
	They have connections.

off, won't try to find new jobs" would be coded as references both to
systemic/structural and personal/dispositional factors. The open-ended
responses were coded by a second rater and Cohen's kappa ranged from
.85 to .98 for the different dilemmas.

The predominant personal/dispositional explanations for poverty, unemployment, and homelessness referenced a lack of effort, motivation, and
especially an individual's failure to work hard in school. References to
difficulties managing money also ranked high as an explanation for poverty, as did drug abuse and gambling as explanations for unemployment.
Systemic/structural attributions primarily referenced a lack of opportunities (i.e., no jobs), national or global economic trends (i.e., inflation, foreign
competition), or government policies (i.e., defense cutbacks). Social backgrounds (i.e., poor people were born into poor families) and a lack of
personal connections were also endorsed as reasons for poverty and homelessness, less so for unemployment.

With regard to explanations for wealth, respondents predominantly
referenced hard work and industry, followed by talent and intelligence, and
diligence in the classroom. Notably, references to racism or prejudice were
almost nil (a total of three for unemployment, three for poverty, one for
homelessness, and two for wealth).

Some responses could not be assigned to the categories used in this study.
For example, the statement, "I feel sorry for them" was coded as empathy and
"the unemployed don't have jobs" as a definitional explanation. The most
frequent of these responses was a general reference to education (i.e., "they
didn't get a good education" or "they aren't trained"). Such uncodable re-

sponses were treated as missing data and, for this reason, a different number of cases were used in the analyses of the four open-ended questions.

After coding, a categorical variable was created based on whether the student's attribution was a reference (a) *only* to personal/dispositional factors; (b) *only* to systemic/structural factors; or (c) to a combination of systemic/structural *and* personal/dispositional factors.

In addition to the open-ended questions, students responded to a set of Likert-type (agree–disagree) items measuring their perceptions of family and school practices. The study focused on two measures of what the authors have termed *cautionary parenting*. The first, "social vigilance," tapped the extent to which parents warned their children to be wary of trusting others who might take advantage of them, and admonished their children to look out for themselves because they could not always rely on others to take care of them. The second measure, "urgency of academic success," assessed the extent to which parents exerted pressure on their children to get good grades and set high goals, and warned them that their future would be jeopardized by not doing well in school. Cronbach's alpha was .60 for the former and .71 for the latter measure.

School practices focused on the adolescents' perceptions of social support at their school. The first, "teacher support," (alpha = .66) tapped the extent to which teachers cared about and respected students. The second, "student alienation" (alpha = .67), was based on adolescents' perceptions of a lack of camaraderie in the student body and a need for self-reliance at their school.

RESULTS

The results of the chi-square tests of independence are presented in Table 4.3. They reveal that the inner-city youth were more likely than their peers in the urban ring or the suburb to attribute both poverty and affluence to personal/dispositional factors (i.e., factors under the individual's control). In contrast, youth from the urban ring and especially from the suburb were more likely to give structural/systemic explanations or to combine structural with dispositional explanations. In terms of unemployment, youth from the inner-city and the urban ring communities were equally likely to hold individuals responsible for their unemployment, whereas those from the suburb blamed the system. There were no significant between-group differences in attributions for homelessness. It should be noted that youth from the inner city did, in fact, endorse structural and systemic arguments. On balance, however, they were more likely than their peers in the other communities to weigh in on the side of individual responsibility.

Table 4.4 presents a comparison of family and school practices in the three communities. This comparison suggests that youth from the inner city perceive a school environment that is more alienating in terms of

TABLE 4.3

Adolescents' Attributions for Poverty, Unemployment, Homelessness, and Wealth

	Inner City		Urban Ring		Wealthy Suburbs		χ^2
	%	N	%	N	%	N	
Unemployment							
Personal/Dispositional	40.3	(25)	25.8	(17)	14.5	(10)	
Systemic/Structural	25.8	(16)	31.8	(21)	52.2	(36)	
Both Categories	33.9	(21)	42.2	(28)	33.3	(23)	16.07*
Poverty							
Personal/Dispositional	49.0	(25)	19.0	(12)	20.0	(12)	
Systemic/Structural	31.4	(16)	46.0	(29)	45.0	(27)	
Both Categories	19.6	(10)	34.9	(22)	35.0	(21)	15.69*
Homelessness							
Personal/Dispositional	26.7	(12)	9.1	(5)	17.0	(9)	
Systemic/Structural	51.1	(23)	61.8	(34)	45.3	(24)	
Both Categories	22.2	(10)	29.1	(16)	37.7	(20)	7.90
Wealth							
Personal/Dispositional	57.1	(28)	24.4	(15)	24.6	(17)	
Systemic/Structural	24.5	(12)	34.3	(23)	20.3	(14)	
Both Categories	18.4	(9)	43.3	(29)	55.1	(38)	24.75**

Note. Number of categories for each set of analyses was based on the total cases referring either to systemic or dispositional causes or to both for the particular social category p (*$p < .01$ and **$p < .0001$).

TABLE 4.4

Comparison of Family and School Practices Reported by Youth in Three Communities

	Inner City		Urban Ring		Wealthy Suburbs		F-statistic
	M	SD	M	SD	M	SD	
Cautionary Parenting							
Social vigilance	5.89	.99[a]	5.41	1.20[a]	5.24	1.16[b]	5.19**
Urgency of academic success	5.70	1.09[a]	5.22	1.21[a,b]	5.17	1.04[b]	4.03*
Social Support At School							
Teachers respect and care about students	4.37	1.53[a]	5.16	1.37[b]	4.93	1.32[a,b]	4.44*
Student alienation	4.82	1.20[a]	3.85	1.28[b]	4.16	1.21[b]	8.04***

Note. Groups with different superscripts differ significantly at $p < .05$ based on Scheffé tests p (*$p < .05$, **$p . < 01$, and ***$p < .0001$).

teacher support and student relationships. Based on a series of Scheffé tests, teacher support was lower in the inner city as compared to the urban ring, and student alienation was higher compared to the urban ring or suburb.

In terms of family practices, urban youth reported more intense messages about the need for social vigilance, self-reliance, and academic success when compared to their peers in the other communities.

DISCUSSION

Why would inner-city youth, whose communities have been most devastated by the combined effects of economic restructuring and cutbacks in social spending, be more likely than their peers from more affluent communities to hold individuals responsible for their social status? Conversely, why would privileged youth more readily hold the social structure or "the system" accountable? To address these questions, the authors begin with a psychological interpretation and then broaden their perspective to discuss differences in the social contract that binds youth to American society.

Blaming the system, the economy, or even the government poses no personal dilemma for adolescents with relatively secure futures. The system tends to work for them and for people like them. In contrast, endorsing the structural or systemic roots of poverty or unemployment implies bleak prospects for youth whose communities have been impacted and whose futures have been compromised by the economic and political changes of the past few decades. In a similar vein, attributing the success of the wealthy to their social connections effectively curtails the possibility of achieving wealth for youth who are disconnected from the mainstream. Compared to their peers in the urban ring and the suburb, the inner-city youth in this study overwhelmingly claimed that people became wealthy because of their own initiative and hard work. This interpretation is supported by the lack of significant differences in explanations for unemployment made by youth in the urban ring and the inner city. Because the urban ring community has been affected by layoffs and plant closings in recent years, youth who live there may be more aware of the possibility of unemployment in their own lives.

As noted earlier, conducting this study in schools has undoubtedly biased the inner-city sample toward those youth with the strongest commitment to education. Statistics show that a disproportionate number of African-American (32%) and Latino (40%) students drop out of school in comparison to White (25%) students (Gibbs, 1988). Because the returns to education are typically lower for African Americans when compared to Whites, African-American youth may be skeptical about whether education will help them achieve their goals (LeCompte & Dworkin, 1991). Furthermore, as has been eloquently described in the work of John Ogbu (1978, 1987), African-American and Latino youth often conceive of education as a mark of assimilation into the dominant White culture. The authors are aware that the attitudes of the minority youth in this study's inner-city sample do not mesh with Ogbu's work. It would seem that these youth are committed to getting an education, a finding the authors will emphasize to make the following points.

First, ignoring within-group variations has, all too often, been a problem with comparative racial studies (Azibo, 1988). Although a disproportionate number of minority students drop out of school, most complete their high school education. This study contends that an intense self-reliance is demanded of those minority students who persist. Second, although minority youth from poor neighborhoods may be aware of the system's failures, it may be necessary for them to disregard those failures in order to remain committed to education and the American dream. As Taylor and his colleagues found, to the extent that Black youth blamed the system for the job ceilings facing African Americans, they were more likely to have given up on their own education (Taylor, Casten, Flickinger, Roberts, & Fulmore, 1994).

There is no empirical support in the literature for stereotypes about African-Americans undervaluing educational achievement, having low educational aspirations, or attributing failure to external causes (Graham, 1994; Kandel, 1970). Reflecting on interviews conducted with minority families in the inner city, Wilson (1988) noted that, contrary to popular media images, the families overwhelmingly endorsed mainstream values for work and family despite the formidable odds they faced. The results of the present study confirm this picture of self-reliance. The urban, predominantly minority youth in this study were more likely than their peers from more affluent communities to endorse beliefs in self-sufficiency and the work ethic. They also heard messages of self-reliance from their families and felt that they received little social support at school.

This sense that minority students voiced about being "on their own" is echoed in a study of social support among African-American male high school students (Jackson, 1993). Seventy-five percent of the students in Jackson's study perceived that they got very little social support either from adults at school (principals, teachers, or counsellors) or from people in the community (whether relatives, ministers, or friends). Instead, these young men relied heavily on themselves.

Representations of reality are social; they are collectively generated and rooted in group experience (Moscovici, 1988). This study contends that, by virtue of their differing degrees of access to opportunities in society, youth develop varying interpretations of how society and its rules work. The authors use the metaphor of a *social contract* to describe how young people interpret the bargain or deal that exists between people and society. Fifteen years ago when Robert Leahy (1983, p. 114) first asked American youth to explain "why some people are rich and others are poor," he found that middle-class youth were more likely than others to hold individuals responsible for their station in life. Leahy also discovered that African Americans were more likely than their White peers to contend that the rich had inherited their money or violated laws to get it. Since that time, there have been significant changes in the American social contract, changes that have attenuated opportunities in American society for minority youth in poor, urban communities. To maintain optimism in the face of formidable odds, these youth may believe that it is incumbent on the individual to create his or her own success and that those who rely on the system may be disappointed.

REFERENCES

Azibo, D. (1988). Understanding the proper and improper usage of the comparative research framework. *Journal of Black Psychology, 15*, 81–91.

Center for Budget and Policy Priorities (1990). *Drifting apart: New findings in growing income disparities between the rich, the poor, and the middle-class.* Washington, DC: Congressional Budget Office.

Cohen, C. J., & Dawson, M. C. (1993). Neighborhood poverty and African-American politics. *American Political Science Review, 87*, 286–302.

Coleman, J. S. (1988). Social capital in the creation of human capital. *American Journal of Sociology, 94*, 95–120.

Danzinger, S., & Gottschalk, P. (Eds.). (1993). *Uneven tides: Rising inequality in America.* New York: Russell Sage.

Gibbs, J. T. (Ed.). (1988). *Young, Black, and male in America: An endangered species.* Westport, CT: Auburn House.

Graham, S. (1994). Motivation in African Americans. *Review of Educational Research, 64*, 55–117.

Harrington, M. (1962). *The other America: Poverty in the United States.* New York: MacMillan.

Jackson, J. (1993). *A comparative study of high and low achieving inner-city African-American sophomore males' expectations of self-, in-school, and out-of-school support.* Unpublished doctoral dissertation, Western Michigan University, Kalamazoo.

Kandel, D. (1970). Race, maternal authority, and adolescent aspiration. *American Journal of Sociology, 76*, 999–1020.

Leahy, R. L. (1983). The development of the conception of economic inequality: II. Explanations, justifications, and conceptions of social mobility and social change. *Developmental Psychology, 19*, 111–125.

LeCompte, M., & Dworkin, A. (1991). *Giving up on school: Student drop-outs and teacher burn-outs.* Newbury Park, CA: Corwin.

Marable, M. (1992). *The crisis of color and democracy: Essays on race, class, and power.* Monroe, ME: Common Courage.

Marable, M., & Mullings, L. (1994). The divided mind of Black America: Race, ideology and politics in the post Civil Rights era. *Race and Class, 36*, 61–72.

Moscovici, S. (1988). Notes towards a description of Social Representations. *European Journal of Social Psychology, 18*, 211–250.

Ogbu, J. U. (1978). *Minority education and caste: The American system in cross-cultural perspective.* New York: Academic Press.

Ogbu, J. U. (1987). Variability in minority school performance: A problem in search of an explanation. *Anthropology & Education Quarterly, 18*, 312–334.

Taylor, R. D., Casten, R., Flickinger, S.M., Roberts, D., & Fulmore, C. D. (1994). Explaining the school performance of African-American adolescents. *Journal of Research on Adolescence, 4*, 21–44.

United States Bureau of the Census (1992). Census of Population and Housing, 1990: Summary Tape File 3 on CD-Rom, Bureau of the Census, Washington, DC.

Wilson, W. J. (1987). *The truly disadvantaged: The inner city, the underclass, and public policy.* Chicago: University of Chicago Press.

Wilson, W. J. (1988, April 26). *The American underclass: Inner-city ghettos and the norms of citizenship.* Godkin lecture, John F. Kennedy School of Government, Harvard University, Cambridge, MA.

Wilson, W. J. (1991). Studying inner-city social dislocations: The challenge of public agenda research. *American Sociological Review, 56*, 1–14.

5

The American Indian Child:
Victims of the Culture of Poverty
or Cultural Discontinuity?

Ardy Sixkiller Clarke

According to the 1990 U.S. Census, American Indians are the most poverty-stricken group in the nation. A recent Census report indicated that more than half of the Indian households earn less than $20,000 annually and that Indian children are three times more likely to be poor than White children. The statistics further point out that American Indians are the only ethnic group in the United States whose average household income has fallen since 1980. In addition, the report shows that not only do Indian households have the highest poverty rate, they also have the highest unemployment rates in the nation. In response to the report, Alan Parker, director of the National Indian Policy Center, commented:

> The poverty on Indian reservations is pervasive and endemic. It's no secret that the government has not responded in any meaningful way to boost reservation economies or by creating tax incentives or a financial structure to address these problems.... It's been going on for at least 20 years and it's only getting worse.

Research clearly shows that poor children are more likely to drop out of school than are their more advantaged peers. Studies have consistently demonstrated the relationship between the number of poor students in a district and the number of dropouts. This does not mean that growing up poor will itself determine whether a child will drop out of school; however, it does indicate that unless the burden of poverty is alleviated by the distribution of resources and the commitment of sympathetic and dedicated teachers and administrators, it is much harder for a child to succeed.

Unfortunately, for American Indian children that assistance has not been generally available. Instead, many educators and researchers have mislabeled the conditions of poverty as the conditions of culture and its incongruence with the school environment. Thus, it becomes very easy, as well as convenient, to blame school failure among American Indian children on the students' culture.

The fact remains that for the American Indian child growing up in a home where the parents are low income or unemployed, or in a home with a single mother on AFDC, the chances are good that the child will receive far less positive attention from teachers and administrators in the school, even when it is a reservation school dedicated to educating American Indians. In any case, poverty is bad enough, but when poverty is combined with insensitive, uncaring teachers, it becomes much more difficult for an Indian child to overcome the hurdles of school.

Robert Coles, in his three-volume *Children of Crisis* (1971), devoted a chapter to teachers and the children of poverty. He maintained that teachers like "well-scrubbed, eager, obedient, responsive" students, which is often a far cry from the characteristics of children of poverty. Furthermore, he questioned the larger issue of poverty and child performance in school based on what he called *family's spirit*:

> Does a [poor] mother give her children a sense of confidence . . .? Mothers . . . who never quite know where the next few dollars will come, have little energy left for their children. Life is grim and hard, and the child simply has to find that out. He does, too; he learns it and learns it and learns it. He learns how to survive. . . . He learns why his parents have given up on school, why they have tried and fallen flat on their faces. He learns about things like racial hatred . . . he learns whether he is an insider or an outsider. . . . By the time a child . . . first arrives at school he has learned so much that his knowledge might perhaps be credited to an account called "the intelligence of the so-called unintelligent as it appears in sly, devious and haunting ways." The average teacher may know all that, but find little time to dwell upon the social and psychological forces that make children so very different before they have had one day of school. (pp. 435–436)

An examination of various national surveys on dropouts further demonstrates the problems encountered by racial minorities. These surveys report that about 13% of the White students in the United States drop out of school, but surveys on minority students report that between 12% and 24% of Black students drop out, and that approximately 40% of Hispanic students and between 35% and 50% of American Indians never complete high school (Hispanic Policy Development Project, 1984; National Foundation for the Improvement of Education, 1986; Peng, 1985; Peng & Takai, 1983; Swisher, Hoisch, & Pavel, 1991; U.S. Government Accounting Office, 1986). As Theodore Sizer (1984) pointed out, many schools in this country assume that minority students will not graduate. In the case of reservation schools, a similar attitude prevails.

Throughout the history of Indian education there have been numerous explanations for the low achievement of Indian students. At first, a common explanation was the genetic defect. American Indian children were from a cultural background that was inherently inferior, both intellectually and morally. In the 1960s, the cultural deficit explanation became popular. Thus, Indian children did not achieve because they were not reared in a cognitively stimulating environment and were "socially disadvantaged" or "culturally deprived." The cultural deficit theory was acceptable to educators in that it enabled them to place the responsibility for school failure outside the school.

In the late 1960s, the culturally relativist position became an explanation for failure of Indian students. This position blamed neither the teachers nor the students, but placed the responsibility for failure of Indian students on cultural differences in communication styles between the teachers and their students. In the mid-1970s, John Ogbu (1974, 1978) argued that school failure was the result of inequity in access to employment and that generations of minorities who had been denied access to opportunities in the American society had simply communicated their cynicism to their children, thus accounting for the school failure of minority children. By the mid-1980s, dropping out and school failure were attributed to multiple variables and students possessing those characteristics were labeled "high-risk" or "at-risk" youth. Many educators have cautioned that those terms are no more than disguised labels for students who were previously regarded as "culturally deprived" or "culturally disadvantaged."

Many of the studies on Indian students suggest that there is a need for a "culturally relevant" curriculum within the schools to keep students in school. In fact, one recent study (Jacob & Jordan, 1987) presented a compelling argument for Indian failure in school by pointing to the cultural differences between Indian cultures and the Euro-American culture. Other researchers have suggested that Indian students receive messages in school that conflict with the messages of their home, thus creating dissonance within the child and a subsequent resistance to school (Bowers & Flanders, 1990; Spindler, 1987).

Although *cultural relevance* is rarely defined, these studies have given rise to bilingual education programs or Indian studies courses within the regular curriculum throughout Indian education. These curriculum efforts have not been without their critics. Gerald Wilkinson (1981) suggested the following:

> For all the talk about the uniqueness of "Indian education" all that has basically been created are White institutions run by Indians. . . . These institutions have not made the leap from the colonial mentality to the development of indigenous concepts based on their own self-interest as people. . . . In the area of curriculum much has been made of bilingual education. Except at the low-grade levels, bilingual education is generally taken to mean native language courses. These courses have about the same effect on the students as if they were taking Latin or Greek. The thing about language is that it can only be successfully taught if it can be used. . . . To succeed a tribe must make a cultural decision that their language is an important part of their life and their future. . . . Another example is the teaching of history. . . . The history of Indian people is not taught as Indian history but as the history of Indian/White relations. This approach gives the impression that Indians would have no past at all if it had not been for the European invasion. . . . It is difficult to see how an Indian young person could get any perspective on himself when his past is presented to him as a mere sideshow in the panorama of human existence. (p. 46)

That a culturally relevant curriculum will ameliorate the problems of Indian students in school is rarely discussed in terms of how the curriculum will improve performance, except in regard to improved self-identity or self-esteem.

What is important for educators is to separate the impact of poverty and the impact of culture on the educational achievement of Indian children and to identify the processes by which poverty and cultural background affect success or lack of success. This chapter deals with the impact of poverty and culture on American Indian children.

THE MYTHS OF THE CULTURE OF POVERTY

At the heart of the problem is the fact that poverty is distasteful not only to most Americans but also to most educators. We do not like to think or talk about this, much less do anything about it. To further complicate the matter, since the early 1980s we have witnessed a rightward shift in the public debate about social welfare regarding the defective nature of poor people, their motivations, behavior, and moral character. Although the majority of attention has focused on Black Americans, American Indians have been the subject of some media attention—the most recent example being "Tragedy at Pine Ridge," a 1991 NBC news two-part special on the social problems of the Oglala Sioux on the Pine Ridge Reservation in South Dakota. Rather than focusing on the poverty, the extremely high unemployment rates, and the lack of economic initiatives on the part of the federal government as the root of the problems, the reservation-specific culture and the pathological behaviors of alcohol abuse became the basis of the news special.

A typical example of the prevailing attitude in this country about the poor is found in the work of Isabel Sawhill (1989), a senior fellow at the Urban Institute, who referred to the poor people of this country as the "underclass." Although Sawhill's work is based on her observations with Blacks, there is an underlying applicability of her treatise to all poor, racial groups in the United States including American Indians. According to Sawhill, the underclass in America exhibits behavior that is "dysfunctional" and she sets about describing the "norms" that society demands of its members:

> First, children are expected to study hard and complete at least high school. Second, young people are expected to refrain from conceiving children until they have personal and financial resources to support them; this usually means delaying childbearing until they have completed school and can draw a regular salary. Third, adults are expected to work at a steady job, unless they are retired, disabled, or are supported by a spouse. Fourth, everyone is expected to obey the laws. (p. 3)

Sawhill (1989) maintained that every citizen should meet these obligations as a part of the American "social contract" and further proclaimed that "the underclass is a subgroup of the American population that engages in behaviors at variance with those of mainstream populations" (p. 5). The most common of the deviant behaviors include dropping out of school, welfare dependency, adult male unemployment or underemployment, and female-headed households.

William Julius Wilson (1987) described the underclass within the accepted *tangle of pathology* litany as individuals involved in crime, abuse, teenaged pregnancy, out-of-wedlock births, welfare dependency, and female-headed households. David Ellwood (1988) characterized the *poor* as those who experience "a frightening array of negative forces: deprivation, concentration, isolation, discrimination, poor education . . . crime, drugs and alcohol, the underground economy, and welfare" (p. 200). He further maintained that this underclass "seem[s] to embrace values that the middle class cannot understand" (p. 200).

The danger in the viewpoints advocated by Sawhill (1989), Wilson (1987), and Ellwood (1988) is that their ideas have been embraced by politicians, middle-class Americans, wealthy Americans, and a wide range of middle-class minority groups. These ideas have also found fertile ground among the younger generation of White Americans who see the chance of having a better life than their parents slipping out of their reach. Because these views often regard poverty status as synonymous with minority status, it opens an entirely new venue for racial hatred and bias. Therefore, the incompetent individual who is unable to find a job blames affirmative action or women or a minority group.

In recent years politicians have fueled the anger against the poor by campaigning against welfare for poor women and children. Becuase the general public's perception of the *welfare recipient* is often defined as a female member of the significant minority group within a state or region, racial issues become intertwined with poverty. A corollary to this perception, in regard to American Indians, for example, is that Indians are poor because of their race, which is intermingled with cultural values incongruent with White, middle-class America. In other words, Indians are poor because they adhere to cultural values that inhibit their movement into affluency. Totally absent from this theory is the recognition that being poor is a major burden for any child to overcome; but when one adds the factor of race, the opportunities become even more limited. Josue Gonzalez (1985), Associate Superintendent of the Chicago Public Schools, suggested that there are actually two school systems in the United States: one that is invested with resources and good teachers and serves middle-class or affluent White youth, another that is a *pauper's system* that educates most of America's poor, minority children.

POVERTY VERSUS CULTURE

Perhaps the most significant feature about these constructs of underclass is that they all focus on behavior, values, and culture, and all center around an overlapping list of behavioral characteristics. These factors serve to perpetuate the idea that Indians are locked into their current situation not by their lack of opportunities, but because of their culture, values, and traditions that are inherently out of sync with mainstream America. In addition, there is an unspoken premise that underlies these beliefs—that the culture itself is responsible for the poverty conditions.

Because American schools have historically been the purveyors of the "American culture" and middle-class Anglo values (even among Indian reservation schools), blaming the culture of the child, the "within-child deficit," has become the norm in Indian education. American Indians have also fallen victim to this type of propaganda and have accepted the cultural discontinuity theories as the reasons for their children's lack of success in schools. Many researchers and educators have alleged that Indian students adhere to alien cultures and values that are incompatible with the school environment, thus creating patterns of behavior that impede success in school. Therefore, it is the child and the child's culture that have failed, not the school. I would assert, however, that it is not the "alien" Indian cultures, traditions, and values, nor the cultural discontinuity between the schools and the home environment but, rather, the state of poverty of American Indian households, the hidden curriculum of the schools, and the stereotypical attitudes toward Indian children that are the major factors impeding the success of Indian youth.

American Indians have, in one sense, compromised their cultures by accepting these explanations for their behavior and their children's failure in school. For example, in general, Indians have come to accept characterizations of behavior as "an Indian thing" or "that's the way Indians are" rather than behaviors that are distinctly a "poverty thing." Whereas characterizing cultural phenomena as the cause of school failure reveals a zeal for validating the need for integration of the culture into the school curriculum and has provided countless opportunities for experts on culturally sensitive curriculum reform, it also betrays a fundamental propensity to ignore the economic conditions on reservations and the implications those conditions may have in the schooling of children. Further, it conceals the real distinction between the behaviors that are related to culture and behaviors that are related to poverty.

THE PROBLEM OF EDUCABILITY AND THE HIDDEN CURRICULUM IN SCHOOLS

The lack of success in school for Indian children is often blamed on the problem of educability; the claim is that American Indian children do not possess the motivations, the orientations, and the skills that are prerequisites for schooling. These prerequisites, which are acquired through early exposure to learning tasks and positive socialization experiences, are often referred to as the *hidden curriculum of schools*. Basically, the hidden curriculum advances four elements of educability.

First, it is expected that on entering school, children will possess a finite set of student behaviors. These behaviors are developed by providing early experiences in which children learn appropriate adult–child relationships (Bloom, 1972). An example might be to teach the child to respond to adult directions. Second, teachers expect that children will enter school with the development of cognitive and perceptual skills appropriate to the school setting. In other words, educators presume that parents will provide their children with activities that will encourage them to explore and analyze their environment (Shipman & Bussis, 1968). Third, educators expect that children will enter school with the motivation to achieve. This motivation is developed by parents encouraging their children to hold positive feelings toward school and about adult praise and approval. Finally, teachers assume that the child understands and speaks standard English (Shaefer, 1970, 1976).

Throughout the literature, these four aspects of the hidden curriculum differentiate between the poor student and the good student. What is perplexing, however, is that the American Indian student who fails to acquire the prerequisites of the hidden curriculum is often quite capable outside of school, and while many American Indian students have difficulty in school, others do not.

Research on the effects of poverty on educability appears to be compromised by two factors: socialization and health. The influence of poverty on the socialization of children is not well documented; however, we know that unemployment among adults often results in withdrawal, depression, apathy, and loss of self-respect (Levin, 1975). With the high rate of unemployment and underemployment on Indian reservations, we can theorize that negative parental behaviors have powerful effects on Indian children.

Furthermore, poor people have less access to the printed media and are restricted in the quality and amount of information they receive (Hurwitz, 1975). In fact, most people of poverty appear to substitute television for printed media. According to Hurwitz, "While television can be a powerful educator, its present programming supports a distorted view of reality and everyday life" (p. 4). This distorted perception may be a distinct effect of poverty that impacts the early socialization of the child and thus his or her educability. Further, in poor families it is unlikely that printed materials or educational materials (paper, crayons, pencils, books) are available. This in itself is another detriment to the child of poverty who, in order to acquire the prerequisites of the hidden curriculum, must have access to those materials in early childhood.

In general, poverty and health are strongly related. Poor people are less likely to seek and obtain proper medical care. In the case of American Indians on reservations who depend mostly on the Indian Health Services for medical attention, the conditions are often quite bleak. Throughout Indian country there is a plethora of accounts of understaffed hospitals, incompetent staff, and insufficient funds for providing adequate care. Indian people suffer from the highest infant mortality rate in the nation, the shortest life expectancy, have a greater risk of prenatal complications associated with low birth rate, and have the highest rate of babies with fetal alcohol syndrome. Some researchers have suggested that poor children have an increased risk of suffering neurointegrative sensory motor abnormalities, which contribute to lack of achievement in school (Birch, 1972; Birch & Gussow, 1970). Other researchers have found a direct relationship between poverty and intellectual development in later life. Although severe malnutrition is not a major problem in the United States, subnutrition is a problem for poor children on Indian reservations. Researchers report that subnourished children are less attentive in school, less responsive, more easily fatigued, and unable to sustain prolonged mental and physical activity (Birch, 1972; Birch & Gussow, 1970; Brock, 1961; Hertzig, Birch, Richardson, & Tizard, 1972). That subnutrition indirectly affects a child's motivation and cognitive skills is, therefore, a given.

There is no question that poverty and ethnic status are inextricably linked in that many people who live in poverty come from minority groups, certainly at a higher proportion than in the mainstream society. But it is important that we separate the issues of poverty from those of culture. Poverty is strongly associated with health problems and socialization factors that have a profound influence on the development and education of children. Should we continue to view poverty and ethnicity as synonymous, however, we will perpetuate an ethnocentric misinterpretation of the educability of Indian children and the subsequent development of inappropriate educational interventions.

CULTURAL DISCONTINUITY THEORY

The cultural discontinuity theory maintains that cultural differences in communication and learning styles of minority students result in conflicts and misunderstandings within the Euro-American culture of the school, leading to failure for students. Underlying the theory is the assumption that language, memory, and other cognitive skills are held in common by American Indian groups or other minorities. Although the demands on the individual may vary depending on the social, physical, and economic requirements of the group, conflicts and differences arise as a result (Cole & Bruner, 1971). Researchers have, therefore, concluded that making the classroom curriculum more culturally relevant will mean success for Indian students.

The basic argument put forth by the cultural discontinuity theorists is that teachers and students differ in their expectations of behavior and that their expectations are derived from experiences outside of school in what sociolinguists call speech communities or speech networks. According to Hymes (1974), culturally distinctive ways of speaking differ from one speech community to the next and tend to run along major social divisions such as race, ethnicity, first language background, or class. Thus, although an Indian child may only speak English, the child is a member of a differing speech community or network that has differing assumptions about ways of communicating approval, disapproval, sincerity, irony, disinterest, and the like. Further cultural differences in ways of listening and speaking between the non-Indian teacher's speech network and the Indian child's speech network lead to recurring, systematic miscommunication within the classroom.

Susan Philips (1983), who studied children on the Warm Springs Reservation in Oregon, examined the differences in communication and interaction patterns between the community and the school. Philips maintained the following:

> The children of the Warm Springs Indian Reservation are enculturated in their preschool years into modes of organizing the transmission of verbal messages that are culturally different from those of Anglo middle-class children. I argue that this difference makes it more difficult for them to then comprehend verbal messages conveyed through the school's Anglo middle-class modes of organizing classroom interaction. (p. 4)

One aspect of the hidden curriculum of schools is the requirement of standard English skills. For an Indian child, the lack of standard English skills is said to result in ineffective communication and thinking skills. Some researchers have suggested that requiring standard English skills ignores the universality of languages and is the product of racial discrimination, and that standard English is not a demonstrated requirement for potential educability of minority children (Baratz & Baratz, 1970; Labov, 1970).

Other researchers have suggested that similar conflicts occur between the behaviors of minority children and the expected behaviors of the teacher or the school. For example, if a teacher comes from a culture or speech network in which attention is measured by direct eye contact and a child comes from one in which it is impolite to look directly at a speaker, the teacher may interpret the child's behavior as unmotivated or disinterested rather than recognizing what is happening in terms of cultural differences. As a result, the teacher further contributes to the dissonance of the child who may react in what is considered inappropriate ways such as withdrawal, silence, or hostility, possibly leading to a teacher diagnosis of student incompetence or inadequacy.

Researchers have reported on similar conflicts between behaviors expected in the home and those expected in the school. For example, one study looked at Hawaiian children and found that both parents and siblings were responsible for the care and safety of children within the home. Further, the study showed that Hawaiian children often look to older siblings or peer groups for help and that they watch and monitor adult behaviors as well as those of other children. In school, however, children are expected to seek help only from the teacher or to pay attention to what the teacher is doing and saying. As a result, the teacher often interpreted the helpful nature of Hawaiian children when they consulted with other children as "cheating" (Gallimore, Boggs, & Jordan, 1974). This difference between expected behaviors in school and those of the home further contributes to the conflict between students and the concept of educability and is applicable to the behavior of Indian children as well as Native Hawaiians.

Although there is considerable empirical evidence to support the communication process explanation of cultural discontinuity, there is little evidence to support the inclusion of culturally relevant materials within the classroom as a solution to improved Indian student achievement (Ledlow, 1992). The following studies are most often cited by researchers in Indian education to support the cultural discontinuity theory.

The Kamehameha Elementary Education Project (KEEP) was developed by Vogt, Jordan, and Tharp (1987) in response to the lack of success of Native Hawaiian children compared to Japanese, Chinese, and students of European ancestry. The project developed a K–3 language arts program based on the socialization practices in Hawaiian homes. As a result of the culturally compatible curriculum, at-risk Hawaiian children demonstrated significant gains in reading achievement. Vogt and colleagues replicated the KEEP project at the Rough Rock Community School on a Navajo reservation in Arizona. Even though researchers concluded that the two studies support the argument for cultural compatibility between school and home as an enhancement for school success, it was found that many of the strategies that were successful for Hawaiian children were ineffective or counterproductive with Navajo students. Other educators have characterized Indian schools as offering an inappropriate curriculum that does not reflect the Indian child's cultural background and consequently results in early school leaving, even though there is little empirical evidence to support these assumptions (Coladarci, 1983; Reyhner, 1992).

On the other hand, a 1983 study of Navajo youth found that the student's first language was not as important a factor to school success as the successful transition into English. Students who were fluent and dominant in English or bilingual in English and Navajo were far less likely to drop out of school, regardless of their first language. Students from less traditional homes, however, dropped out at much higher rates (Chan & Os-thimer, 1983). It is important to note, according to the premises of the cultural discontinuity theory, that the more traditional Navajo and those who spoke their language or were bilingual should, for all intents and purposes, have difficulty in school. Yet the opposite was found to be true.

In a 1989 study of Navajo and Ute dropouts, it was found that students who came from traditional Navajo homes and who spoke their Native language and participated in social and religious activities did not feel that the school curriculum was inappropriate for Indian students. Deyhle (1989) found that Ute students, who were less traditional than the Navajo students, experienced the highest dropout rates and the most problems academically and socially. These students reported that the curriculum was not relevant to them as Indians. Deyhle concluded that "a culturally non-responsive curriculum is a greater threat to those whose own cultural 'identity' is insecure" (p. 42).

CULTURAL DIFFERENCES AND EDUCABILITY

Perhaps one factor that is being overlooked in this debate is that the problems of educability of Indian students may lie between the child's attitudes developed within one setting and the expectations and requirements of schooling. For example, schooling requires obedience and assent on the part of students. It requires that students accept that knowledge is important to their survival and their future. It may be that education is not viewed in that context by Indian students who drop out. In fact, there is evidence to suggest that Indian students have developed a resistance to learning.

One explanation for the failure of minority students that has received a great deal of attention in the last decade is found in the work of John Ogbu, who maintains that students, as well as their peers and their parents, are convinced that graduation from school will not help them break out of the cycle of poverty. Ogbu defines these students as members of *castelike* minority groups such as Black Americans, American Indians, Chicanos, and Puerto Ricans. These minority groups have resided in the United States for generations in situations of oppression and share a fatalistic perspective that there will never be opportunities or jobs for them. Therefore, these students develop the attitude or belief that there is no reason to try to succeed in school (Ogbu, 1982).

Ogbu (1978) criticized the cultural discontinuity theory as an explanation for school failure and suggested that the theory results from the work of anthropologists who conducted research to demonstrate that cultural discontinuities cause failure rather than to seek out the causes of failure. His most powerful argument against the cultural discontinuity theory is based on the failure of the theory to explain why immigrant children are successful in school. He maintained that cultural discontinuity among immigrant children and their homes and the schools is just as severe as that encountered by castelike minorities. However, he suggested that members of immigrant minorities are much more optimistic about their chances for opportunities in the American society and that they and their parents believe that effort should be applied to school success as it will pay off in future employment and opportunities. Ogbu (1982) further suggested that just as there are different types of minorities, castelike minorities, and new immigrant minorities, there are different kinds of cultural discontinuities: (a) universal discontinuities experienced by all children; (b) primary discontinuities experienced as a transitional phenomenon by immigrants and non-Western peoples being introduced to Western-type school; and (c) secondary discontinuities, which are more or less enduring among castelike or subordinate minorities within Western nations (p. 291).

Ogbu defines universal discontinuities as the experiences all children encounter in school concerning what is taught, how it is taught, and how it differs from the home environment. Primary discontinuities result when non-Western students or immigrants attend Western schools. Ogbu believes that students who experience primary discontinuity are more motivated to overcome difficulties they encounter because they do not perceive success as a threat to their cultural identity, but rather as a means to opportunity and financial gain. Secondary discontinuities are ascribed to castelike minorities that "develop after members of two populations have been in contact or after members of a given population have begun to participate in an institution such as a school system, controlled by another group" (p. 298). As a result, Ogbu maintains, castelike minorities define themselves in opposition to the Anglo culture and develop "coping behaviors" as a response to oppression. These behaviors, according to Ogbu, may work against student achievement in school in that students may actively resist the attempts of the school to confer on them knowledge and values that they view as important to the Anglo culture—a culture that has consistently denied them access to opportunity.

THE POLITICS OF SCHOOL FAILURE AND SUCCESS

Indian students, whether in school or at home, are learning constantly. When Indian students fail in school, teachers assume that they are not learning. But what this actually means is that the students are not learning what teachers expect them to learn; it does not mean that students are not learning.

According to Frederick Erickson (1987), a long-time defender of the cultural discontinuity theory, learning what is taught in school may be viewed as a form of political assent, whereas not learning may be seen as a form of political resistance. This premise is based on Ogbu's concept of secondary discontinuity. Erickson went on to suggest that assent to authority within the school involves trust which he describes as a

> leap of faith—trust in the legitimacy of the authority and in the good intentions of those exercising it, trust that one's own identity will be maintained positively in relation to authority, and trust that one's own interests will be advanced by compliance with the exercise of authority. In taking such a leap of faith one faces risk. If there is no risk, trust is unnecessary. . . . To learn is to entertain risk, since learning involves moving just past the level of competence, what is already mastered, to the nearest region of incompetence, what has not yet been mastered . . . as new learning takes place with a teacher, the student again engages risk because the student reenters the zone within which the student cannot function successfully alone. If the teacher is not trustworthy the student cannot count on effective assistance from the teacher; there is high risk of being revealed as incompetent. (p. 334)

Erickson (1987) suggested that communication between student and teacher can often lead to an "entrenched, emotionally intense conflict" over time, resulting in regressive relationships where teacher and student do not bond with each other. Consequently, there is trust neither on the part of the teacher nor on the part of the student and, according to Erickson, students become more alienated by school, less likely to be persistent in their schoolwork, and fall further behind academically. In the end, these students become either passively or actively resistant, both characteristics of high-risk youth.

Moreover, Erickson (1987) acknowledged that trust and political assent are the "most fundamental factors in school success," and concluded that culture and cultural differences have varying influences on school success or lack of success:

> A much more prevalent pattern . . . is for cultural differences to make a negative influence, (1) because they contribute to miscommunication in the early grades and (2) because those initial problems of miscommunication escalate into student distrust and resistance in later grades. . . . In the absence of special effort by the school, the deep distrust of its legitimacy that increases among students as they grow older and the resources for resisting by developing oppositional identity that the school provides . . . pose serious threats to the school's perceived legitimacy. . . . Culturally responsive pedagogy is not a total solution. (pp. 354–55)

According to Gerald Wilkinson (1981), much of the rebellion against authority is not a rebellion at all, but rather a struggle on the part of Indian students to create a sense of identity and a context for themselves within a global society:

> Many students learn to conceive of all learning as "honky." A great many of these students reject all formalized learning and then con themselves into

thinking they have done the Indian thing. For all their rejection of what they perceive as White ways they end up falling prey to the shoddiest of the White radical ideas. They are concerned about Indian people and devoted to the Indian cause, but because they have not developed a sufficient critical ability to appraise nor gained the intellectual experience to distinguish, they fall for the radicals' worst ideas, not their best. Another group may conceive of learning as "honky" and as a result pursue it with a vengeance. They view a degree from a university not as a tool to get more involved in the Indian community but as a passport out of it. To the American mind, these people have succeeded; to the Indian mind, they are the most tragic. (p. 49)

AMERICAN INDIANS AND THE CULTURE OF POVERTY

Various factors associated with family background (single-parent households, educational levels of parents, and socioeconomic status) have been used as explanations for the success or lack of success of American Indian students. Many researchers have demonstrated a correlation between dropping out and socioeconomic status of the family, whereas others have suggested that cultural differences between the home environment and the school environment place the students at risk. Others have maintained that parents' educational levels and female heads of households are deciding factors in premature school leaving.

These factors are the consequences of poverty. Whether an individual is a reservation Indian, an African American living in the ghetto, a Hispanic from the barrio, or an Appalachian White, these are not behaviors characteristic of an ethnic group, but rather behaviors resulting from the culture of poverty. Therefore, when we define *Indian culture* as lacking future orientation and living day-to-day, it appears as though we have added legitimacy to the observations of outsiders who have stereotyped a people on the basis of race, rather than the economic conditions forced on a people by segregation on reservations. Thus, when a child is late for school because she or he had to help a single working mother feed younger siblings, we define that child's tardiness as *Indian time*. When someone fails to get to a meeting on time because the car broke down, we explain the incident as "living on Indian time," rather than confronting the real reason for the situation, which is most often linked to poverty.

This legitimacy of stereotypes about American Indian people was expressed in various forms by Indian women who participated in a major study conducted among Northern Plains Tribal groups (Bowker, 1993). For example, women in the study originally expressed the belief that "taking one day at a time" was characteristic of the Indian culture. When the suggestion was offered to a group of women that the philosophy was more characteristic of the creed of Alcoholics Anonymous, many of the women immediately made the connection that origins of the characteristics are embedded in the subculture of recovering alcoholics. This subculture can be found among all classes and racial groups and is definitely not an "Indian trait." One woman commented:

> We have accepted the philosophy of living one day at a time as characteristic of Indian behavior . . . it is not true at all. Traditionally, Indians had to plan and look toward the future for their very survival. Food was stored, tribes moved with the seasons . . . social gatherings were planned because it often required travel to distant places. (p. 134).

Clearly there is a relationship between dropping out of school and poverty for American Indian females. Often teachers misinterpret poverty as a cultural attribute and explain away student behaviors as "being Indian." Perhaps even more enlightening to this discussion is the fact that American Indians themselves have embraced many of their behaviors and events in their lives as "being Indian" rather than recognizing that the basis is actually related to poverty conditions.

It is more convenient for school personnel to attribute tardiness to "Indian time," or to make negative judgments about parents' lack of interest or appreciation for school by insinuating that they are embedded in the traditions of an oral culture and language rather than in the White, Anglo written tradition. It is much easier to assign inappropriate behaviors—such as boredom, idleness in class, or daydreaming—to traditional, carefree, permissive Indian parenting than to address the attitudes of teachers or the lack of proper nutrition.

Over and over again, American Indians have allowed researchers and writers to explain away behaviors as the truths of culture. In other words, American Indians have, in a sense, cooperated by attributing their own behaviors to culture.

PARENTS' EDUCATIONAL LEVEL

Research tells us that poverty and educational level are directly related. A number of researchers have maintained that socioeconomic status and educational level of parents are more influential than school factors in determining whether or not a student stays in school or drops out. Throughout the literature, girls whose mothers dropped out of school are reportedly more at risk than girls whose mothers graduated from high school.

From Bowker's (1993) work, it would appear that parental support and involvement is the key to a child's success in school. A parent with an eighth-grade education can be just as supportive as a parent with a graduate degree. On the other hand, parents in both of those categories can neglect their children, be too much involved in their own lives and work, and fail to recognize the importance of parental guidance and support in a child's life.

Clearly, girls whose mothers dropped out of school are more at risk than girls whose mothers graduated from high school. There is, however, another intervening factor, according to Bowker. Many women whose mothers dropped out often reported their mothers returning to school and completing high school requirements and, in some cases, college degrees. This type of role modeling certainly impacts American Indian girls. When parents, either verbally or by modeling, set expectations for girls to complete school and reinforce the message that school is important, the girls react positively.

It has also been reported by many researchers that the number of American Indian youth growing up in one-parent homes far exceeds the national norm. Research also tells us that children from one-parent homes are more at risk than children who grow up in the traditional homes of two-parent families. In the case of American Indian children, although there may be only one parent in the family, there often are other adults in the household, including grandparents, aunts, uncles, and even live-in mates.

Although being raised in a single-parent home does not mean that a girl will drop out of school, Bowker (1993) found a correlation between dropping out and single-parent homes. However, she theorized that this may be the result of the economic status of single-parent homes rather than family structure. Furthermore, Bowker reported that the stability of family structure appears important to all women. Women from divorced homes or single-parent homes, in some cases, were less likely to find the support and encouragement they needed to remain in school. Yet the absence of birth parents (girls raised by relatives or guardians) in itself seemed to be less important unless poverty was a major problem.

Because single parenting is much more common among American Indians than among other groups in the country, it is evident that support for single mothers is critical to the welfare of children. Whether this support comes in the form of tribal assistance, opportunities for increased training and jobs, or family support, it must be recognized that single-parent families are on the increase within American Indian communities and more teenage girls are having babies. As a result, this problem is likely to increase, thus placing larger numbers of children at risk.

CONCLUSION

Senator Carol Moseley-Braun recently labeled the welfare legislation passed in Congress as the "Pontius Pilate approach." Basically, Congress has voted to wash their hands, so to speak, of the poor. If lawmakers really wanted to address the issues of poverty in America they would have to deal with the gross disparity of wealth, income, and power in this country. Everyone but the rich will suffer from the destruction of federal programs, especially the American Indian who is already labeled "the poorest of the poor."

The question remains as to what should be done for American Indian children to encourage them to be all that they can be. First, it is imperative that we reject the assumption that poverty and race are synonymous. If we accept that a percentage of all people in the United States have children out of wedlock, that they drink alcohol, take drugs, live on welfare, get divorced, and are unemployed, then we can recognize that such behaviors exist across all classes and all groups of people, and dispel the idea that race produces pathological behaviors. Throughout the research on American Indians, the discussions suggest that pathological behaviors are attributed to cultural characteristics, traits, values, and differences within tribal societies. Other writers would lead us to believe that those same characteristics found in racial groups are typically found among the poor, who also tend to be minority as well.

Moreover, we should distinguish between those issues and behaviors that are truly cultural and those that are not, rather than legitimizing stereotypical views of our people and our tribal groups. We should fight for policy changes that will provide opportunities for our children, for better housing, economic development of reservations, better health care for our children and our elderly, and for the kind of substance abuse treatment and rehabilitation that is available to the affluent in American society. Educators interested in the problems of American Indian students must examine the effects of restricted socialization and health factors on the acquisition of the hidden curriculum and its implications for our children.

If we accept that our children are unsuccessful because they are Indian and that our culture is incompatible with the White culture, then we are blaming ourselves and our children for their lack of success, rather than placing the blame where it rightfully belongs.

REFERENCES

Baratz, S., & Baratz, J. (1970). Early childhood intervention: The social science base of institutional racism. *Harvard Educational Review, 40*(1), 29–50.

Birch, H. G. (1972). Malnutrition, learning, and intelligence. *American Journal of Public Health, 62*(6), 773–784.

Birch, H. G., & Gussow, J. D. (1970). *Disadvantaged children: Health, nutrition, and school failure.* New York: Harcourt Brace.

Bloom, B. S. (1972). Innocence in education. *School Review, 80*(3), 333–352.

Bowers, C. A., & Flanders, D. J. (1990). *Responsive teaching: An ecological approach to classroom patterns of language, culture, and thought.* New York: Teachers College Press.

Bowker, A. (1993). *Sisters in the blood: The education of women in Native America.* Newton, MA: WEEA Publishing Center.

Brock, J. (1961). *Recent advances in human nutrition.* London: Churchill.

Chan, K. S., & Osthimer, B. (1983). *Navajo youth and early school withdrawal: A case study.* Los Alamitos, CA: National Center for Bilingual Research.

Coladarci, T. (1983). High school dropout among Native Americans. *Journal of American Indian Education, 23*(1), 15–22.

Cole, M., & Bruner, J. (1971). Cultural differences and inferences about psychological processes. *American Psychologist, 26*(10), 867–876.

Coles, R. (1971). *Children of crisis: Vol. 3. The south goes north.* Boston: Little, Brown.

Deyhle, D. (1989). Pushouts and pullouts: Navajo and Ute school leavers. *Journal of Navajo Education, 6*(2), 36–51.

Ellwood, D. T. (1988). *Poor support: Poverty in the American family.* New York: Basic Books.

Erickson, F. (1987). Transformation and school success: The politics and culture of educational achievement. *Anthropology and Education Quarterly, 18*(4), 335–356.

Gallimore, R., Boggs, J., & Jordan, C. (1974). *Culture, behavior, and education.* Beverly Hills, CA: Sage.

Gonzalez, J. M. (1985). Renegotiating society's contract with the public schools. *Carnegie Quarterly,* p. 4.

Hertzig, M. G., Birch, H. G., Richardson, S. A., & Tizard, J. (1972). Intellectual levels of school children severely malnourished during the first 2 years of life. *Pediatrics, 49*(6), 814–824.

Hispanic Policy Development Project. (1984). *Make something happen.* Washington, DC: National Commission on Secondary Schooling for Hispanics.

Hurwitz, N. (1975, May). Communications networks and the urban poor. *Equal Opportunity Review,* 1–5.

Hymes, D. H. (1974). On ways of speaking. In P. Bauman & J. Sherzer (Eds.), *Explorations in the ethnography of speaking.* New York: Cambridge University Press.

Jacob, E., & Jordan, C. (1987). Explaining the school performance of minority students. *Anthropology and Education Quarterly, 18*(4), 259–392.

Labov, W. (1970). The logic of nonstandard English. In F. Williams (Ed.), *Language and poverty: Perspectives on a theme.* Chicago: Markham.

Ledlow, S. (1992). Is cultural discontinuity an adequate explanation for dropping out? *Journal of American Indian Education, 31*(3), 21–36.

Levin, H. (1975). *Work: The staff of life.* Paper presented at the American Psychological Association Conference, New York.

National Foundation for the Improvement of Education. (1986). *Dropping out: The quiet killer of the American dream.* Washington, DC: National Education Association.

Ogbu, J. U. (1974). *The next generation.* New York: Academic Press.

Ogbu, J. U. (1978). *Minority education and caste: The American system in crosscultural perspective.* New York: Academic Press.

Ogbu, J. U. (1982). Cultural discontinuities and schooling. *Anthropology and Education Quarterly, 13*(4), 290–307.

Peng, S. S. (1985, March). *High school dropouts: A national concern.* A paper prepared by the U.S. Department of Education for the Business Advisory Commission, Education Commission of the States, Denver, CO.

Peng, S. S., & Takai, R. T. (1983). *High school dropouts: Descriptive information from high school and beyond.* Washington, DC: National Center for Educational Statistics.

Philips, S. U. (1983). *The invisible culture.* New York: Longman.

Reyhner, J. (1992). American Indians out of school: A review of school–based causes and solutions. *Journal of American Indian Education, 31*(3), 21–56.

Sawhill, I. V. (1989, Summer). The underclass: An overview. *Public Interest, 96,* 3, 5.

Shaefer, E. S. (1970). Need for early and continuing education. In V. H. Denenberg (Ed.), *Education of the infant and young children.* New York: Academic Press.

Shaefer, E. S. (1976). Parents as educators: Evidence from cross-sectional, longitudinal, and intervention research. In W. W. Hartup (Ed.), *The young child* (Vol. 2). Washington, DC: National Association for the Education of Young Children.

Shipman, J., & Bussis, A. (1968). The impact of the family. *Disadvantaged children and their first school experience: ETS-OEO longitudinal study.* Princeton, NJ: Educational Testing Service.

Sizer, T. R. (1984). *Horace's compromise: The dilemma of the American high school.* Boston: Houghton Mifflin.

Spindler, G. D. (1987). Why have minority groups in North America been disadvantaged in their schools? In G. D. Spindler (Ed.), *Education and cultural process: Anthropological approaches* (pp. 160–172). Prospect Heights, IL: Waveland Press.

Swisher, K. G., Hoisch, M., & Pavel, D. M. (1991). *American Indian/Alaskan native dropout study.* Washington, DC: National Education Association.

U.S. Census. 1990. Washington, DC: U.S. Government Printing Office.

U.S. Government Accounting Office. (1986). *Dropouts: The extent and nature of the problem.* Washington, DC: U.S. Government Printing Office.

Vogt, L., Jordan, C., & Tharp, R. G. (1987). Explaining school failure, producing school success: Two cases. *Anthropology and Education Quarterly, 18*(4), 276–286.

Wilkinson, G. (1981, January/April). Educational problems in the Indian community: A comment on learning as colonialism. *Integrateducation, 19,*46–50.

Wilson, W. J. (1987). *The truly disadvantaged: The inner-city, the underclass, and public policy.* Chicago: University of Chicago Press.

II

Family and Peer Contexts and Adolescent Adjustment

6

Parents and Peers in the Lives of African-American Adolescents: An Interactive Approach to the Study of Problem Behavior

Craig A. Mason
Ana Marie Cauce
Nancy Gonzales

It has become almost impossible to open a newspaper or turn on the evening news without being reminded of the ever-increasing levels of violence and various problem behaviors that afflict today's youth. Between 1980 and 1990, the frequency with which youths between the ages of 10 and 17 committed serious crimes grew at an astonishing rate. For example, the number of youths arrested for murder increased by 90%, compared to a 10% increase for adults (FBI Uniform Crime Statistics, as cited in the *Seattle Times*, August 30, 1992). What's more, drug use, which had declined for nearly a decade, is regaining popularity. Although these increases and their attendant effects cut across ethnicity, they are particularly pronounced for African-American youth, who are more likely to be involved as participants and victims of such behaviors. Not surprisingly, there has been a growing call from policymakers and citizens alike for research to help us understand what factors lead to these problematic behaviors, especially among African-American youth.

The types of behavior of most concern have been referred to variously as *conduct disorder, delinquency, externalizing,* and *deviant* and *antisocial* behavior, depending on the age of the offender, the severity of the behavior, and the preference of the researcher. This constellation of behavior problems, which has been called *problem behavior syndrome* (Jessor & Jessor, 1977), includes fighting, stealing, alcohol and drug use, defiance of authority at home or at school, and aggression; it will be referred to throughout this chapter simply as *problem behavior*.

Research suggests that problem behavior is remarkably stable, with the presence of such behaviors during childhood and early adolescence predicting later levels of problem behavior and delinquency (Dishion & Loeber, 1985; Farrington 1987; Robins, 1966, 1978). Given this stability, one promising area for research is the family environment. For example, harsh parenting strategies and coercive family interactions have been consistently found to predict adolescent problem behavior (Conger, Conger, Elder, Lorenz, Simons, & Whitbeck, 1992; Dishion & Loeber, 1985; Forgatch & Stoolmiller, 1994).

THE FAMILY ENVIRONMENT:
WARMTH AND CONTROL

The centrality of family relationships in the development of behavior problems during early childhood is undisputed. A growing body of research suggests that this continues to be the case through adolescence (Dishion & Loeber, 1985; Forgatch & Stoolmiller, 1994; Henggeler, 1989). Beginning with the work of Schaefer (1965), Becker (1964), and Baumrind (1968), two constructs—parental warmth and parental control—have been traditionally used to describe parenting practices or childrearing styles. Variations on this dimensional schema continue to be reflected in more current descriptions of parent–child relationships during adolescence (e.g., Allen, Hauser, Eickholt, Bell, & O'Connor, 1994; Conger et al., 1992).

In general, *parental warmth*, or a close affective bond between parent and child, is related positively to healthy psychological adjustment in children and adolescents (Grotevant & Cooper, 1985; Powers, Hauser, & Kilner, 1989). The relationship between control and adjustment is less straightforward. Overly harsh and restrictive forms of control have generally been considered harmful to healthy adjustment and are positively related to problem behavior (Conger et al., 1992; Steinberg, 1990). On the other hand, *firm* or *behavioral* control (the absence of which is sometimes referred to as *lax* control) is most often negatively related to problem behavior (Dornbusch & Gray, 1988; Forgatch & Stoolmiller, 1994; Patterson & Stouthamer-Loeber, 1984). That is, when parents exercise firm control, their children are *less* apt to engage in problem behavior.

A great deal of research undergirds this two-dimensional schema for conceptualizing childrearing. The literature supporting the relationship of control and warmth to social adjustment and problem behavior is likewise impressive. Nonetheless, almost all the research in this area has been conducted within White families. Recent work with multicultural samples has suggested that childrearing within African-American families can be described in terms of Baumrind's (1968) schema, which used warmth and control dimensions to categorize families as authoritative, authoritarian, or permissive (Steinberg, Dornbusch, & Brown, 1992). Interestingly, this same body of work suggests that in contrast to White families, childrearing practices in African-American families are not predictive of educational attainment, which has been strongly related to problem behavior (Steinberg et al., 1992).

This lack of predictive ability may be due in part to the possibility that the same childrearing practices that lead to either healthy or problem behaviors in White children may not be related to the same behaviors in African-American children. For example, Baumrind (1972) found that African-American children raised in authoritarian homes fared better academically than those in authoritative homes. This finding calls into question the applicability to African-American families of research on links between authoritative or authoritarian parenting and school achievement that has been based primarily on White families; this issue has been raised by others (Cauce, Hiraga, Graves, Gonzales, Ryan-Finn, & Grove, in press).

Steinberg and colleagues (Steinberg et al., 1992) have suggested an alternative explanation. They found that African-American adolescents' peer groups often eschew academically oriented goals. Such peer groups, they suggest, short-circuit the potentially positive influence of the family. Based largely on this work, the National Research Council (1993) proposed that "[deviant] peer influences are overwhelming and undermining the positive impact of good parenting" (p. 55).

THE PEER ENVIRONMENT AS A CONTEXT FOR PARENTING

Research clearly implicates the peer environment in the development of adolescent problem behavior (Dryfoos, 1990; Elliott, Huizinga, & Ageton, 1985). Youths who say their friends steal, get into fights, or use drugs, for example, are more apt to be involved in these same activities themselves (Dishion & Loeber, 1985; Henggeler, 1989; Rutter & Giller, 1983). Indeed, Patterson and his colleagues (Patterson, Reid, & Dishion, 1992) at the Oregon Social Learning Center have noted that although the family provides basic life training, avoiding or engaging in problem behavior is ultimately a group activity.

In short, adolescence is a time of changing social relationships during which peers play an increasingly central role. Given the influence of peer relationships on healthy adolescent adjustment and behavior (Cauce & Srebnik, 1991; Hartup, 1983), it is not surprising that association with peer groups that engage in problem behavior should be related to less optimal adjustment. Indeed, association with such peers is perhaps the single most robust and consistent predictor of problem behavior. For example, Oetting and Beauvais (1987) reported that "initiation and maintenance of drug use among adolescents is almost entirely a function of peer clusters" (p. 136). Further, in a classic study focusing on general problem behavior, personality, and environmental influences, Jessor and Jessor (1977) found that youth aged 12 to 22 were more likely to exhibit problem behavior if they accepted such behavior in their peers or if their peers engaged in such behavior.

Association with problem peers is often viewed as an intermediary step in a longer causal process, beginning with the family (Patterson, Reid, & Dishion, 1992). In *coercion theory*, based on the extensive research and clinical work by Patterson and his colleagues at the Oregon Social Learning Center (Patterson, Reid, & Dishion, 1992; Patterson & Stouthamer-Loeber, 1984), too much harsh control interferes with a child's ability to form healthy, prosocial friendships. Not enough firm control, however, leads to association with problem peers in adolescence. Although the rationale is somewhat different, Eccles and colleagues (Eccles, Buchanan, Flanagan, Fuligini, Midgley, & Yee, 1991) also proposed that poor parenting may lead to problem behavior by increasing adolescents' vulnerability to negative peer influences.

The formulations previously discussed above essentially suggest a mediational model. In this model, the effect of one predictor on an outcome is mediated by a second, intermediate variable. In other words, while A predicts C, in reality, A influences B, which then influences C. For example, in the simple model presented in Fig. 6.1, parenting behaviors influence peer group association which, in turn, leads to adolescent problem behavior.

In contrast to the mediational approach, the ecological perspective presented by Steinberg et al. (1992) entails a moderator model. Rather than viewing peer relationships as the mechanism through which earlier family influences are carried forward into adolescence, they view the peer environment as a contextual factor that must be taken into account when gauging the influence of parenting. Fig. 6.2 is a visual representation of the moderator model, in which A and B interact *to produce* C.

Though Steinberg et al. (1992) suggested a moderator model of family and peer influences, that model is never directly tested in their work. Instead, because their focus is on explaining ethnic group differences in achievement-related behavior, they essentially employ ethnicity as a proxy variable for peer group practices—Asian-American peer groups value achievement, African-American peer groups devalue achievement, and White and Hispanic/Latino peer groups lie somewhere in the middle. The use of ethnicity as proxy for a behavioral or environmental variable, while perhaps effective at the group level, overlooks the fact that

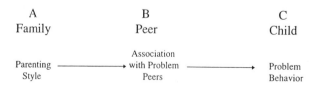

FIG. 6.1. A mediational model of family and peer influences.

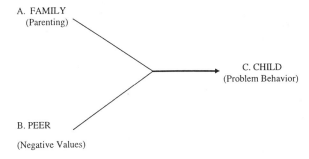

A. FAMILY
(Parenting)

C. CHILD
(Problem Behavior)

B. PEER
(Negative Values)

FIG. 6.2. A moderator model of family and peer influences.

there is typically as much, if not more, variation within groups as between groups.

Although African-American adolescents as a group may engage in (and are victims of) problem behavior more often than White youths, many—quite likely most—do not engage in problem behavior at all. The focus of this chapter is not on why or how African Americans are different from Whites, Hispanic/Latinos, or Asian Americans, but on African Americans themselves. Hence, the goal of the following research is to examine how family and peer influences interact to explain the development and maintenance of problem behaviors *within* a sample of African-American adolescents.

THE BASIC STUDY

Beginning in 1989 and ending in 1993, the authors interviewed African-American adolescents and their parents as part of the Family and Adolescent Study of School Transitions (FASST). All the adolescents were in either the seventh or eighth grade at the start of the study; they ranged in age from 12 to 15 (mean = 13.5). The sample was skewed with regard to gender, with females comprising almost two thirds of the group.

Families were recruited from a variety of formal and informal community systems (e.g., schools, churches, and youth groups) to represent a broad spectrum of the African-American community in the greater Seattle area, where they make up approximately 20% of the larger population. Data obtained at the start of the study suggested that the families were primarily working-class, but socioeconomically diverse. Most of the mothers (91%) were high school graduates, although few graduated from college (11%). When household income was examined, most families could not be categorized as *poor* (e.g., 58% reported incomes above $20,000 per year), but relatively few reported incomes that could be considered as falling within the medium-to-high range (e.g., less than 20% reported household incomes greater than $40,000 per year).

Initial interviews were conducted with 144 adolescents and their families. Four families were headed by a single father, and in seven, neither parent was present. The remaining families were almost equally divided into two-parent families (52%) and mother-headed, single-parent families (48%). Sixty-four percent of the two-parent families included both biological parents.

The retention rate over the course of the study was approximately 75%, with families whose incomes were lower less likely to be retained. It should be noted that adolescents and families who underwent changes in their custodial arrangements were dropped from some prospective analyses; consequently, some included as few as 85 families. For complete details of the analyses discussed here, see Mason, Cauce, Gonzales, and Hiraga (1994), Mason, Cauce, Gonzales, and Hiraga (in press), and Mason, Cauce, Gonzales, Hiraga, and Grove (1994).

The questionnaires that were administered tapped into key dimensions of parenting style, including parental warmth, or the affective quality of the parent-child bond, and two broad types of parental control: negative, manipulative/guilt-based control, referred to as *restrictive control*, and a more positive form, referred to herein as *firm control*. Questionnaires also assessed the adolescents' involvement in problem behavior and the degree to which their peer groups were involved in problem behavior (e.g., the deviant peer group construct). In contrast to Steinberg and his colleagues (Steinberg et al., 1992), who administered questionnaires in schools to adolescents only, the authors' questionnaires were individually administered at home to include parents. All the analyses presented here draw from this multiple-informant format.

As noted previously, the type of problem behavior assessed varied from minor problems, including fighting (without a weapon) and skipping school, to more serious problems, such as stealing, using alcohol or drugs, and fighting with a weapon. To place this behavior in its proper context, it should be noted that the sample mean (about 54) on the externalizing scale of the Achenbach Child Behavior Checklist (Achenbach & Edelbrock, 1979) was close to the normative mean of 50. This normative sample of African-American youths is relatively rare in research to date (Cauce, Hiraga, Graves, Gonzales, Ryan-Finn, & Grove, in press).

AN INTERACTIVE CONTEXTUAL MODEL
OF PARENTING

The sine qua non of an interactive contextual model of parenting is that the effects of specific parenting behaviors, or a specific parenting style, vary according to other contextual variables, for instance, the peer group context.

In other words, like parenting behaviors may have different effects given different contextual environments. Statistically, such differences are assessed via an interaction between the contextual factor and parenting; theoretically, the contextual factor is said to "moderate" the effect of parenting.

In this examination, the peer group was the contextual factor that the authors believed would moderate the effects of parenting, which was examined in terms of warmth and control. The first step in examining an interactive model entailed assessing the main effects of variables that will later be examined jointly. (Main effects assess the degree to which predictors affect the outcome directly; an interactive model can "work" regardless of whether main effects are found.) In terms of warmth and control, our results were mixed.

When examined directly, the relationship between parental warmth, as reported by parents, and problem behavior was only marginally significant.[1] When adolescents were the source of reports on the closeness of the parent–child relationship, the examination evidenced no direct relationship to problem behavior. In contrast, when parental control was examined, a strong link with problem behavior was found. Higher levels of adolescent reports of parental *firm* control were related to lower levels of problem behavior; however, parent reports of *restrictive* control were found to have a curvilinear effect on levels of problem behavior. The highest levels of problem behavior were evidenced when parents reported using either very high or very low levels of restrictive control. The optimal level of control—that which is associated with the lowest amount of problem behavior—was located somewhere near the middle of two extremes, neither too high nor too low.

Nonetheless, the direct association between control and problem behavior is, at best, modest. Regardless of the statistical index examined (e.g., simple correlations, percentages of variance, beta weights, or path coefficients), the effect size is small. This suggests that consideration of other factors—examined in isolation or in combination with parenting—is needed to better understand adolescent problem behavior.

As noted previously, a promising avenue of study is the nature of the adolescent's peer group or whether the adolescent associates with deviant peers. This idea was confirmed in the present study, as adolescent reports of their friends' involvement in deviant activities proved a robust predictor of their own problem behavior. In contrast to the small direct effect of parenting, the direct effect of the peer group could be qualified as falling within the moderate-to-large range.

If these analyses were ended here, one might conclude, as did the

---

[1]Our use of the terms *parents* and *parenting* throughout is consonant with the tradition of research in that field. However, the overwhelming number of parents that participated in this study were mothers. Thus, the numbers represented here are most applicable to mothers and mothering.

National Research Council (1993), that in light of the powerful effects of peer groups, parenting style has little impact on African-American adolescents. Today, research examining interactive, contextual relationships is still relatively uncommon; the path most traveled begins and ends with the examination of main effects and direct relationships. Expanding the current study to include contextual effects, however, has yielded interesting results—not only did the peer group influence problem behavior directly, it also influenced how parenting affected problem behavior.

SIMPLE LINEAR MODERATORS

Although the closeness of the parent–child relationship was not found to directly influence problem behavior, its effects emerged in interaction with peer group behavior. Specifically, for adolescents in "good" peer groups, the affective quality of parent–child relationships was unrelated to whether they engaged in problem behavior. Simply put, such youth did not engage in much problem behavior. Among those adolescents in more problematic peer groups, however, mother–child relationships factored much more heavily. Close relationships with their mothers provided these children with buffers against the harmful influences of problem peers. This effect is evidenced by the lower rates of problem behavior exhibited by these youth as compared to those who were partners in weaker mother–child dyads.

The interactive nature of the relationships described previously is relatively simple in construct. As illustrated by the model represented in Fig. 6.3, variable A (e.g., the peer group) is said to moderate the effects of variable B (e.g., the parent–child relationship). An example of a more extreme form of the model, shown in Fig. 6.4, was suggested by Baldwin,

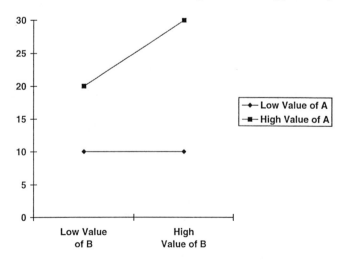

FIG. 6.3. Ordinal or noncrossover interaction.

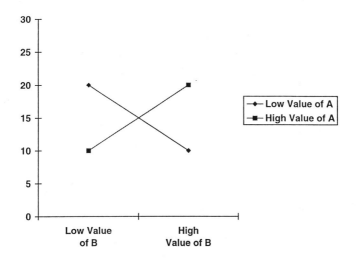

FIG. 6.4. Disordinal or crossover interaction.

Baldwin, and Cole (1990). They found that in high-risk environments, adolescents demonstrated higher levels of cognitive competence when their parents exercised higher levels of control. In low-risk environments, higher levels of cognitive competence were found when parents exercised lower levels of control. As such, this suggests that regression lines based on high and low values of the moderator cross. These types of interactions have been referred to as *disordinal/crossover interactions* (Fig. 6.4), as opposed to *ordinal/noncrossover interactions* (Fig. 6.3), in which regression lines do not cross within the possible range of data values (Aiken & West, 1991; Lubin, 1961).

CURVILINEAR MODERATORS

Although the effects of parental warmth were readily captured by a simple linear model, a more complex model was needed to render the influence of parental control. A curvilinear model was tested. Although still relatively rare, in recent years there has been a growing interest in curvilinear relationships between parenting and child behavior and adjustment. Typically, in a curvilinear model, it is predicted that some moderate level of a parenting behavior is optimal for adolescent outcomes; levels above or below this optimal level are associated with negative adolescent outcomes. Thus, when graphed, this type of a curvilinear relationship resembles a "U" when the outcome in question suggests problem behavior, or an upside-down "U" for more adaptive behavior.

Curvilinear relationships of this nature are statistically examined by a quadratic term in the predictive equation. The quadratic term, parenting^2, indicates the curvilinear nature of the relationship. It is possible to have linear interactions, curvilinear interactions, or both between contextual variables and curvilinear parenting variables. Statistically, these interactions are evident in two ways. First, a significant interaction between a context variable and the linear term of a curvilinear parenting variable (e.g., context X parenting) generally indicates that the optimal level of parenting changes according to the contextual variable. The location of the "U" changes, depending on the contextual, moderator variable. This type of interactive relationship is presented in Fig. 6.5.

In contrast, a significant interaction between a context variable and the quadratic term of a curvilinear parenting variable (i.e., context X parenting^2) generally indicates that the strength or shape of the curve changes based on the level of the contextual variable. The location of the "U" also may change across values of the contextual moderator (depending on other terms in the regression equation), but, more significantly, the shape of the "U" may range from being very shallow—or even inverse—to very steep. The profundity of this curve depends on the level of the contextual variable. An example of this type of interactive relationship is presented in Fig. 6.6.

Both types of interactive curvilinear relationships were found in the examination of the peer environment and parental control as predictors of behavior problems in African-American adolescents. With regard to firm control, both the optimal level and the strength of the curvilinear effect increased when adolescents were part of a more negative peer group. With restrictive control, the curvilinear interaction reflected a strengthening in the curvilinear effect, rather than an actual change in the optimal level. Restrictive control had no effect on levels of problem behavior for youth in

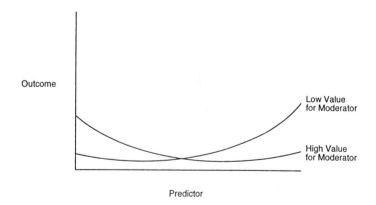

FIG. 6.5. Graph of a moderator variable interacting with the linear term of a curvilinear variable (i.e., $y = b_3mx + b_2x^2 + b_1x + b_0$).

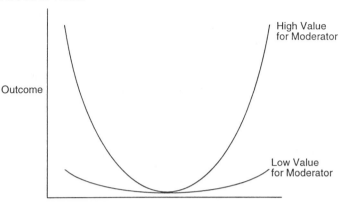

FIG. 6.6. Graph of a moderator variable interacting with the quadradic term of a curvilinear variable (i.e., $y = b_3 mx^2 + b_2 x^2 + b_1 x + b_0$.

less problematic peer groups, although it had a strong curvilinear effect when youths reported that their peer groups engaged in more deviant behavior.

PRACTICAL IMPLICATIONS OF INTERACTIVE, CONTEXTUAL MODELS OF PARENTING

On a theoretical level, this study suggests that the effects of parenting behaviors are linked to the context in which they take place. Examining parenting without also examining the peer environment tells an incomplete and possibly misleading story. Furthermore, even when considered simultaneously, their relationship is not straightforward and linear, making for an extremely complex situation that has received relatively little attention. Increasingly complex models, however, are being introduced in the literature, especially now that structural equation modeling techniques have become so accessible. These models can readily provide important insights into why African-American parents parent the way they do (see McLoyd, chap. 2, this volume, and Mason, Cauce, Gonzales, Hiraga, & Grove [1994] for two examples). Moderator models such as those examined in this chapter have no such explanatory function; they do not help us understand why parents parent in specific ways.

Instead, moderator models such as these help us understand why two parents behaving in identical manners can have different impacts on their children. They warn us that although typologies suggesting that any one type of parenting is better than others may prove sufficient to describe parenting in the context of the White middle class, they are too simplistic to capture the challenges facing parents of African-American children.

The term *precision parenting* has been used to describe the difficulty African-American parents face in finding the right amount of control to exert in the face of a peer environment which may influence their children in undesirable ways. Indeed, one mother in our study said her task as a parent was like "threading a needle in the dark." If she was too lenient, she believed her daughter would run wild, like some of her peers who were pregnant, in trouble with the law, or had dropped out of school. On the other hand, she feared that if she was too strict, her daughter would grow distant and begin to "sneak around," ultimately getting into trouble anyway.

In her search for the "golden mean" of parenting, this mother cultivated a close relationship with her daughter and maintained a vigilant stance toward not only her behavior, but also that of her peer group. This is consistent with what the authors' research suggests to be optimal parenting behavior. To be sure, this ideal is extremely difficult to establish, and even more difficult to maintain; it is much more challenging than what is required of parents in more benign and circumscribed contexts.

Researchers and policymakers have been overly critical when characterizing the so-called failures of African-American parents. In a tradition established by the Moynihan report (1965), the problems of African-American youth are blamed on deficiencies in the family environment, whether in terms of structure or parenting behaviors. A brief look at the research literature of the last several decades reveals that African-American parenting styles have been described as overly authoritarian, permissive, and controlling. The research outlined in this chapter, however, suggests that such characterizations are too simplistic. For example, at least insofar as problem behavior is examined, what may be too authoritarian in one context may be too permissive in another.

In their work with African-American families during the last several years, the authors have noted that parents struggle with a number of basic questions: Should I allow my daughter to go out in the afternoon, or make her wait for me to come home from work? Is eleven o'clock too late to let my son stay out with friends? Is a month-long grounding too harsh a punishment for skipping a class? Unfortunately, there are no simple answers to these concerns. Parenting is not like a t-shirt—one size does not fit all.

Effective parenting is not simply a matter of knowing adolescents and gauging their level of maturity; parents must also take into account adolescents' peer groups, and the types of behaviors in which they engage. As our research programs increasingly reflect the diversity of the U.S. population, it is likely that other contextual factors of importance will emerge. The neighborhood environment comes immediately to mind as an important consideration that is only recently beginning to get the attention it merits. Our challenge as researchers is finding models that are not so complex as to be uninterpretable, but not so simple as to be misleading. When it comes to African-American youth and their families, this task is just beginning.

REFERENCES

Achenbach, T. M., & Edelbrock, C. S. (1979). The Child Behavior Profile: I. Boys aged 12–16 and girls aged 6–11 and 12–16. *Journal of Counseling and Clinical Psychology, 47*(2), 223–233.

Aiken, L. S., & West, S. G. (1991). *Multiple regression: Testing and interpreting interactions.* Newbury Park, CA: Sage.

Allen, J. P., Hauser, S. T., Eickholt, C., Bell, K. L., & O'Connor, T. G. (1994). Autonomy and relatedness in family interactions as predictors of expressions of negative adolescent affect. *Journal of Research on Adolescence, 4*(4), 535–552.

Baldwin, A. L., Baldwin, C., & Cole, R. E. (1990). Stress-resistant families and stress-resistant children. In J. Rolf, A. Masten, D. Cicchetti, K. Nuechterlein, & S. Weintraub (Eds.), *Risk and protective factors in the development of psychopathology* (pp. 257–280). Cambridge, England: Cambridge University Press.

Baumrind, D. (1968). Authoritarian vs. authoritative control. *Adolescence, 3*(11), 255–272.

Baumrind, D. (1972). An exploratory study of socialization effects on Black children: Some Black–White comparisons. *Child Development, 43*(1), 261–267.

Becker, W. C. (1964). Consequences of different types of parental discipline. In M. L. Hoffman & L. W. Hoffman (Eds.), *Review of child development research* (Vol. 1, pp. 756–761). New York: Russell Sage.

Cauce, A. M., Hiraga, Y., Graves, D., Gonzales, N., Ryan-Finn, K., & Grove, K. (in press). African-American mothers and their adolescent daughters: Closeness, conflict, and control. In B. J. Leadbeater & N. Way (Eds.), *Urban adolescent girls: Current research and future trends.* New York: New York University Press.

Cauce, A. M., & Srebnik, D. S. (1991). Returning to social support systems: A morphological analysis of social networks. *American Journal of Community Psychology, 18*(4), 609–616.

Conger, R. D., Conger, K. J., Elder, G. H., Lorenz, F. O., Simons, R. L., & Whitbeck, L. B. (1992). A family process model of economic hardship and adjustment of early adolescent boys. *Child Development, 63*(3), 526–541.

Dishion, T. J., & Loeber, R. (1985). Adolescent marijuana and alcohol use: The role of parents and peers revisited. *American Journal of Drug and Alcohol Abuse, 11*(1–2), 11–25.

Dornbusch, S. M., & Gray, K. D. (1988). Single-parent families. In S. M. Dornbusch & M. H. Strober (Eds.), *Feminism, children, and the new families* (pp. 274–296). New York: Guilford.

Dryfoos, J. G. (1990). *Adolescents at risk: Prevalence and prevention.* New York: Oxford University Press.

Eccles, J. S., Buchanan, C. M., Flanagran, C., Fuligini, A., Midgley, C., & Yee, D. (1991). Control versus autonomy during early adolescence. *Journal of Social Issues, 47*(4), 53–68.

Elliott, D. S., Huizinga, D., & Ageton, S. S. (1985). *Explaining delinquency and drug use.* Beverly Hills, CA: Sage.

Farrington, D. P. (1987). Early precursors of frequent offending. In J. Q. Wilson & G. C. Loury (Eds.), *From children to citizens: Families, schools, and delinquency prevention* (pp. 136–143). New York: Springer-Verlag.

FBI Uniform Crime Statistics. (1992, August 30). *The Seattle Times,* p. 689.

Forgatch, M. S., & Stoolmiller, M. (1994). Emotions as contexts for adolescent delinquency. *Journal of Research on Adolescence, 4*(4), 601–614.

Grotevant, H. D., & Cooper, C. R. (1985). Patterns of interaction in family relationships and the development of identity exploration in adolescence. *Child Development, 56*(2), 415–428.

Hartup, W. W. (1983). Peer relations. In P. H. Mussen (Ed.), *Handbook of child psychology* (Vol. 4, pp. 103–196). New York: Wiley.

Henggeler, S. W. (1989). *Delinquency in adolescence.* Newbury Park, CA: Sage.

Jessor, R., & Jessor, S. L. (1977). *Problem behavior and psychosocial development: A longitudinal study of youth.* New York: Academic Press.

Lubin, A. (1961). The interpretation of significant interaction. *Educational and Psychological Measurement, 21*(4), 807–817.

Mason, C. A., Cauce, A. M., Gonzales, N., & Hiraga, Y. (1994). Adolescent problem behavior: The effect of peers and the moderating roles of father absence and the mother-child relationship. *American Journal of Community Psychology, 22*(6), 723–743.

Mason, C. A., Cauce, A. M., Gonzales, N., & Hiraga, Y. (in press). Neither too sweet nor too sour: Antisocial peers, maternal control, and problem behavior in African-American adolescents. *Child Development.*

Mason, C. A., Cauce, A. M., Gonzales, N., Hiraga, Y., & Grove, K. (1994). An ecological model of externalizing in African-American adolescents: No family is an island. *Journal of Research on Adolescence, 4*(4), 639–655.

Moynihan, D. P. (1965). The tangle of pathology. In R. Staples (Ed.), *The Black family* (pp. 37–57). Belmont, CA: Wadsworth.

National Research Council. (1993). *Losing generations: Adolescents in high-risk settings.* Washington, DC: National Academy Press.

Oetting, E. R., & Beauvais, F. (1987). Common elements in youth drug abuse: Peer clusters and other psychosocial factors. *Journal of Drug Issues, 17*(1–2), 133–151.

Patterson, G. R., Reid, J. G., & Dishion, T. J. (1992). *Antisocial boys.* Eugene, OR: Castalia.

Patterson, G., & Stouthamer-Loeber, M. (1984). The correlation of family management practices and delinquency. *Child Development, 55*(4), 1299–1307.

Powers, S. I., Hauser, S. T., & Kilner, L. S. (1989). Adolescent mental health. *American Psychologist, 44*(2), 200–208.

Robins, L. N. (1966). *Deviant children grown up: A sociological and psychiatric study of sociopathic personality.* New York: Krieger.

Robins, L. N. (1978). Sturdy childhood predictors of adult antisocial behavior: Replications from longitudinal studies. *Psychological Medicine, 8*(4), 611–622.

Rutter, M., & Giller, H. (1983). *Juvenile delinquency: Trends and perspectives.* Harmondsworth, England: Penguin.

Schaefer, E. S. (1965). A configurational analysis of children's reports of parent behavior. *Journal of Consulting Psychology, 29*(6), 552–557.

Steinberg, L. (1990). Interdependency in the family: Autonomy, conflict, and harmony in the parent-adolescent relationship. In S. Feldman & G. Elliott (Eds.), *At the threshold: The developing adolescent* (pp. 255–276). Cambridge, MA: Harvard University Press.

Steinberg, L., Dornbusch, S. M., & Brown, B. B. (1992). Ethnic differences in adolescent achievement: An ecological perspective. *American Psychologist, 47*(6), 718–729.

7

Educational and Occupational Aspirations and Expectations Among Parents of Middle School Students of Mexican Descent: Family Resources for Academic Development and Mathematics Learning[1]

Ronald W. Henderson

Underachievement and disproportionate rates of school failure among Latino populations have been widely documented (e.g., Haycock & Navarro, 1988; Orum, 1986; Valencia, 1991). Although much of the research intended to understand and ameliorate this problem has focused on literacy (Moll, 1992), a pattern of generally low levels of mathematics achievement and participation among populations of Mexican descent is an equally distressing matter. In fact, recent efforts to reform mathematics instruction have generated an emphasis on communication as a goal of mathematics instruction, resulting in an increased commonality of purpose with literacy instruction (Henderson, Landesman, Nur, & St. John, 1992).

The discrepancy between Latino and majority group performance in mathematics is especially striking for tasks that require a strong conceptual grasp of subject matter, as contrasted with skill in computation. This particular pattern of underachievement in mathematics imposes a severe constriction of opportunity for Latino populations in the United States, especially in light of predictions that an increasing portion of career opportunities in coming years will be in what Labor Secretary Robert Reich (1991) has called "symbolic-analytical services." Thus, competence in mathemat-

[1]The work reported in this chapter was made possible by a grant to the National Center for Research on Cultural Diversity and Second Language Learning from the U.S. Department of Education, Office of Educational Research and Improvement. No endorsement is implied nor should be inferred. Sincerest thanks are expressed to the families who participated in the study and to Professor Edward M. Landesman, June Sison, Estella Mejía, and Maria Castro.

ics will be required for an increasing number of jobs in the new economy. Consequently, the task of preparing students for productive roles in the workforce poses a major challenge to schools seeking to accommodate rapid demographic changes.

This chapter reports on a study of families of seventh-grade students in a middle school in which we assisted teachers as they adopted instructional practices congruent with goals of recent mathematics reform efforts. Our work in the school focused on helping teachers provide meaningful connections between student experience, mathematical skills, and conceptual understanding by contextualizing instruction (Henderson, 1995). This work was part of a larger program of research aimed at (a) gaining a better understanding of the sociocultural, instructional, and motivational dynamics that influence learning outcomes in mathematics among students of Mexican descent; and (b) developing instructional practices responsive to cultural, linguistic, and individual variations among this population of students at the middle school level (see Henderson et al., 1995).

Latino students constitute a rapidly growing segment of the school population in California. Although much of this population resides in urban centers, a substantial segment can be found in smaller communities in the state's agricultural heartland. The schools of these communities have long histories of serving students of Mexican descent, but the proportion of Mexican-descent students within the entire school population has increased dramatically within a relatively short period of time. The challenge of providing an effective educational experience for these students has only rarely been successfully met. Although many children of Mexican descent achieve well in school, this group is disproportionately represented among low achievers (Valencia, 1991). These students are plagued by high dropout rates (Rumberger, 1991), and those who do remain in school often find themselves in classes that do not afford them the same opportunities to learn as those students with Euro-American backgrounds. In short, large numbers of students of Mexican descent have been exposed to what McKnight and his associates (McKnight et al., 1987) have called "the underachieving curriculum."

Educators are often admonished to think of increasing diversity in their classrooms not as a problem, but as an opportunity. However, many well-intentioned educators who agree with that admonition are unsure of how to take advantage of the opportunities presented to them by diversity in the classroom. Whereas social critics and researchers often blame teachers for poor achievement among students of Mexican descent, many middle school teachers acknowledge the need for change in instructional organization and content, but tend to fix the blame for poor achievement on mediating factors that diminish the results of their efforts. In part, these teachers fault the elementary schools, whose standards they consider too lax. To an even greater degree, however, they blame students and their families for low achievement and motivation, citing lack of parental interest and lack of support of schooling. These widespread beliefs about families of Mexican descent are often based on very fragmentary and selective experiences with the parents of the students in their classes. This is especially true in middle school, where teachers are responsible for the instruction of large numbers of students during the course of a school day, with little opportunity to develop personal relations with more than a few students.

The research presented here represents our efforts to identify and describe family characteristics of seventh-grade students of Mexican descent who participated in our collaborative effort to reform mathematics instruction at the middle school level. The characteristics and activities in which we were interested were those that supported school learning and motivation, with a particular emphasis on mathematics.

The association between family environment and school achievement has been demonstrated in a substantial body of research, some of which has been conducted with Latino populations (Henderson, 1972, 1981; Henderson & Merritt, 1968; Laosa & Henderson, 1991; Martinez-Pons & Zimmerman, 1989). Our intent was to describe the aspirations and expectations parents had for their children, parents' knowledge of the instrumental means by which these aspirations might be realized, and the nature of the resources available to support and facilitate the children's learning and motivation. The research incorporated a demographic sample that reflected the proportional mix of student backgrounds with which the teachers in our collaborative venture were working.

METHOD

Sample

Thirty students were selected at random from the population of seventh graders enrolled in the classrooms in which we were involved in a research collaborative to explore a contextualized approach to instruction in mathematics. All such classes were being taught in English. Although some students in these classes were not highly proficient in English, we shall refer to this sample as the English-only (EO) group. Two families in the randomly selected sample were Euro-American; the remainder were Latino, and specifically, were of Mexican descent. This distribution of ethnicity was typical of the EO mathematics classes that were exploring the use of contextualized instruction.

A second sample of families was drawn at random from two classes in which mathematics was being taught in Spanish. These students were not involved in the larger study of thematic instruction, but were included in the interview sample for purposes of comparison with families whose children were assigned to EO classes. We interviewed 22 of the families selected for this second sample. The school district classified these students as having limited English proficiency (LEP)[2].

Together, these two samples appear to be fairly representative of the population served by the middle school in which our work was being conducted, and in many other schools in this and other California communities with a similar economic base.

Mothers of the target students were the principal respondents in 49 of the 52 interviews. In one family, however, the principal respondent was the child's father; in another, the respondent was the child's stepfather; and, in a third family, the respondent was the child's aunt, who served as surrogate parent. For the sake of convenience, both natural and surrogate parents were referred to as "parents" during the study.

Interviews were conducted in the respondents' homes. Aside from the principal respondent, there were often other people in the room in which the interview took place and, in 14 cases, a second person participated in the interview conversation. In most instances, the secondary respondent was the child's father. However, in a few cases, the secondary respondent was an older sibling or an aunt.

In all cases where a second person participated in the interview, the primary respondents' answers were coded as the primary data for the analyses. Additional comments from the second respondent, however, were also recorded and accounted for in the qualitative analyses.

Procedures and Data Sources

Families were interviewed by female graduate students of Latino descent who were familiar with the primary language of the families and the demographics involved in the study. Each interviewer was assigned approximately half the families in the sample. Initial contact was made by telephone; the purpose of the study was explained, and the family's participation was solicited. An interview time and date were then set for each participating family.

The Interview. The principal instrument used in this study was an interview schedule that included a mix of open-ended questions and forced-choice responses. Open-ended questions were accompanied by suggested prompts that elicited in-depth responses and provided additional information whenever initial responses were insufficient. Interviews were conducted in the preferred language of the respondent. Two Mexi-

---

[2]Some researchers (i.e., Waxman, Huang, & Padron, 1995) attempt to avoid the deficit connotation of terms such as *limited English proficiency* by substituting the term *English learners.* For purposes of clarity, we have elected to use the term used by the schools themselves. Because the meaning of the terms used to identify groups of people is socially constructed, we believe any advantage gained by substituting new terms is temporary, pending basic changes in the social construction of meaning within the larger society.

can-descent mothers, as well as the two Euro-Americans, chose to be interviewed in English. All other interviews were conducted in Spanish.

Interviewers took notes during the interview, and attempted to record responses verbatim. Where necessary, the interviewers elaborated their notes immediately after the interview. The interviews were also tape recorded for later reference, thereby enabling us to confirm or expand the interviewers' notes later.

Mathematics Achievement. In some analyses, we used mathematics scores from the Stanford Achievement Test. Achievement data from school district files were available only for the students in EO classrooms.

Goal Orientation. Recent literature has shown that student goal orientations are potentially important contributors to academic achievement in general (Dweck, 1986; Dweck & Leggett, 1988; Elliot & Dweck, 1988), and to achievement in mathematics (Peterson, 1988). According to Dweck's model, goals that reflect learning orientation are superior to goals that merely involve performance and reflect the desire to please others (teachers or parents) by getting a "correct" answer or earning a good grade. A characteristic of students whose goals reflect a learning orientation is the inclination to seek intellectual challenge and to persist in the face of scholastic difficulty. Challenge-seeking and persistence traits were measured by a self-report instrument developed for this purpose (Henderson, 1991).

Mathematics Attitudes. A measure of student attitudes toward mathematics was developed to determine the effects of curricular integration of student experience, mathematical skills, and conceptual understanding. The measure was administered by project personnel during mathematics classes and included items that formed five subscales. The Mathematics Attitudes subscale assessed to what degree each student enjoyed mathematics. The Mathematics Self-Concept subscales assessed the relationship between the students' own self-confidence levels and their mathematical capabilities. The Stereotypes of Mathematicians subscale assessed the degree to which students held negative stereotypes of mathematicians, or regarded their work as incompatible with family life and social relations. The Mathematics Future subscale measured the extent to which students thought their future life as adults would require work with mathematics. Finally, the Parental Encouragement subscale assessed the students' perceptions of the degree to which their parents provided support and encouragement for study and achievement in mathematics. This latter scale was comprised of selected items from Fennema and Sherman's (1976) mathematics attitude scales. Items for the other scales were either developed specifically for the present study or adapted from items used in the National Assessment of Educational Progress.

Demographic Questionnaire. A demographic questionnaire was appended to the student attitude measure. This questionnaire requested information on students' ethnic identity and country of birth, as well as parents' birthplace and level of educational attainment.

RESULTS

Family Characteristics

Ethnic Identity, National Origin, and Family Constellation. Of the 50 students for whom ethnic self-identification data were available from the demographic questionnaire, all of the LEP students identified themselves as Mexicano. None chose the term Chicano or Latino. Twelve of the students in the EO mathematics classes classified themselves as Chicano. Nine EO members identified themselves as Mexicano, four as Latino, and three as Latino of mixed ethnicity.

Of the parents for whom birthplace data were available (51 Latino mothers and 43 Latino fathers), all of the mothers and fathers of LEP students were born in Mexico. Ninety-three percent of the mothers and 96% of the fathers of Latino students in EO mathematics classes were of Mexican birth. Thus, the parents of both groups were remarkably similar with regard to their national origin. However, there was a difference in birthplace for the students themselves. Eighty-six percent of the LEP students were born in Mexico, as compared to 23% of the students in the EO mathematics classes.

Although the number of children in these families ranged from four to ten, the median number was four. And although the household size ranged from three to thirteen members, the median household size was six. Most households consisted of two adults and their own children, although the range of adults in the household was from one to six.

Educational Attainment of Parents. We were especially interested in parents' educational attainment, because previous research had demonstrated that parental education is a good predictor of children's school achievement (Laosa & Henderson, 1991; Valencia, Henderson & Rankin, 1981, 1985). In particular, the educational level of mothers was shown to contribute to student intellectual performance (Gándara, 1982; Laosa, 1980; Valencia et al., 1981, 1985). Complete data were available on the formal education of all mothers, and comparable data were reported for all but 10 of the fathers. The number of years of schooling was then coded to represent the equivalent level of schooling in the United States.

The level of formal educational attainment among families in both Latino samples was very low. The educational attainment model category for parents of both EO and LEP students was some elementary education short of elementary school completion. Many parents in this category had no more than one or two years of elementary school education. Two mothers and three fathers had no formal education. Two LEP mothers attained the highest level of education for their category—some high school, short of graduation. Among EO mothers, the highest level of educational attainment was achieved by three women who had all completed some college work. The highest level of education completed by any LEP or EO father was some high school, short of graduation. Both Euro-American mothers had completed some college postgraduate work, while one Euro-American father had completed some undergraduate college level study, and the other had completed some graduate work.

Income and Occupations. Whereas both of the Euro-American families reported an annual income in excess of $50,000 per year, the median family income for both Mexican-descent groups, LEP and EO, was between $10,000 and $20,000 per year. In the aggregate, three families reported earning less than $5,000 per year, and 14 earned between $5,000 and $10,000. No family with children in the LEP sample earned more than $20,000 per year. Six families with children in EO mathematics classes earned from $20,000 to $30,000, and three such families earned between $30,000 and $40,000 per year. To put these income levels in perspective, it should be noted that the cost of living in this area is among the highest in the United States.

Respondents were asked to identify their current and former occupations. The Occupational Classification System of the U.S. Bureau of the Census was used to categorize parental occupations. Employment data were not available for 7 mothers and 17 fathers. The missing data on the fathers' employment was generally associated with female-headed, single parent households.

Although the occupational status level of fathers of LEP and EO students did not differ, mothers of EO children tended to be employed in higher status occupations than did LEP mothers ($F = 5.68$, p .02). The current and usual occupations were generally the same. However, one mother of an LEP student and one father of an EO student were identified as unemployed.

Among LEP and EO mothers, only one woman listed her usual occupation as "homemaker." The majority of the Mexican-descent mothers' occupations were classified as "Operatives (Nontransportation)"; most of these women worked in canneries. The "Farm Laborer" occupational category was a close second in frequency; most of the mothers in this category worked in the agricultural fields. The number of mothers employed as either farm laborers or cannery workers was roughly divided between the LEP and EO groups. A few Latino mothers were employed in other occupations, but generally no more than a single individual per specific job category. Two mothers were employed as food service workers and three were engaged in various clerical occupations. Among the Latino families, the three mothers who had clerical jobs and the one mother who worked as an office manager were all from the EO sample. These were the highest status occupations in the distribution of Latino mothers' occupations.

The employment situation for Latino fathers was similar to those for EO and LEP mothers, except that the frequencies were reversed for the cannery and farm labor occupations. The vast majority of the fathers with known occupational statuses were farm laborers, with cannery workers comprising the next most frequent category. However, the number of fathers employed as cannery workers was less than half the number of those engaged as farm laborers.

The small group of Euro-American parents in the sample all worked at professional-level occupations. One Euro-American mother was a teacher. The other mother and both fathers were classified as "Manager/Administrators (Nonfarm)."

Occupational Aspirations and Expectations

Aspirations and expectations were of special interest in this investigation because these variables have been found to strongly predict educational achievement in the general population (Otto & Haller, 1979). Moreover, as previously mentioned, some teachers involved in the project cited lack of parental support and low parental aspirations as the source for low academic achievement and motivation among students of Mexican descent. This perception runs counter to findings from a number of studies that report high educational and occupational aspirations among Latino populations (Chacón, Cohen, & Strover, 1986; Henderson & Merritt, 1968; So, 1987). Because research suggests that motivation is a primary contributor to achievement among immigrant populations (Duran & Weffler, 1992), parents' aspirations for their children's achievement among recent Mexican immigrants would also be expected to contribute to the variance in actual student achievement.

Few studies have actually examined the association between aspirations and achievement outcomes for this population. However, those studies that have examined the relationship between parental aspirations and student achievement in various Hispanic subgroups have generally found positive associations (Buriel & Cardoza, 1988; Martinez-Pons & Zimmerman, 1989). In their study of sociocultural correlates of achievement among three generations of Mexican-American high school students, Buriel and Cardoza (1988) found that student aspirations (among the several background variables examined) were the only significant predictor of mathe-

matics achievement among first and second generation students, accounting for 35% and 26% of the variance, respectively. Student aspirations were
also among the significant predictors of mathematics achievement among
third generation students.

The association between student and parent aspirations seems likely to
develop, at least in part, out of the dialogue and interaction that take place
between parent and child. The majority of the Mexican-descent parents in
our samples said they did talk with their child about his or her future as an
adult. However, 32% of the parents of LEP students and 28% of the EO
parents said they did not have such conversations. The frequency of such
dialogue or interactions was determined by asking parents, "How often
does your child talk with you or your husband/wife about his/her hopes
for the future?" Responses were structured by a 5-point Likert scale format
with options ranging from "very often" (defined as almost every week) to
"almost never" (defined as not more than twice per year). Of the Mexican-
descent parents who responded ($n = 48$), half reported having such conversations "very often" or "fairly often." Twenty-seven percent talked with
their child about their hopes for his or her future "now and then," although
the remaining 21% had such conversations "not often" or "almost never."

Parents were then asked about their own aspirations for their child's
future occupation. In order to focus attention on eventual occupations for
their child when he or she reached maturity, parents were asked, "What
kind of job or occupation would you like to see your child have when he or
she is about 40 years old?" That question was followed with a probe to
determine why the parents had such occupational aspirations and whether
they believed their aspirations matched those of their child. The occupations named in response to these questions were coded using the Occupational Classification System of the U.S. Census and were scored for
socioeconomic status (SES) using the Nam-Powers SES scale (combined
sexes). The latter scale provides a composite measure, based on the proposition that measures of objective status conditions do a reasonable job of
indexing life chances (Miller, 1991).

In general, there was a low degree of correspondence between the
parents' *specific* occupational aspirations for their child and their child's
own aspirations, as perceived by his or her parents. However, the difference between parental and child aspirations (as indexed by Nam-Powers
scores) for the 28 cases for which comparable parent and child data were
available was not significant ($t = 1.701$, *ns*). These results suggest comparability in the SES of occupational aspirations among parents and children,
if not in the specific occupational choices.

Mothers and fathers did not differ from one another in their occupational
statuses ($t = .042$, *df* 28, *ns*), as measured by Nam-Powers scores. The
occupational aspirations these parents held for their children were significantly higher than mothers' ($t = 16.208$, *df* 38, $p < .0005$) or fathers' ($t = 13.874$,
df 31, $p < .0005$) own occupational statuses. The Nam-Powers scores indexing

parents' aspirations for their children exceeded the scores for fathers' usual occupations by 64 points, and those for mothers by 63 points. To put this difference in perspective, it is instructive to note that the possible range of scores on the Nam-Powers scale, from lowest to highest among the occupations indexed, is 99 points.

It is not surprising that the parents' occupational aspirations for their child generally exceeded their own occupations. A more interesting contrast, however, is that between the parents' aspirations for their child's eventual career and their expectations for the kind of career their child might actually achieve. For the 23 respondents for whom both aspiration and expectation data could be coded, aspiration scores exceeded expectation scores by 30.71 points ($t(22) = 3.72, p < .001$).

Recent literature has suggested that Mexican-American girls may have special barriers to overcome in the study of mathematics because of attitudes and stereotypes within the Mexican culture that discourage female participation (MacCorquodale, 1988). A comparison of the distributions of aspirations and expectations for boys and girls is shown in Fig. 7.1. The aspirations' interquartile ranges for boys and girls are fairly comparable. However, the boys' median lies very near the top of the distribution, whereas the girls' median is significantly lower.

The picture is quite different for occupational expectations. For boys, the Nam-Powers scores display a symmetrical distribution, although the distribution for girls is tightly clustered around one central value, with only a few outliers toward both ends of the distribution. The occupations represented by the median value for girls can best be characterized as clerical. These data should be interpreted with caution because the number of cases with available data in the cells for expectations is small (15 for boys, 12 for girls).

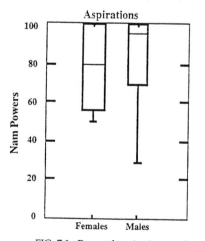
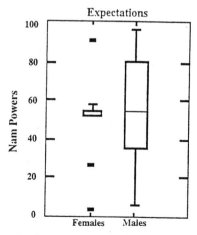

FIG. 7.1. Parental aspirations and expectations for their sons' and daughters' future occupational attainment.

Parents most frequently aspired for their children to become, in order of preference, doctors, lawyers, teachers, and nurses. Qualitative analysis of interview data suggest that the principal motive behind parental aspirations for children was the parents' desire for their child to do better professionally than they themselves had done. As mentioned earlier, the majority of parents, fathers and mothers alike, worked either in the fields or in canneries. Many who were employed in the canneries had, at various times in their lives, worked in the agricultural fields, and vice versa. Characteristically, parents did not want their children to have to endure the hardships of working either in the fields or the canneries. As one mother and cannery worker said, "I don't want [my children] working in the fields or the cannery. It's too hard and pays too little." This sentiment was expressed by many parents. One Mexican-born mother with 3 years of formal education had no specific aspirations for her son aside from the hope that he would work at "something easy. Not in the field . . . *not* in the field." Another was sure that her son would have a better future if he studied. If children would only study, she asserted, "they wouldn't have to work like us in the fields." Another woman stated that she wanted her daughter to work with computers, "so she doesn't [have to] work in the fields. My body hurts, and I tell her to study so she don't have to work like I do." This response, phrased in terms of physical working conditions, was typical of many parents. One woman hoped her son would do some kind of work in an office, saying, "We [parents] want the best for our children. I want him to have a good career, like in an office. I want him to have a better future so that he doesn't have to work like me in the fields."

Instrumental Knowledge for Occupational Attainment

The high aspirations identified among the parents in these samples are consistent with the results of other research with Latino populations. Given the high aspirations these parents have for their children, it is important to determine the nature and extent of the parents' instrumental knowledge of the means by which the occupational aspirations they have for their children might be achieved. A number of items in the interviews were designed to yield information regarding parental knowledge of these instrumental means. Parents were asked to determine what qualities would be important for the occupational aspirations they had for their children and the aspirations their children had for themselves. In addition, parents were asked to assess their child's strengths and limitations relative to those qualities. The parents' knowledge of the nature and extent of the education necessary to attain these aspirations was also used in coding the interviews for Instrumental Knowledge. Responses to all relevant questions were collated into typescripts for each respondent. In addition, a rating scale was constructed to quantify the responses. Explicit criteria were stated for each of eight points on the scale. A second reader scored a random sample of 20% of the interviews. The interrator reliability coefficient was .90.

A qualitative analysis of interview data revealed that most parents had only the most general instrumental knowledge of how their career aspirations for their children might be attained. The distribution of instrumental knowledge scores was virtually identical for the LEP and EO samples. A regression analysis performed to determine if parents' instrumental knowledge was predictive of their child's year-end performance on a standardized test of mathematics achievement yielded nonsignificant results. In addition, the correlation between parents' instrumental knowledge and the child's perception of parental support and encouragement for their study of mathematics was also insignificant.

The most salient insights into parents' instrumental knowledge came from conversations that were not formally part of the interview schedule. Inquiries relating to instrumental knowledge often elicited questions from the parents, who seemed starved for school-related information on matters such as how to get into college. Parents seemed to be particularly impressed by the fact that the interviewers were both Latinas who "had made it"; that is, who had not only attended college, but also were pursuing graduate degrees. Lengthy conversations often followed the interviews. To the extent permitted by the situation, parents called on the interviewers as a resource, often saying that their children needed opportunities to talk with role models, such as these Latina graduate students.

When speaking of the qualities their children exhibited that would prove important in preparing for an aspired-to occupation, parents often mentioned intelligence, responsibility, studiousness and motivation, patience, and tenacity. A Mexican-descent mother with a high school education who worked as a cashier thought her son was well-suited to become an engineer because he was "a fast learner" who was "very intelligent" and could do "many things well and quickly." Another Mexican-born mother with 6 years of formal education and a GED also wanted her son to become an engineer. He liked to work with people, she said, and, "wants to do more than we do, someday." She went on to explain that "he does well in school because he doesn't want to be a worker. He wants to be someone well-known." In a family in which both parents were born in Mexico, the mother's assessment that her daughter would make a good lawyer was based on the observation that "she argues very much, is stubborn, thinks things out thoroughly, and thinks of many good things. She is a good student." Another mother was confident that her daughter would make a good psychologist because "she likes to help friends with their problems. She has solved serious problems with her friends, like runaways."

When asked about the education or training required to realize a given occupational aspiration for their child, many parents commented on the need to be responsible and punctual, to study and, where applicable, to go to college. Few parents, however, could say much about the specific kind of education required to realize their aspirations. Some mentioned a specific community college or university within the region. Others alluded to the need to study specific subjects; most prominently mathematics, English (or reading and writing), and science.

Resources for Support and Guidance in the Study of Mathematics

This project was particularly concerned with the priority that the study of mathematics was given in these families, and the types of resources available to support the child's schoolwork, particularly in mathematics. In their study of home educational processes and academic achievement among three Hispanic groups in the U.S. (Puerto Rican, Cuban, and Central and South American), Martinez-Pons and Zimmerman (1989) found that the effect of aspirations on achievement was an indirect one, mediated by the amount of time spent on homework. Other research with Latino populations has demonstrated that parental involvement in the child's academic life, through such activities as monitoring homework, is instrumental to success in school (Delgado-Gaitan, 1988, 1990). To explore the nature and extent of academic support and guidance in the homes of students involved in this study, parents were asked whether their child talked with them about his or her schoolwork. The vast majority of the Latino samples (86% of LEP, 83% of EO) responded in the affirmative. When asked for more specific information on the frequency of these conversations, 55% of the Latino respondents reported talking with their child about school work "very often" (e.g., more than once per week), and an additional 18% said they engaged in such conversation "quite often." Seven parents said they "almost never" had such conversations with their child (i.e., no more than a couple of times during a school year). Two respondents reported that they did not have such conversations often, and six had such conversations only "now and then." Thus, although the majority of the parents in the sample appeared to talk with their children about schoolwork with some frequency, 27% engaged in this kind of interaction with their child only occasionally, or even less frequently.

All parents responded in the affirmative when asked if they believed mathematics would play a significant role in their child's future. When probed for specifics, typical responses focused on the usefulness of mathematics in everyday life and as preparation for jobs. Work with computers was frequently identified as an area in which the study of mathematics would be useful, although the limitations of computers and calculators were also mentioned. An example of the latter kind of comment came from a family in which both parents were born in Mexico and their child was born in the United States. These parents felt mathematics was an important area of study which prevented excessive dependence on computers. As the mother said, "Now they use computers and if the batteries die then people are helpless. If you don't know math, everything stops." The father agreed, saying, "You have to learn you can't depend on a calculator or a computer."

Many responses to the follow-up probe regarding the role of mathematics in a child's future were very general. When asked for what purpose their child should learn mathematics in the school, some parents responded, "For everything." A rather atypical response, emphasizing the fundamental value of mathematics, came from a mother who said, "I've heard it is the root of all other studies." In this instance, the parents and their child were born in Mexico. The parents stated that they wanted their daughter to become a doctor, an interest motivated, at least in part, by the fact that the mother had serious health problems and acknowledged that she "might not live long." Despite both parents' occupational aspirations, however, the mother believed her daughter aspired to become a beautician.

Some parents believed that the study of mathematics was important for practical rather than professional reasons. One parent said, "If you don't know math, you can't keep track of your money. It's important for everything." Other parents mentioned that mathematics would prove helpful in performing routine tasks such as budgeting household finances and balancing a checkbook. And, at least one mother thought the study of mathematics was important because her daughter enjoyed it. Of her daughter's interest in mathematics the mother said, "She likes numbers. They don't bore her. Most people don't like math."

However, the majority of the parents' comments focused on the professional usefulness of mathematics. Many parents' posited that math was "the basis for a career" and believed that "for everything you need math; you need math for every job." One Mexican-born mother, who had completed 2 years of college and was employed as an office manager, hoped her son would eventually become a doctor, saying, "Math is one of the primary skills he has to master for his profession and for daily use." Another mother believed that proficiency in mathematics was important for her son, because "with math he can obtain at least a cashier's job. I know math is good for him, even though I don't understand it." And two Mexican-born parents believed that mathematics would help their American-born son become a carpenter. The father, who was employed in the field of construction, commented, "The way things are going, [mathematics] will be critical for him to succeed." The mother added, "If he can't solve problems, how can he work?"

Considering the broad-based sentiment that mathematics is important for daily life and future careers, we were especially interested to know what resources were available to these students when they needed help with mathematics. When asked who in the home helped the child with mathematics assignments, parents named a variety of different family members: mother, father, older brother or sister, friend, teacher, cousin, aunt, and uncle. The relationship of each person mentioned as a source of help in mathematics was recorded. Most respondents named only one person in response to the initial query, but some named more than one person to whom the student typically went for help with mathematics.

Older sisters were the most frequently mentioned source of help in mathematics. Older brothers and fathers were also mentioned, but each was named as a resource only about half as often as were older sisters. Teachers were also frequently named and, for some students, teachers were the only source of help in mathematics. Many parents expressed frustration or a sense of helplessness because their own limited educational experience prevented them from helping their child with mathematics assignments. In some cases, parents said that their efforts to help often confused their child; they cited cultural differences between Mexicans and Americans as a source of this confusion. These cultural differences appeared to occur on the procedural level, such as the algorithm used for long division.

Although parents often were concerned about their inability to help their child with mathematics, more than two thirds said their child "rarely" or "never" needed help with mathematics homework, an interesting response indeed, considering the concerns teachers had expressed about Mexican-descent students' failure to complete assigned homework.

Examples of Study Environments

Two contrasting cases provide valuable insight into student work conditions in the home. In the first case, the mother reported that her daughter was very interested in school, and was always trying to find ways to "balance study and work." Both parents in this family seemed very supportive of their daughter's education, but their living conditions and work situations made it difficult to provide an environment conducive to school work. Both parents worked at different times; the father at night, and the mother during the daytime. Because of their divergent work schedules, both parents were home together for only a short time during the day.

The family resided in a converted garage, where there were many children. The daughter had a heavy schedule of household chores and found it difficult to find the time and place for study. Often, she went outside to sit and work in the car while one parent slept inside the apartment. Living in this cramped space, the family often became embroiled in parent–child arguments, fighting over whether the light should be left on while the daughter studied or off while the father slept. Although both parents recognized the importance of their daughter's education, the daughter was constantly involved in a balancing act; she coordinated her own child-care responsibilities for the care of younger siblings and school and housework activities with her parents' home and work schedules and sleeping arrangements.

In the second case, to the consternation of her mother, the student was not at all interested in school. The single mother apparently resided with a live-in boyfriend, not in a converted garage, but in a typical home. In addition to the mother, daughter, and boyfriend, an estimated six families resided in the house, each using one room as an "apartment" and sharing the kitchen and bathroom facilities. Even if the daughter were interested in school, one wonders where she could find the space to study.

Perceptions of the Value of Schooling and Mathematics Achievement

In spite of the practical difficulties involved in providing support for school work in the home environment, parents of Mexican descent clearly believed in the value of education. Parents' responses were unanimously affirmative when asked, "In the long run, do you think it really matters whether your child does well in school?" When prompted to explain their responses, almost all parents expressed the belief that doing well in school was important for a future career. Of the importance of her son's success in school, one mother said simply, "It's his future." In another family, in which both parents were respondents, the father expressed the hope that his daughter might become a doctor while the mother mentioned nursing as a career possibility. Regarding the importance of her daughter's school success, the mother commented, "It's the road to her career . . . [and] the base to do something for the future." Other parents agreed, and expressed their hope that school success could help their children achieve high-level professional careers. However, not every parent aspired to a high-prestige occupation for his or her child. As one respondent said, "I think that education is the foundation to do something in life. Without it, it is impossible. My main illusion [sic] is that [my children] have good careers, but not necessarily great careers."

A majority of respondents emphasized the importance of doing well in school in order to procure jobs later on. Many parents expressed the hope that their children could have better, less difficult lives than they themselves had led. One father said of his children, "All of that [schooling] will be of use to them and life is getting hard—for every job you need to get schooling. Now it is hard to get a job even with a high school education." One mother explained that she and her husband wanted their son "to have a good job so he can do more than we've done. So he can have more than we do." Another woman repeated the admonishment she gave her son. "I say that I didn't study. Do you want to work in the fields [like me]?" The boy's father, who also participated in the interview, added, "I don't want to see him washing dishes." It was clear that both parents believed their son had to study if he wanted to have a better life than either of them had led.

Although most parents wanted their children to prepare for good jobs to ensure their future success, a few also expected assistance from their children later on. One mother commented that it was important to both her and her husband that their son could "help us later when we can no longer work." Some parents were less specific about job preparation, but emphasized the future in a more general way. When asked why her daughter should continue her education, one mother replied, "Because she'll have a better future and studying will help her." Another mother agreed, saying that she wanted her daughter "to have a better future of her own."

In addition to wanting their children to do well in school to help ensure success in the job market, many parents expressed a strong desire to see their children achieve personal success and status. The phrase "to be somebody" was often used to express this desire. As one woman explained, "I think a mother wants her child to succeed. I want him to be somebody and not do the work we've had to do." Another said, "It is something good for her. For her to be functional and be somebody. It all depends on her." The mother of a child who was born in Mexico said that she wanted her son to "be a success. I want him to go to college." The parents in this family had attained more than the average level of formal education for their group, having both gone to the equivalent of their first year of high school. Another mother said simply, "I want [my daughter] to have a good job and be somebody."

An occasional respondent expressed that he or she valued school learning in its own right. For example, one woman thought it was important to do well in school because "the school is set up to teach valuable academic and social skills." Another said, "There's nothing better than an education. Jobs come and go, but an education is very important." This comment came from a family where the parents' wanted their daughter to become a secretary.

Parent Perceptions of Children As Students of Mathematics

Parents responded to several items pertaining to the target child's achievement and attitude toward mathematics. The results reported here are aggregated for the Mexican-descent parents because differences in the responses of the two groups were nonsignificant. More than one third of the parents thought their child was "good" or "very good" at doing math problems. Only 6% thought their child was either "not very good at all" or "fairly good." The majority (59%) believed their child to be "pretty good" at doing math problems. When asked how their child's work in mathematics compared to that of other students of the same age, just over half of the respondents (53%) believed that their child's mathematics achievement was about average. Forty percent considered their child to be "better than most" or "among the very best," while 7% were at the other end of the scale, indicating that their child was "far below average," or "somewhat below average."

To determine whether EO parents were reasonably accurate in their knowledge of their child's mathematics achievement, the correlation between the two relevant items and the posttest standardized mathematics achievement was examined. Both items were significantly correlated with posttest standardized mathematics achievement. Comparable results were obtained when the Euro-American subjects were eliminated from the computation. The actual level of achievement, as indexed by the mean of the Normal Curve Equivalent (NCE) scores on the standardized mathematics test used as a posttest measure was 42.6 (SD = 13.1) for the EO Latino samples. Because NCE scores have a mean of 50 and a standard deviation of approximately 21 points, the mean for this sample falls approximately one third of a standard deviation below the normative mean.

Interestingly, when asked how they expected their child to do in mathematics next year, the majority of the parents (72%) expected their child to do "very well" or "extremely well." No parent expected poor performance ("not well at all") and relatively few expected their child to do "fairly well" (9%) or "quite well" (19%). A comparison of estimates of current performance in mathematics and expectations for mathematics achievement next year showed that the difference between these two variables was significant (t = 4.436, p < .0005).

Typically, when there was an obvious discrepancy between parental perceptions of present performance and expectations for future performance, parents explained that they anticipated an improvement in their child's school performance because they expected greater academic effort. One mother said that she expected her son to do better "because I want him to try harder. He's a little lazy." Another expected her son's academic performance to improve "because I have hope. I see him very enthusiastic at school." And another described the action she and her husband planned to take, saying, "We're going to punish him and we're going to talk to his teacher because this year he surprised us—his grades went down."

Some parents explained their expectations in terms of teachers' efforts. One mother stated that her children "now have a strong, energetic teacher of math, so I think they'll be more responsive." Another believed that her daughter's teachers would "help her more, given that she doesn't understand. With their help, she will improve."

Another mother believed that her child's present grades were the result of a temporary situation that would reverse itself when the child adjusted to a change in school. The mother explained, "When he changed schools his grades went down and the switch of schools was the problem—change of friends, etcetera."

Given these perceptions of current and anticipated performance, parents were asked to rate the level of importance for doing well in mathematics.

Well over two thirds felt that it was "important" or "most important" for their child to do well in mathematics. No one believed that doing well in mathematics was "not important" or only "fairly important."

When asked to what degree their child enjoyed the study of mathematics, more than 50% thought their child liked math "quite a bit" or "very much," while only 22% reported that their child liked math "very little" or "not much at all." Twenty-seven percent gave a middle-of-the-road response that their child liked math "somewhat."

Plans and Academic Guidance

Parents were asked to respond to the open-ended question, "What math classes will your child probably take in high school?" Both sets of Euro-American parents were able to answer in considerable detail with the names of specific high school mathematics classes they expected their child to take. In general, parents in both the EO and LEP samples displayed little knowledge of the specific mathematics classes their children might take in high school. Responses to this item were dichotomized into two groups, one comprised of families in which the respondent could name one or more high school mathematics class anticipated in the child's future education, and the other comprised of those families in which the respondent was unable to name any mathematics class. A one-way ANOVA was performed to compare these two groups on the posttest mathematics score. The comparison demonstrated significantly higher mathematics achievement for those students whose parent or parent surrogate could name at least one mathematics course in their plans for their child's educational future ($R = .52$, $R^2 = .27$, $p < .006$. With Euro-American families deleted from the analysis, the difference between the groups dropped to a marginally significant level ($R = .38$, $R^2 = .15$, $p < .06$).

With regard to parents' knowledge of their child's academic achievement in mathematics, 76% knew what grade their child had received in math for the previous two semesters. Only six parents did not know what grades their child had received in either of the two previous semesters. When parents were asked what kind of a mathematics student their child had been during elementary school, there was a fairly marked difference in response patterns for parents of children in LEP and EO classes. Sixty percent of the parents of LEP children reported that they were either "not good at all" or "fair" as mathematics students in elementary school, whereas 62% of parents of students in EO classes reported that their children were either "very good" or "extremely good." The difference between the responses of the two groups was statistically significant ($t = 3.64$, $p < .001$).

Two home environmental variables were entered into a step-wise regression analysis to determine whether or not they served as predictors of achievement on the mathematics posttest. The first of these variables, labeled "parental knowledge of the school," was a composite of responses to items that assessed the parents' knowledge of (a) the classes their child was taking in school, and (b) the school contact for information or academic assistance. The second variable, "homework guidance," was determined by items that indexed (a) the frequency with which parents helped their children with homework, and (b) the parents' own reports of their efforts to monitor their children's homework assignments. It should be noted that this variable reflects the frequency of homework assistance by the parent, not including the additional sources of assistance discussed earlier. Together, "parental knowledge of the school" and "homework guidance" accounted for 30% of the variance in mathematics posttest scores (R (2, 24) = .55, $p < .01$).

Relationship of Student Characteristics to Mathematics Attitudes and Achievement

Latino students enrolled in EO and LEP classes were compared on several subscales of a Mathematics Attitude Scale administered to the classes in which these students were enrolled. Attitudes toward mathematics were more positive among students born in Mexico than among students born in the United States (t (41) = 6.70, $p < .02$). Students born in Mexico also expressed a higher level of expectation that they would be involved with work requiring mathematics than the Latino students born in the United States (t (44) = 2.57, $p < .01$). The groups were not significantly different in their perceptions of parental support for mathematics study, stereotypes of mathematicians, mathematics self-concept, or beliefs about the nature of mathematics.

Achievement Attributions

Some researchers have suggested that cultural beliefs may contribute to the discrepancy between mathematics achievement in the United States and Asian nations (Stigler & Baranes, 1989). The research suggests that, more than American mothers, Asian mothers tend to attribute their children's learning problems in mathematics to instructional inadequacies, insufficient effort on the part of the child, or insufficient support in the home. To determine whether parents in our sample attributed mathematics achievement to ability or effort, and to ascertain whether parents considered mathematics learning to be more dependent on effort or ability than other subjects, we reminded parents that some children do better than others in certain school subjects. With that caveat in mind, parents were asked to judge the relative importance of ability and effort for success in different school subjects: reading/language arts, science, arithmetic/mathematics, and physical education. The response format was a 5-point Likert scale where answers ranged from parental emphasis on the importance of effort (scored 5) to parental emphasis on the importance of ability (scored 1), with equal effort and ability attributions located at the midpoint on the scale.

Results of t tests indicated that Latino parents' attributions of mathematics achievement to ability versus effort differed only for the contrast between science and physical education (t (46) = 2.56, $p < .01$). Parents believed that science required more effort, as compared to physical education, which required more natural ability.

The relation between parents' mathematics achievement attributions to students' own goal orientations and their preference for challenge-seeking and persistence in mathematics assignments was examined by Pearson correlations. Parents' attributions of mathematics outcomes were significantly and negatively related to students' own challenge-seeking/persistence scores ($r = -.39$, $p < .0005$ for the total sample; $r = -.387$, $p < .0005$ for the Latino sample). Contrary to research expectations, this negative correlation indicated that parents who attributed successful performance in mathematics school work to ability, rather than to effort, had children who scored higher on the Challenge-Seeking/Persistence scale of the self-perception measure.

Peer Influences

Peers exert a potentially powerful influence over the educational and career aspirations of children. In addition, peer associations are instrumental in the adoption of academic values and achievement behaviors (Delgado-Gaitan, 1988; Rumberger, 1991). Because parents may play an instrumental role in the formation and maintenance of their child's friendship associations, a number of questions were asked to determine the nature of parental guidance in students' choice of peers. Thirty-nine parents provided responses that were coded to the question, "Do you approve of your child's school friends?" The vast majority answered in the affirmative. A series of follow-up questions attempted to determine the qualities parents consider important in their child's choice of friends. Additional probes were used in an attempt to determine the goals, achievement status, and personal qualities of the child's actual friends. One of the Euro-American mothers voiced especially strong approval of her daughter's friends, asserting that "most of them are much like her, regardless of their race. Their families are interested in [their children] doing well in school." In describing the kinds of friends her daughter had, she said, "Most are on the honor roll. They are planning to go to college."

Except for the explicit reference to college, this response was not unlike those of a large proportion of the Latino parents. Many spontaneously mentioned that "being a good student" was an important quality in choosing school friends. One such parent observed that her son's friends were "in the same grade as him. He says they're good students." This woman thought the important qualitative characteristics of her child's school friends were trust and communication and believed that it was important that the children talk to one another about "their thoughts, their future, and their present. And that they trust each other."

Friends who were not involved with drug or alcohol use and who stayed off the streets were often mentioned in the responses of Mexican-descent parents. One woman approved of her daughter's friends because "they're like her, not involved in drugs or bad things." Another mother described her daughter's friends as "good students with good grades and no problems." When asked what qualities she thought were important in her child's choice of friends, this woman replied that her daughter "has good friends—serious. They don't hang out in the street. She has lots of friends. It's important that they study and don't have bad habits—smoking or drinking."

Shared values were also important, as was the case with a mother who based her approval of her son's friends on the perception that "he hangs around kids like him. The same kind of student, same kind of family. He is a good judge of character, and picks his friends well." Later, she elaborated that it was important that a school friend be "someone that comes from a family with the same values and moral instructions that I have." Another boy's mother described her son's friends as "good students. They study and I think they don't have any interest in drugs." In characterizing the qualities that would be important in a school friend she said that her son "looks for someone who he can be friends with. I want him to have friends that have fun in a healthy way. There are many bad things out there, like drugs."

A few parents said their child had few friends outside of the family. When asked if she approved of her child's friends, one mother replied, "He has few friends, so we don't know for sure." In response to further probes, the mother indicated, "From what we know, he has few friends. He had one friend but we didn't approve of him and he stopped seeing him. I don't know—he plays with his cousins. I want him to get along with others. I prefer a friend who don't lead him astray."

Several families were less explicit about the qualities desired in their children's friends or the specific qualities to be avoided, commenting instead on general personal qualities and good behavior. Without mentioning bad influences in specific terms, these parents wanted friends who were well-behaved. One mother said of her son's friend, "I know his mother. He's a good boy." When asked what kinds of student her son's friend was, she replied, "More or less an okay student," after which she repeated her earlier assessment, "He's a good boy."

A small proportion of the sample did not appear to know who their children's friends were, and did not seem to be actively involved in the formation or maintenance of their children's friendships.

Parent Participation and Involvement in the School

Parental academic involvement has been identified as a major influence on children's academic performance (Rumberger, 1991). The parents of students who stay in school and who are academically successful tend to be more involved, not only in monitoring homework, as mentioned previously, but also in attending school functions and teacher conferences. But research on parent involvement in schools suggests that recent immigrants often feel insecure because they lack the knowledge, time, and resources to participate in school activities (Delgado-Gaitan, 1988, 1990). In order to assess the nature and degree of parental involvement with the schools, parents were asked to respond to a series of items structured in a Likert format. These items explored the frequency of parents' meetings with teachers or counselors, attendance at meetings of school groups (i.e., School Site Council or the Parent-Teacher Association), frequency of volunteering at the school, attendance at events such as "back to school nights" or "open house," and attendance at or participation in school-based social activities, such as school fairs or carnivals. Scores for each item ran from 1 through 5. A composite score of school participation was computed and entered into a regression equation to determine whether such activities were predictive of student achievement. The result of the analysis was significant, with school participation accounting for 23% of the variance in scores on the standardized mathematics achievement test administered at the end of the school year $(R (1, 25) = .48, df 1,25, p < .01)$. The result was still significant when the analysis was rerun after eliminating the Euro-American subjects $(R (1, 25) = .43, p < .03)$. Consistent with other research on this topic, parents often expressed concern about their ability to interact with school personnel because of their limited facility with English, or lack of knowledge of the curriculum. Many expressed doubts that they were really welcome at the school, and some specifically stated that they had not been invited. As one mother said when asked if she ever attended meetings of school groups, "It's held in English, so what's the point?"

CONCLUSIONS AND DISCUSSION

The samples studied in this investigation are typical of the classroom composition of many middle schools in small to midsize California communities that depend heavily on an agricultural economic base. The school in which our present research was conducted is committed to heterogeneity in the classroom, although this resolve has been somewhat compromised by the formation of "accelerated" mathematics classes in response to parental pressure. With this exception, mathematics classes in the school in which our research took place were of two varieties.

Seventh-grade students with little facility in English were assigned together in LEP classes. Our LEP sample is representative of the constituents of those classes, where over three quarters of the students and all of the parents were born in Mexico. Standardized achievement data were not available for this student group because the Stanford Achievement Test, administered as part of the school district's testing program and used as a posttest measure of program effectiveness, is inappropriate for LEP students. However, data on mathematics attitudes and goal orientations, administered in the student's preferred language, were available for this sample. The availability of data determined which analyses included or excluded the LEP sample.

Seventh-grade students with a greater knowledge of English were enrolled in the EO classes. Although the vast majority of EO students were of Mexican descent, 86% were born in the United States. The range of mathematics achievement in these classes can be understood, in part, by noting that the scores of the Mexican-descent students were normally distributed around a mean that was approximately one third of a standard deviation below the norms for the test. In contrast, the two Euro-American students in the sample had scores that fell more than one standard deviation above the test norms. This comparison is not intended to contrast the achievement of Euro-American and Mexican-descent students. Given the disparity in their backgrounds and educational histories, such a comparison would be inappropriate. The achievement information on Euro-American students is presented in this research to indicate the broad range of student achievement with which teachers were attempting to cope in these heterogeneously grouped classes. In this school, like many others that are attempting to remove restrictions on learning opportunities by detracking, teachers are faced with a tremendous range of student achievement and language ability. Seldom are they provided with appropriate training to teach such a diverse range of instructional needs or a suitable curriculum to replace the traditional textbooks. Without provision for appropriate training, materials, and curriculum, it is reasonable to ask whether the goal of equity in learning opportunities is being realized effectively.

In past research and educational policy literature, students of Mexican descent have often been treated as a homogeneous group. The problem of treating the population as undifferentiated is evident in our samples, in which within-group variations in self-identification, similar to those documented by Matute-Bianchi (1986) at a high school in this same community, are already evident at the middle school level. All of the LEP students identified themselves as Mexicano, although Mexican-descent students from EO classes were more likely to identify themselves as Chicano. If Matute-Bianchi's results hold, these differences may have important long-range implications for school behavior and achievement.

The Mexican-descent households in both samples were considerably larger than households in the general population. Although the largest family in either sample had 10 children, households generally consisted of nuclear families, with an average of 4 children per family. However, many parents and children lived in crowded quarters shared with other families. They often maintained extended relationships with kinfolk left behind in Mexico.

Although there was some range in the various characteristics that comprise the usual markers of SES, the majority of the Mexican-descent families were near the lowest possible levels of these variables. A large majority of parents of both EO and LEP students had completed less than an elementary school education.

In most households, both parents were employed. This is consistent with other data indicating that Latinos in California participate in the laborforce to a degree that exceeds the participation of Euro-Americans, as well as other minorities (Hayes-Bautista, Hurtado, Valdez, & Hernandez, 1990). Although both parents were employed, they tended to be concentrated at the lowest socioeconomic levels of the occupational scale. Fathers of EO and LEP students did not differ with regard to the SES level of their occupations, as indexed by the Nam-Powers Scale, but there was a significant difference in the employment levels of EO and LEP mothers. Mothers of EO students tended to be employed in higher status occupations than LEP mothers. Consistent with a pattern of employment in unskilled, low-status occupations, the median income level of the Mexican-descent households was far below the poverty level. Households of EO students had a significant income advantage over LEP families.

Most parents reported that they spoke with their child on a regular basis about his or her future occupational achievement. However, it is interesting to note that a sizable minority reported that they did not have such conversations with their child.

As we would expect on the basis of findings from previous research, these parents held high aspirations for their children. In a few cases, parental aspirations for their children were influenced by the parent's own occupational experience. For example, a mother who was employed as an office cleaner wanted her child to work with computers. She was impressed with what she knew of computers because, from her vantage point, they appeared to provide a work environment free of the demanding physical labor of the fields or canneries.

Other parents aspired for their children to work as supervisors. Their knowledge of supervisory work was based on observations of their own supervisors in the canneries. Interestingly, they did not appear to want their child employed in this capacity in the canning industry. One woman was explicit about this, expressing the hope that her child might work as a supervisor, but "not in the cannery."

Although direct work experience played a role in some parents' aspirations for their children, a large majority of the parents hoped for their children to work at an occupation with which they had little personal contact. These parents wanted their children to enter prestigious medical or legal occupations. It is interesting to note that law and medicine are among the few professions portrayed as prestigious and lucrative in the media, which seems a likely source of these parents' occupational perceptions and aspirations. It would be interesting to understand more of what parents actually know about the occupations they aspire to for their children, and the source of the parents' perceptions.

As would be expected, parents' aspirations for their children's occupations were considerably higher than for their own occupations. In addition, there was a significant discrepancy between parents' *aspirations* for their child's future occupation, and their *expectations* of what occupation their child would actually attain. Most parents realized that their aspirations were unrealistic. They often noted the lack of resources to support their child's education, and their own limitations in helping their child achieve academically. It is noteworthy that parental aspirations were unrelated to mathematics achievement although expectations *were* significantly related to achievement. The relationship was substantial, with expectations accounting for 32% of the variance in mathematics achievement.

Given the limited formal education and restricted first-hand contact with higher status occupations, it is unsurprising that parents had little instrumental knowledge of how their child should prepare for the occupations they had hoped he or she would achieve. The degree to which parents did possess such instrumental knowledge was not predictive of achievement. This finding is congruent with our expectations, because instrumental knowledge does not appear to support the kinds of studies in which students are involved at the middle school level. Nevertheless, we regard instrumental knowledge of the requirements necessary for achieving aspired-to occupations to be an important variable that we expect will take on increasing importance as the child progresses through school. This hypothesis remains to be tested in future studies.

In contrast, knowledge of the mathematics classes their children might take in high school was significantly associated with mathematics achievement. This suggests that parents with more knowledge of the mathematics curriculum were in a better position to guide and support their children's study of mathematics.

There were no mean differences in the aspirations and expectations parents had for their sons and daughters. However, there were marked gender contrasts for expectations, with a great deal of spread in the distribution for boys, in contrast to a tight clustering for girls. The median value indexing expectations for girls could best be characterized as representing clerical occupations. Such recognition of restricted occupational opportunities for females of Mexican descent suggests that occupational expectations may be a better variable than aspirations for the study of gender differences in educational and work opportunities among Mexican-descent populations.

As parents described their aspirations for their children, their chief hope was that the children could have better, less difficult lives than they themselves had experienced. Parents did not want their children to have to endure the hardships of the fields or the canneries. Income was also seen as important, but that seemed secondary to achieving a life that was less physically strenuous and demanding. Quite spontaneously, many parents placed a strong emphasis on the importance of studying in order to achieve a life free of hardships.

The high value placed on education by parents in both the EO and LEP samples was pervasive. Reese, Gallimore, Goldenberg, and Balzano (1995) have shown that some studies of the association between children's academic achievement and parents' educational aspirations and expectations for their children may be misleading because different cultural groups construe these concepts in different ways. Specifically, the Mexican term *educación* implies an inseparable link between formal study and moral upbringing. However, it was very clear in the interviews on which the present work is based that the expressions of faith in the efficacy of education as a means to a better life referred specifically to formal study. Parents were quite articulate in stating their beliefs that education, and the study of mathematics, in particular, was important for jobs and careers. Some explicitly noted changes in the kinds of jobs that would be available in the future, and observed that jobs which presently required relatively little formal education would require at least a high school education in the future. The value that families of Mexican descent place on education and their high rate of participation in the work force distinguish this population from groups characterized as an "underclass" (Hayes-Bautista et al., 1990).

Although popular belief in the United States has held that a common school experience fosters upward social mobility, it has not served that function equally well for all ethnic groups. Likewise, not all immigrant groups have bought into this belief system. Education has served this function, to a substantial degree, for groups such as Greeks, Eastern European Jews, and Japanese. However, the schools were viewed with suspicion by other groups, such as Italians and, to some extent, Slavs, Poles, and Irish (Silberman, 1970). Likewise, the desire for children to have better lives than their parents may not be a universal goal of immigrant groups. Glazer and Moynihan (1963) called attention to this fact by citing a south Italian proverb that says "don't make your child better than you are" (cited in Silberman, 1970, p. 55).

Most parents reported talking with their children about school work and more than half said they engaged in such conversations very often. However, there were a few who said they rarely or never talked with their children about school work. When parents were probed to learn what school subjects were discussed in these conversations, mathematics was spontaneously mentioned by only a small minority. But when asked specifically about mathematics, all parents said they thought it would play an important role in the child's future—both in the demands of everyday living and in the workplace.

Mothers were infrequently identified as the person the child could go to for help with mathematics. Older sisters appeared to serve as a primary source of assistance. This seems consistent with the role of "little mother" assigned to the older girls in many Mexican-descent households, combined with the fact that older sisters had probably been exposed to the curriculum their younger siblings were now experiencing. Although fathers were mentioned as a possible resource more often than mothers were, parents often spoke of their inability to help with the mathematics assignments their children brought home from school. In many cases, parents simply explained that they couldn't help because they had little or no education themselves. In a few cases, parents felt they didn't understand their children's mathematics because it was done differently in the United States than in Mexico. This difficulty was apparently based on differences in the computational procedures taught in the two countries, and in the conception of mathematics as an arithmetic operation. Although curricular reform efforts have attempted to move away from an emphasis on computation and toward higher order thinking processes, what these parents knew of the curriculum from their children's actual school experiences almost certainly confirms the conception of mathematics as computation.

Parents generally thought that their children enjoyed learning mathematics in the classroom. Moreover, most parents thought their children were actually doing quite well or very well in mathematics. Nevertheless, when asked how they expected their child to do in mathematics during the subsequent year, most parents reported that they anticipated substantially improved performance. When asked to provide a reason for the expected improvement in performance, many anticipated greater academic effort from their child. Some parents described their plans to place greater pressure for achievement on their child, while others hoped to find new auxiliary resources outside of the school.

The Euro-American parents, all of whom had at least some college-level education, answered in considerable detail when asked about their plans for their child's high school education. In particular, the Euro-American parents, with their extensive experience with American educational institutions, were well informed about the mathematics classes their children would be taking in high school. The Mexican-descent parents, however, were unable to discuss future plans in anything approaching the knowledge of particulars demonstrated by the Euro-Americans.

The general intentions of Mexican-descent parents were not so different from those of Euro-American parents, with most reporting that they expected their child to take more mathematics than required for graduation. The discrepancy between intent and having the instrumental knowledge to guide the child in his or her course choices has important implications. It underscores the importance of appropriate counseling and guidance within the school. Yet, there has been a history of Mexican-descent students being counseled to leave mathematics courses that would potentially expand rather than constrict their future options. These students tend to be "tracked" into mathematics courses that are a "dead end" with respect to preparation for well-paying, professional careers (College Entrance Examination Board, 1990; Ford Foundation, 1981; Rendón & Triana, 1989).

Both EO and LEP families demonstrated more similarities than differences on most issues explored in this study. However, there were a few interesting disparities between the two groups. First, the parents of children in EO classes thought their children were better mathematics students than did parents of children in LEP classes. We have no achievement data for LEP students comparable to that available on the EO students, so there is no direct way to judge the accuracy of those parental perceptions. However, from classroom observations it did seem to be the case that instruction in LEP classes was targeted at a lower level than was the case in EO classes. We do not know whether that was a function of differences in the achievement level of the students or differences in teacher expectations.

Students of Mexican birth were the majority in LEP classes and the minority in EO classes. The students born in Mexico expressed more positive attitudes toward mathematics than did those born in the United States. This difference was significant. In addition, students of Mexican birth expressed higher expectations of working in occupations requiring mathematics than did students of American birth. However, there were no differences in student perceptions of parental support for the study of mathematics, in stereotypes of mathematicians, in mathematics self-concept, or in beliefs about the nature of mathematics among the LEP and EO groups. Of all these variables, parental encouragement for the study of mathematics appeared to be especially important, and was significantly associated with actual mathematics achievement.

Parents of both EO and LEP students tended to recognize the importance of ability and effort in mathematics, science, reading/language arts, and physical education performance. The only significant difference was for the contrast between science and physical education. Parents of both groups believed that achievement in science resulted from student effort, although achievement in physical education resulted from the child's natural ability. Contrary to what we might expect from the literature that emphasizes parental beliefs about effort as an important factor in mathematics achievement, children whose parents saw achievement in mathematics as the result of ability in lieu of effort tended to be higher achievers than those whose parents attributed achievement more to effort. This does not mean that parents minimized the role of factors other than ability. Throughout the interviews there was a strong sense of the important role played by effort and learning opportunity in mathematics achievement. This was especially evident when parents explained the discrepancy between their child's current performance and the performance expected for the subsequent year.

The overall picture presented by data from our interviews with parents of middle school students of Mexican descent is one of caring parents who want better lives for their children than the lives they themselves have had. For most of the parents in our samples, those desires have found concrete expression in the high aspirations and expectations they hold for their children's future occupations. Most of the Mexican-descent parents had little instrumental knowledge of the requirements necessary for their children to enter the professions which parents hoped they would enter, and many parents demonstrated their desire for such information in conversations with the interviewers. It was clear that these parents had placed their faith in education as the route by which their aspirations and expectations for their children could be realized. They also recognized that preparation in mathematics was an important access route to many of the professions to which they aspired for their children, but they had little specific knowledge of the courses their children should take in high school if those avenues of choice were to be kept open. Lacking such knowledge, these parents will be entirely dependent on whatever information and guidance is made available to their children through high school counselors who, under normal conditions, carry extremely heavy caseloads. This would be problematic in the best of times, but it is particularly troubling because counseling resources in the school district were cut very heavily during recent budget reductions.

Children whose parents had some specific knowledge of mathematics courses in high school were already achieving at higher levels than those whose parents lacked such information. Although parents attempted to support their child's mathematics learning as best they could, a minority reported that they did not interact with their children about such matters, or seldom did so. Many parents said they did not feel prepared to help their children because of their own limited educational backgrounds.

For most parents of Mexican descent, lack of interest did not appear to limit the support they provided for their children's learning. Support and guidance appeared to be a function of the school and its curriculum, and the instrumental means by which parental aspirations were realized. It should not be surprising that parents who were not socialized in this system would have limited knowledge of its workings.

Parents' sense of efficacy in supporting their children's mathematics learning seems to have been firmly linked to their conception of mathematics. Among many parents of Mexican descent, it was apparent that mathematics was purely a matter of computation. For example, in our current work, a parent who accompanied one of our project members to an orientation session for trainers for the Family Math program was overjoyed to learn that many of the things he had been doing at home, such as playing lotto and dominos with his children, promote skills that are relevant to the California Mathematics Framework. This knowledge seemed to give him a new sense of empowerment. We believe the broad involvement of parents in the Family Math program will promote both their sense of efficacy and their ability to conduct mathematics activities at home that directly support the reformed curriculum being taught at school. It should also promote knowledge of the alternatives available to their children when they move on to high school. As an added benefit, parent involvement in the Family Math program may help immigrant parents feel more comfortable in the school setting and become more involved in other school activities.

Almost all of the parents of students in both the LEP and EO classes, mothers and fathers alike, were participants in the work force. Most worked long, physically demanding hours for little pay. Therefore, parent–teacher conferences and other school activities that acquaint parents with their children's academic progress and the school curriculum were nearly impossible to attend. Despite this, the importance of the parents' participation in school activities and their knowledge of the school curriculum was underscored in this study. Both of these variables were significant predictors of mathematics achievement among children of Mexican descent. Measures that can be adopted to ameliorate this situation include scheduling conferences in the evenings to accommodate parents' work schedules, conducting meetings in Spanish or providing Spanish translation, and instituting programs such as "Family Math" which serve to acquaint parents with the mathematics curriculum and with informal family activities that support mathematics learning (Henderson & Landesman, 1995).

It also seems important to search for ways to help parents acquire the instrumental knowledge they obviously crave regarding the job preparation and professional requirements necessary for achieving desirable occupations. Moreover, there should be a way to acquaint parents and students alike with the nature of occupations of which they have no knowledge. New work emphasizing a thematic approach to mathematics instruction in the context of a university–school business partnership is currently being carried out in a community whose population is comparable to the population in the present research (Henderson et al., 1995). The initial focus for the business partner in collaboration with teachers and mathematicians is the development of a thematic curriculum that brings practical, job-related uses of mathematics into the classroom. Future planning will explore ways of involving parents in the practical application of mathematics so that they can expand their knowledge of occupations and the ways in which they are attained.

REFERENCES

Buriel, R., & Cardoza, D. (1988). Sociocultural correlates of achievement among three generations of Mexican-American high school seniors. *American Educational Research Journal, 25* (2), 177–192.

Chacón, M. A., Cohen, E. G., & Strover, S. (1986). Chicanas and Chicanos: Barriers to progress in higher education. In M. A. Olivas (Ed.), *Latino college students* (pp. 296–324). New York: Teachers College Press.

College Entrance Examination Board. (1990). *Changing the odds: Factors increasing access to college*. New York: Author.

Delgado-Gaitan, C. (1988). The value of conformity: Learning to stay in school. *Anthropology and Education Quarterly, 19* (4), 354–381.

Delgado-Gaitan, C. (1990). *Literacy for empowerment: The role of parents in children's education*. London: Falmer.

Duran, B. J., & Weffler, R. E. (1992). Immigrants' aspirations, high school process, and academic outcomes. *American Educational Research Journal, 29* (1), 163–181.

Dweck, C. S. (1986). Motivational processes affecting learning. *American Psychologist, 41* (10), 1040–1048.

Dweck, C. S., & Leggett, E. L. (1988). A social-cognitive approach to motivation and personality. *Psychological Review, 95*, 256–273.

Elliot, E. S., & Dweck, C. S. (1988). Goals: An approach to motivation and achievement. *Journal of Personality and Social Psychology, 54* (1), 5–12.

Fennema, E., & Sherman, J. (1976). Fennema-Sherman mathematics attitude scales: Instruments designed to measure attitudes toward the learning of mathematics by females and males. *Catalog of Selected Documents in Psychology, 6*, 1–32.

Ford Foundation. (1981). *Minorities and mathematics*. New York: Author.

Gándara, P. (1982). Passing through the eye of the needle: High-achieving Chicanas. *Hispanic Journal of Behavioral Sciences, 4* (2), 167–179.

Glazer, N. & Moynihan, D. P. (1963) *Beyond the melting pot*. Cambridge, MA: MIT Press and Harvard University Press.

Haycock, K., & Navarro, M. S. (1988). *Unfinished business: Fulfilling our children's promise*. Oakland, CA: The Achievement Council.

Hayes-Bautista, D., Hurtado, A., Valdez, R. B., & Hernandez, A. C. R. (1990). *Redefining California: Latino social engagement in a multicultural society*. Los Angeles: Chicano Studies Research Center, University of California, Los Angeles.

Henderson, R. W. (1972). Environmental predictors of academic performance of disadvantaged Mexican-American children. *Journal of Consulting and Clinical Psychology, 38* (2), 297.

Henderson, R. W. (1981). Home environment and intellectual performance. In R. W. Henderson (Ed.), *Parent–child interaction: Theory, research, and prospects* (pp. 3–32). New York: Academic Press.

Henderson, R. W. (1991, December). *Development of a measure of motivational goal orientations for mathematics learning* . Santa Cruz, CA: University of California, National Center for Research on Cultural Diversity and Second Language Learning.

Henderson, R. W. (1995, April). *Middle school mathematics for students of Mexican descent: A thematic approach to contextualization of instruction*. Presented as part of a symposium at the Annual Meeting of the American Educational Research Association, San Francisco, CA.

Henderson, R. W., & Landesman, E. M. (1992, December). *The role of instrumental and social competence in the development of higher order cognitive processes in mathematics among language minority students*. [Final report to the Office of Educational Research and Improvement, U.S. Department of Education, under Cooperative Agreement No. R117G10022]. Santa Cruz, CA: University of California, National Center for Research on Cultural Diversity and Second Language Learning.

Henderson, R. W., Landesman, E. M., Nur, D. K., & St. John, L. (1995, June). *Equity in access to the mathematics curriculum: Crossing the great theory-practice divide*. [Technical Report]. Santa Cruz, CA: University of California, National Center for Research on Cultural Diversity and Second Language Learning.

Henderson, R. W., & Merritt, C. B. (1968). Environmental backgrounds of Mexican-American children with different potentials for school success. *Journal of Social Psychology, 75* (1), 101–106.

Laosa, L. M., (1980). Maternal teaching strategies in Chicano and Anglo-American families: The influence of culture and education on maternal behavior. *Child Development, 51* (3), 759–765.

Laosa, L. M., & Henderson, R. W. (1991). Cognitive socialization and competence: The academic development of Chicanos. In R. R. Valencia (Ed.), *Chicano school failure and success: Research and policy agendas for the 1990s* (pp. 164–199). New York: Falmer.

MacCorquodale, P. (1988). Mexican-American women and mathematics: Participation, aspirations, and achievement. In R. R. Cocking & J. P. Mestre (Eds.), *Linguistic and cultural influences on learning mathematics* (pp. 137–160). Hillsdale, NJ: Lawrence Erlbaum Associates.

Martinez-Pons, M., & Zimmerman, B. J. (1989, April). *Differences in home educational processes and achievement among three Hispanic groups in the U.S.* Paper presented at the Annual Meeting of the American Educational Research Association, San Francisco.

Matute-Bianchi, M.E. (1986). Ethnic identities and patterns of school success and failure among Mexican-descent students in a California high school: An ethnographic analysis. *American Journal of Education, 95* (1), 233–255.

McKnight, C. C., Crosswhite, J., Dossey, J., Kifer, E., Swafford, J., Travers, T., & Cooney, T. (1987). *The underachieving curriculum: Assessing U.S. school mathematics from an international perspective.* Champaign, IL: Stipes.

Miller, D. C. (1991). *Handbook of research design and social measurement* (5th ed.). Newbury Park, CA: Sage.

Moll, L. C. (Ed.). (1992). *Vygotsky and education: Instructional implications and applications of sociohistorical psychology.* New York: Cambridge University Press.

Orum, L. S. (1986). *The education of Hispanics: Status and implications.* Washington, DC: National Council of La Raza.

Otto, L. B., & Haller, A. O. (1979). Evidence for a social psychological view of the attainment process: Four studies compared. *Social Forces, 57* (3), 887–914.

Peterson, P. L. (1988). Teaching for higher-order thinking in mathematics: The challenge of the next decade. In D. A. Grouws, T. J. Cooney, & D. Jones (Eds.), *Perspectives on research on effective mathematics teaching* (Vol. 1, pp. 2–26). Reston, VA: National Council of Teachers of Mathematics.

Reese, L., Gallimore, R., Goldenberg, C., & Balzano, S. (1995). Immigrant Latino parents' future orientations for their children. In R. F. Macías & R. G. García Ramos (Eds.), *Changing schools for changing students: An anthology of research on language minorities, schools & society* (pp. 206–230). Santa Barbara, CA: Linguistic Minority Research Institute, University of California.

Reich, P. B. (1991). *The work of nations: Preparing ourselves for 21st century capitalism.* New York: Knopf.

Rendón, L. I., & Triana, E. M. (1989). *Making mathematics and science work for Hispanics.* Washington, DC: American Association for the Advancement of Science.

Rumberger, R. W. (1991). Chicano dropouts: A review of research and policy issues. In R. R. Valencia (Ed.), *Chicano school failure and success: Research and policy agendas for the 1990s* (pp. 64–89). New York: Falmer.

Silberman, C. E. (1970). *Crisis in the classroom: The remaking of American education.* New York: Random House.

So, A. Y. (1987). The educational aspirations of Hispanic parents. *Educational Research Quarterly, 11*(3), 47–53.

Stigler, J. W., & Baranes, R. (1989). Culture and mathematics learning. In E. Z. Rothkopf (Ed.), *Review of research in education* (Vol. 15, pp. 253–306). Washington, DC: American Educational Research Association.

Valencia, R. A. (Ed.). (1991). *Chicano school failure and success: Research and policy agendas for the 1990s.* New York: Falmer.

Valencia, R. R., Henderson, R. W., & Rankin, R. J. (1981). Relationship of family constellation and schooling to intellectual performance of Mexican-American children. *Journal of Educational Psychology, 73* (4), 524–532.

Valencia, R. R., Henderson, R. W., & Rankin, R. J. (1985). Family status, family constellation, and home environmental variables as predictors of cognitive performance of Mexican-American children. *Journal of Educational Psychology, 77* (3), 323–331.

Waxman, H., Huang, S-Y. L., & Padron, Y. N. (1995, April). *Motivation and learning environment differences between resilient and nonresilient Latino middle school students.* Paper presented at the Annual Meeting of the American Educational Research Association, San Francisco.

8

Attitudes Toward Sexuality and Sexual Behaviors of Asian-American Adolescents: Implications for Risk of HIV Infection[1]

Connie Chan

INTRODUCTION

Until 1990, Asian Americans represented an ethnic minority group that was perceived to be at lower risk than African Americans or Hispanics/Latinos for HIV infection, the presumed causal agent for AIDS (Centers for Disease Control, 1989). Reasons cited for this perception include behavioral differences in intravenous drug use (Centers for Disease Control, 1989), sexual behavioral habits (Cochran & Mays, 1988), and underidentification of AIDS cases (Aoki, Ngin, Mo, & Ja, 1989). However, in urban areas such as San Francisco, Toronto, New York, Boston, Los Angeles, and Seattle, where Asians have immigrated and settled in large numbers, cases of HIV infection and AIDS have begun to increase dramatically (Aoki et al., 1989), perhaps reflecting the rise in the number of AIDS cases in Asia. In 1994 the World Health Organization estimated the number of adult HIV infections in East, Southeast, and South Asia at 3 million, compared to 1 million in North America.

In San Francisco, Americans of Asian and Pacific Island descent (APIs) represent 33% of the population and, in 1988, recorded the largest percentage increase in reported AIDS cases in comparison to other ethnic minority groups (Mandel & Kitano, 1989). Although the number of Asian-American AIDS cases was relatively low before 1990, a review of existing data indicates that the number of reported cases is increasing.

There has been little empirical research focusing on sexual behaviors of Asian Americans and their risk for HIV infection and other sexually trans-

---

[1]Funding for this study was provided by the Institute for Asian American Studies at the University of Massachusetts Boston and The Center for Education in the Inner Cities at Temple University.

mitted diseases (STDs). There is reason to believe that the extent of the AIDS epidemic in the Asian-American community is not well understood and that the actual number of Asian Americans who may test HIV-positive has not been accurately measured. The extent to which cultural beliefs and types of behaviors may contribute to or protect against HIV infection in the Asian-American population is still unknown.

Even less is known about Asian-American adolescents' perceptions of "risky" behavior that leads to HIV infection, the social factors underlying these perceptions, and their knowledge of AIDS (Strunin, 1991). There are several factors which may contribute to this lack of information about Asian Americans and AIDS.

First, the methods by which surveillance data on AIDS have been collected and reported give an incomplete picture of the epidemic among Asian Americans. In most reports, Asians are combined with Pacific Islanders or placed with Native Americans in an "other" category. When there is a category of Asians, linguistically, racially, and culturally different Asian groups are combined into one general category. This general grouping of Asians makes it impossible to distinguish trends, modes of transmission, or other variables in the Asian ethnic groups or communities (Aoki et al., 1989).

Second, the diversity of the API group is extraordinary. There is no single "Asian-American" community in the United States; rather, it consists of many subcommunities of ethnic Asian-American groups such as Chinese, Japanese, Filipino, Indians, Koreans, Vietnamese, Cambodians, Samoans, and so forth. According to the 1990 U.S. Census (U.S. Bureau of the Census, 1992) the "Asian" category covers 29 different groups and the "Pacific Islander" category comprises 20 distinct racial and ethnic groups. Collectively, these groups speak more than 100 languages and dialects. Even within specific ethnic groups—for example, between fifth-generation Chinese and new immigrants—there can be great cultural, social, economic, religious, political, and geographic differences.

Impediments to gathering adequate data on the HIV status of the Asian-American population include the diversity of the population, its relatively small size in this country (3% of the total population), and the inability to make inferences at the national level about the community as a whole. In the few state and local studies that address the health status of Asian Americans, generalizations about the entire Asian-American community cannot be made because of the diversity of the community and differences in their geographic distribution. Moreover, APIs currently comprise the third-largest U.S. minority group, and are the fastest growing community of color, with annual growth rates that may exceed 40% during the 1990s. By the year 2050, it is predicted that the API population in the United States will grow to 41 million.

Of the 242,146 AIDS cases documented in the United States through September 1992, the Centers for Disease Control (1992) reported that 1,525 (0.6%) were identified as APIs. The male-to-female ratio of AIDS cases and deaths is approximately 11 to 1. Of the AIDS cases in the API community, 74% were contracted by men who have had sex with men, compared with 58% for all races. The 1992 data resembles data collected at the beginning of the epidemic for other racial groups, leading to speculation that the API communities are still in the early stages of a growing HIV epidemic. Given the relative geographic and psychosocial isolation of many API communities, the effect of an infectious disease may be magnified and spread more quickly once it takes hold. The course of the epidemic in these communities may well begin to resemble that of the African-American and Hispanic/Latino communities, with increases among the heterosexual population, women, and children. It is imperative that culturally aware and effective prevention methods and education be implemented as quickly as possible, especially with adolescent youth who are sexually active.

Even with reports of increased seroprevalence in communities with large API populations such as San Francisco, where it was estimated that 35% (2,034 individuals) of homosexual and bisexual API men are infected with HIV, there has been a sense among local, state, and federal agencies, as well as AIDS organizations, that APIs have lower risk for contracting AIDS. As a result, little attention has been given to APIs regarding AIDS prevention programming, sexual practices, AIDS knowledge, beliefs, and attitudes toward AIDS and sexuality.

ASIAN-AMERICAN ADOLESCENTS

In 1992, 20% of all reported AIDS cases were in the 16- to 29-year-old age group, and rates among 11- to 24-year-olds have doubled each year (Centers for Disease Control, 1992). Because the AIDS incubation period is estimated to be from 2 to 7 years, this group is likely to have been infected during adolescence (Strunin, 1991). Surveys of U.S. adolescents demonstrate that approximately 50% of teenagers have had sexual intercourse by the age of 16, and more than 70% by age 19 (Zelnik & Kanter, 1980). Yet all of these sexually active teenagers are not at equal risk for HIV infection and other STDs. Those adolescents who have intercourse at an earlier age, or whose patterns of sexual behavior include more partners and anal sex, those who use alcohol and drugs, as well as those who drop out of school or are of low socioeconomic status (SES) may be at greater risk. Research has demonstrated that the age at which sexual activity begins differs by racial and ethnic background, with earlier sexual experience correlated with higher risk of contracting an STD (Irwin, 1985). Although African Americans have the highest rates for most STDs, and rates for Hispanics/Latinos fall between the rates for African Americans and White adolescents (Irwin et al., 1985), the rates for Asian-American adolescents were not measured in these studies.

Although some studies of adolescents suggest that knowledge concerning transmission of HIV is increasing, few adolescents in the early years of the AIDS epidemic (1986–1989) considered themselves at risk for contracting HIV—nor did they report changing their behavior to reduce the risk of contracting the virus (Di Clemente, Zorn, & Temoshuk, 1987; Strunin, 1991; Strunin & Hingson, 1987). In Strunin and Hingson's survey of 860 Massachusetts adolescents, 54% were not worried about contracting AIDS and 61% did not think it was likely that they would get AIDS in their lifetime. Only 15% of sexually active adolescents reported changing their sexual practices to avoid contracting HIV. In 1988, Weisman and colleagues found that 90% of a sample of 400 adolescent girls knew that "unprotected sex" was a high risk activity for contracting the AIDS virus, but fewer than 40% of the girls had used condoms the last time they had had intercourse. However, as AIDS awareness and education have increased both in the public view and in some educational settings, adolescents today may be more knowledgeable about AIDS risks.

Racial and ethnic differences in knowledge and perceived risk were found by Di Clemente in a 1988 sample of 261 White, 226 African-American, and 142 Hispanic/Latino students. The adolescents who knew less about AIDS transmission were more likely to perceive themselves at higher risk for contracting the virus, with white adolescents the most knowledgeable and Hispanic/Latino adolescents the least knowledgeable about AIDS.

Although it is sparse, research on Asian-American adolescents' knowledge of AIDS transmission and perceived risks, their attitudes toward sexuality, and reported sexual activity indicates that Asian- American students may be less knowledgeable about AIDS than their non-Asian peers. A 1987 survey of San Francisco-area high school students found that Asian-American students were the least knowledgeable racial group of students regarding AIDS information (Di Clemente et al., 1987). Telephone and high school surveys, conducted in Massachusetts in 1988 with more than 2,000 adolescents, demonstrated that ethnicity was an important predictor of knowledge about AIDS (Strunin, 1991). Strunin's study found that Asian-American adolescents knew significantly less about the ways in which the virus can be transmitted sexually, and about drug-use transmission of the HIV virus, than did the White, African-American, or Hispanic/Latino adolescents. Although the percentage of Asian-American respondents in the survey was very low (3% of the total sample), this study found that significantly more Asian-American adolescents (94% compared to 73% of Whites and Hispanics/Latinos, and 69% of African Americans) were worried about getting AIDS. This finding is even more remarkable in that significantly fewer numbers of Asian Americans reported having heterosexual intercourse in the past year—only 19%, compared with 61% of Hispanics/Latinos, 63% of Whites, and 74% of African Americans. Strunin suggested that because the majority of her Asian-American sample consisted of recent U.S. immigrants, they may adhere more closely to ethnic cultural expectations of abstinence, and may not have been exposed to AIDS education in school or at home.

Indeed, some research indicates that cultural pressures may result in reduced behavioral risk for HIV, as it describes a "sexual conservatism" among Asian-American young adults. Research has reported that Asian Americans are significantly less likely to talk about sex than Whites, African Americans, and Hispanics/Latinos (Erickson & Moore, 1986), and are more disapproving of marital infidelity (Christensen, 1973). However, as Cochran et al. (1991) commented, not outwardly expressing one's sexuality is not necessarily the same as not engaging in HIV-related risk behavior. Cochran's study of 153 Asian-American college students at the University of California, Los Angeles (UCLA) found that previously reported sexual conservatism within this ethnic group may be limited to the initiation of sexual activity. Once sexually active, sexual behaviors appear to be similar to that of their non-Asian counterparts. They found that Asian-American students were practicing sexual behaviors that were risky, including low rates of condom use (11%), and sexual behaviors that would transmit the HIV virus if present. According to the study, Asian-American college students at UCLA are at the same risk for transmission of HIV as are their non-Asian counterparts. If this is true, the potential transmission of HIV within the Asian-American population is likely to be greater than previously assumed.

Any discussion of sexuality and sexual behaviors within Asian-American cultures is complex and problematic. There is no one Asian-American culture but, rather, many separate and distinct ethnic and cultural groupings within the Asian-American community. Even if one were to believe that Asians share a common cultural expectation that reinforces sexually conservative behaviors due to the traditional Asian values of family unity and the desire to not bring shame on the family, the extent to which these cultural values affect Asian-American adolescents who are also exposed to the hegemonic American cultural values is unknown and must be taken into consideration. In addition, lumping all Asian-American subgroups into one is not useful in measuring AIDS knowledge and sexual behaviors, which may differ dramatically depending on ethnicity, length of stay in the United States, socioeconomic status, and education, among other factors. Future research measuring attitudes, knowledge, risk factors, and behaviors of specific Asian-American ethnic and cultural groups rather than combining all groups into a single Asian category would be more applicable to AIDS education strategies.

IMPLICATIONS FOR AIDS EDUCATION

Because Asian cultures have a tradition of keeping the issues of sexuality, sexual expression, and sexual identity within the private realm and discouraging discussion of sexuality in public forums, the majority of Asian Americans may not consider themselves as having a sexual identity such as homosexual, heterosexual, or bisexual (Chan, 1994). This lack of a sexual identity, combined with the taboo of not discussing sexual activity or sexuality in public, may contribute to the perception that Asian Americans are at lower risk for HIV infection and other STDs.

This chapter assesses Asian-American adolescents' knowledge about AIDS transmission, their attitudes about AIDS, their sexual behaviors, and explores whether there are differences between a Cambodian group, which comprises half of the sample, and an "Other Asian" group, which is comprised of adolescents from Chinese, Vietnamese, and South Asian backgrounds. Although the original design called for equal numbers of each ethnic group, in this pilot study we were unable to survey large enough numbers of Chinese, Vietnamese, and South Asians to do analyses by separate ethnic groups. Thus, these three groups are combined into an "Other Asian" category in comparison with a Cambodian group comprised of participants in a youth project. In addition to ethnic and cultural differences, there is a difference between the groups with regard to socioeconomic class (the Cambodian group is based in Revere, a working-class city north of Boston, whereas the "Other Asian" group comes from more varied socioeconomic backgrounds in the Boston metropolitan area).

METHOD

Questionnaires were completed by 80 adolescents (40 boys and 40 girls) in the Boston and Revere geographic areas from July through December, 1994. Participants were recruited from a neighborhood youth program called ROCA-Revere, and from two Asian-American youth programs in the Boston Area. Approximately 17% were born in the United States, 49% in Cambodia, 13% in China, 6% in Vietnam, and 5% in Thailand. The length of time this sample group had lived in the United States ranged from 1 year to 17 years (since birth). An overwhelming majority (90%) of this sample speak a language other than English, with 60% speaking Khmer (the language of Cambodia), 13% Cantonese, 5% Vietnamese, and 4% Korean. Participants ranged from 14 to 19 years old (median = 16.1), and all were enrolled in high school (median grade = 10.1).

PROCEDURE

Questionnaires consisting of 35 items were administered to 96 high school students of Cambodian, Chinese, Vietnamese, and Indian descent. The items included demographic data collection, and assessed AIDS knowledge, attitudes toward AIDS, and personal sexual behaviors, including frequency of sexual contact with males and females, use of condoms, and prior sexual experiences of the respondents. All questionnaires were completed anonymously and on a volunteer basis. Ninety-six questionnaires were distributed, 16 of which were discarded because the respondents did not complete at least half of the questions, or provided obviously false data (such as giving their age as 50 or listing 500 sexual partners in the past year). Eighty participants, comprising the sample group, completed the entire questionnaire with valid data.

The questionnaire included questions from two AIDS awareness and attitude surveys conducted previously in Massachusetts high schools and among adolescents (Strunin, 1991), and by adding additional questions concerning sexual behaviors (regarding anal and oral sex), as well as questions concerning ethnicity and primary language.

One-way ANOVA tested the significance of differences in responses among the Cambodian Americans and the other Asian-American groups. The one-way ANOVA also evaluated any significant differences by gender in the other variables.

RESULTS

Knowledge of HIV Transmission

As a group, this sample of Asian-American adolescents was generally knowledgeable about AIDS and how it is transmitted, although there are some gaps in their knowledge. Table 8.1 summarizes the knowledge about HIV transmission of Cambodian and non-Cambodian Asians.

To measure overall knowledge about HIV transmission, we calculated a "knowledge index" score, a composite score of the number of correct answers to the items in Table 8.1. The mean scores for each group, by ethnicity, as well as the results of a test to measure differences between

TABLE 8.1
Knowledge of HIV Transmission

Can you get AIDS from (% responding correctly)	Cambodia (n = 55)	Other Asian (n = 25)
Toilet seats	91%	95%
Sharing eating utensils	85%	86%
Kissing	82%	85%
Germs in the air	92%	91%
Being in the same room with a person who has AIDS	94%	98%
Sex between two men	100%	100%
Sex between a man and a woman	100%	100%
Male semen	97%	98%
Female vaginal fluids	82%	80%
Giving blood	88%	90%
Injecting drugs	84%	87%

TABLE 8.2

Knowledge Index by Groups

	N	M	SD	SE	t	df	2-tail prob
Group 1 (Other Asians)	25	15.41	2.765	0.564	1.82	51.65	0.074
Group 2 (Cambodians)	55	14.10	3.281	0.442	1.82	51.65	0.074

Note: Composite groups score—Number of items answered correctly (perfect score is 16).

groups, are summarized in Table 8.2.

The results show that Group 1, the Other Asian group, scored higher than Group 2, the Cambodian youths. Although the difference is not highly significant ($p = .074$), the difference in mean scores does indicate that Cambodian adolescents are less knowledgeable about HIV transmission than other Asian-American adolescents.

Discussion of AIDS and Sexual Behavior

This sample of Asian-American adolescents has a much better knowledge of the methods of AIDS transmission than did the Asian group in Strunin's 1991 Massachusetts study (data gathered in 1988). It seems that AIDS education and knowledge about AIDS overall has increased over the past 7 years among high school students. One reason may be that AIDS is discussed far more openly now than it was 6 years ago. When asked if they had ever discussed AIDS with anyone, 72% responded "Yes" and 28% responded "No." The former were asked to indicate with whom they had discussed AIDS (e.g., teacher, friend).

This finding indicates that adolescents are receiving their information about AIDS in schools and from counselors in teen programs, but that there is little discussion about AIDS (and, perhaps, sex) with their parents.

In addition to finding out whether they discussed AIDS, we were interested in how open the adolescents were in talking about sex and sexual behavior with their friends. Thirty-three percent responded that they do talk about sex and sexual behavior with their friends, although 67% said they do not. These results suggest that there is, among this group of Asian-American adolescents, more openness about discussing AIDS in a structured setting, such as in school or in a group program, than there is about discussing sex and sexual behavior with their friends.

Concern About Getting AIDS

Because we wanted to explore whether adolescents felt they were at risk for AIDS and, if so, how high, we asked them a question regarding their perception of risk (see Table 8.3).

These data indicate that there is quite a range in terms of individual worry about personal risk for AIDS; half the sample is quite concerned about getting AIDS, while the other half is only marginally or not at all concerned. To determine whether those who responded positively to being sexually active in the past year were more concerned about getting AIDS, a one-way ANOVA was calculated on this question with sexual activity defining the two groups. No significant difference was found between these two groups. The individuals who reported being sexually active in the past year were no more likely to worry about getting AIDS than those who were not sexually active. Perhaps those who had not been sexually active in the past year abstained from sexual activity because of their concerns about AIDS.

Behavior Changes Due to AIDS Awareness

TABLE 8.3
Perception of Risk

How much do you worry about getting AIDS?	Cambodians	Other Asians
A great deal	24%	31%
Somewhat	20%	26%
A little	31%	20%
Not at all	25%	21%

In response to a direct question as to whether they had changed any of their sexual behaviors because of concerns about getting AIDS, 45% of the overall

TABLE 8.4
Behavior Changes

Behavior Change	Cambodian (n = 16)	Other Asian (n = 20)
Use condoms	50%	60%
Abstain from sex	25%	20%
Check partner out more carefully	25%	30%
No anal sex	25%	0%
Stay with one partner	25%	40%

TABLE 8.5
Sexual Behavior

Number and Percent Responding "Yes" to	Cambodian	Other Asian	Total	F-Values
Sexual contact in the past year	20 (50%)	6 (15%)	26 (33%)	8.01**
Anal sex	10 (25%)	2 (5%)	12 (15%)	5.97**
Oral sex	14 (35%)	4 (10%)	9 (22%)	5.15**
Having sex with someone of the same gender	2 (10%)	0 (0%)	5 (5%)	

Note. *p < .05 and **p < .01.

sample responded "Yes" (40% of the Cambodian group and 50% of the Other Asian group). Those who responded positively to making behavior changes reported changes in the categories listed in Table 8.4.

Risky Behaviors for HIV Infection

Because other studies have found that knowledge about AIDS does not necessarily lead to changing behaviors to reduce the risk of transmission of the virus (Cochran et al., 1991; Strunin, 1991), it was important to find out about the adolescents' past and current sexual behavior (see Table 8.5). One-way ANOVAS measuring differences between groups showed significant differences in some sexual behaviors between the Cambodian and Other Asian groups. Overall, the number of those who indicated that they had engaged in sexual contact in the past year made up 33% of the entire group.

These results show that 26 adolescents, almost one third of the total sample, reported having sexual contact in the past year. The data demonstrate a significant difference between the Cambodian group and the Other Asian group, with the Cambodian group being notably more active during the previous year. The Cambodian group's mean age for first becoming sexually active was 15.4; for the other Asian group the mean was 16.1. Twelve out of the 26 adolescents who were sexually active (46%) reported using condoms during sexual contact, a higher percentage than reported in previous studies of sexually active Asian-American groups. There were no significant gender or ethnic group differences with regard to condom use.

DISCUSSION

In the few published studies measuring AIDS knowledge and sexual behaviors of Asian-American adolescents and young adults, this population has been found to be less knowledgeable about AIDS, to discuss sex and sexuality less and, in some studies, they are found to be less sexually active than their White, African-American, and Hispanic/Latino counterparts. The results of this study reveal that some of these previously held assumptions about Asian-American adolescents may no longer be accurate. As AIDS awareness and educational efforts increase, Asian-American adolescents are much more knowledgeable about how AIDS is transmitted and discuss AIDS more frequently with their friends and adult educators and counselors. Greater numbers of Asian-American adolescents seem to be translating that knowledge into behavioral change in terms of reducing risky behaviors during sex (with increased use of condoms)—although, of the youths who have been sexually active in the past year, only 46% use condoms during oral, anal, or vaginal intercourse.

The results of this study show that a sample of Cambodian adolescents from Revere, Massachusetts differ from their Chinese, Vietnamese, and South Asian counterparts from the metropolitan Boston area only in sexual activity, where significantly more Cambodians report being sexually active in the past year. Possible explanations for this difference are ethnic cultural beliefs, immigrant status, and SES. Cambodian culture, with younger ages for marriage in traditional Cambodia, may—if not openly sanctioning sexual activity at earlier ages—not be as prohibitive as the other Asian cultures.

Although there were no significant differences between groups in terms of immigration status, the majority of both groups were first-generation immigrants who would be expected to adhere more closely to traditional cultural expectations than would more "Americanized" adolescents (i.e., those born in the United States or living here longer). Socioeconomic class may also be a factor in understanding the difference in level of sexual activity between groups. Research has demonstrated that lower SES is correlated with higher behavioral risk for HIV transmission, and the Cambodian group is from a working-class community. However, because AIDS knowledge and attitudes toward AIDS were similar between groups, this socioeconomic factor may play less of a role in this study than in others where low socioeconomic class results in less knowledge about AIDS.

Finally, as this is a pilot study, and these are preliminary results, we expect that a larger sample group which allowed comparison between the three largest Asian ethnic groups in Massachusetts (Cambodian, Vietnamese, and Chinese) would explore these factors in greater contextual depth.

REFERENCES

Aoki, B., Ngin, C. P., Mo, B., & Ja, D. Y. (1989). AIDS prevention models in the Asian-American communities. In V. M. Mays, G. W. Albee, & S. F. Schneider (Eds.), *Primary prevention of AIDS: Psychosocial approaches* (pp. 290–308). Newbury Park, CA: Sage.

Centers for Disease Control. (1989). *Report on AIDS.* Atlanta, GA: Center for Disease Control.

Chan, C. S. (1994). Cultural issues in the development of sexuality and sexual expression among Asian-American adolescents. In J. Irvine (Ed.), *Sexual cultures: Adolescence, community, and the construction of identity* (pp. 88–99). Philadelphia, PA: Temple University Press.

Christensen, H. T. (1986). Attitudes towards marital infidelity: A nine-culture sampling of university student opinion. *Journal of Comparative Family Studies, 4*(20), 197–214.

Cochran, S. D., & Mays, V. M. (1988). Issues in the perception of AIDS risk and risk reduction activities by Black & Hispanic/Latina women. *American Psychology, 43*(11), 949–957.

Cochran, S. D., Mays, V. M., & Leung, L. (1991). Sexual practices of heterosexual Asian-American young adults: Implications for risk of HIV infection. *Archives of Sexual Behavior, 20,* 381–391.

DiClemente, R. J., Boyer, C. B., & Mills, S. J. (1988). Prevention of AIDS among adolescents: Strategies for the development of comprehensive risk-reduction health education programs. *Health Education Research, 2,* 287–291.

Di Clemente, R. J., Zorn, J., & Temoshuk, L. (1987). The association of gender, ethnicity, and residence in the Bay Area to adolescents' knowledge and attitudes about Acquired Immune Deficiency Syndrome. *Journal of Applied Social Psychology, 17,* 216–230.

Erickson, P. I., & Moore, D. S. (1986). *Sexual activity, birth control use, and attitudes among high school students from three minority groups.* Paper presented at the meeting of the American Public Health Association, Las Vegas, NV.

Irwin, C. E., Shafer, M. A., & Millstein, S. G. (1985). Pubertal development in adolescent females: A marker for early sexual debate. *Pediatric Research, 19,* 112A.

Mandel, J. S., & Kitano, K. J. (1989). San Francisco looks at AIDS in Southeast Asia. *Multicultural Inquiry and Research in AIDS: Quarterly Newsletter, 3*(1–2), 7.

Strunin, L. (1991). Adolescent perception of risk for HIV infection: Implications for further research. *Social Science and Medicine, 32*(2), 221–228.

Strunin, L., & Hingson, R. (1991) Knowledge about HIV and behavioral risks of foreign born public school students. *American Journal of Public Health, 81*(2) 1638–1641.

U. S. Bureau of the Census (1992). 1990 Census of population and housing.

Weisman, C. S., Teitelbaum, M. A., & Nathanson, C. A. (1988). *AIDS knowledge, perceived risk, and prevention in adolescent clients of a family planning clinic.* Paper presented at American Public Health Association Annual Meeting, Boston, November 13–17, 1988.

Zelnik, M., & Kantner, J. F. (1980). Sexual activity, contraceptive use, and pregnancy among metropolitan-area teenagers, 1971–1979. *Family Planning Perspectives, 12,* 230–237.

9

African-American Adolescents and Academic Achievement: Family and Peer Influences

Melvin N. Wilson
Deanna Y. Cooke
Edith G. Arrington

Prior to adolescence, a person is primarily dependent on his or her family for care and guidance. It is during adolescence that he or she becomes individuated from the family and that relationships with peers become more salient. During this developmental period, adolescents learn a set of functional skills that are needed for a successful transition into, and survival during, adulthood. In other words, adolescence can be viewed as the "launching pad" into adulthood. A crucial part of the formula for successful adult functioning is one's level of school performance. Arguably, the nature of adolescents'; relationships with family and peers has an effect on their academic performance. Adolescents learn many of their functional skills from both parents and peers, and these relationships have a profound relationship to success. The transition to and through adolescence is obviously a tenuous one that can be affected by a variety of stressors. For African Americans, adolescence is further complicated with issues of race, ethnicity, and, more often than not, socioeconomic status. African-American adolescents must learn to come into adulthood in a society that devalues critical aspects of their identity. This societal phenomenon can indeed have negative effects on adolescents' overall functioning, particularly academic achievement. The purpose of this chapter is to examine the influences of families and peers on African-American academic achievement within a greater social context.

FAMILY INFLUENCES

When attempting to assess family influence on the academic achievement of African-American adolescents, it is important to understand that the socialization process of African Americans necessarily reflects living in a bicultural world (Boykin, 1979, 1983; Brookins, 1985, 1993; Spencer & Markstrom-Adams, 1990). The ecological reality for many African-American families is that they are both a part of and apart from the dominant American culture. African-American socialization, then, refers not only to the way that children are reared, but also to the ecological context of an ethnic lifestyle in American society (Harrison, Wilson, Pine, Chan, & Buriel, 1990). Here, the term *ecological context* signifies the way in which one's life is orchestrated and guided by both internal resources and external limitations. The goals, values, and beliefs given to children within African-American communities are coded, then, for both an understanding of the child's cultural background and for the dominant culture. Accordingly, in order to understand academic achievement among African-American adolescents, we must understand the social systems in which they grow and develop (Harrison, 1987). The primary source of growth, development, and socialization during childhood is the family; one of the most important functions of the family is the preparation of its children for adult roles (Wilson, 1989).

African-American families have traditionally instilled in their children values which constitute a foundation for achievement, including discipline, hard work, self-sacrifice, patience, and love. However, many African-American parents of school-aged children have expressed feelings of futility toward the school system. These feelings may contribute significantly to the now well-documented lower achievement levels of African-American children. The evidence, though complex and inconclusive, generally supports the existence of a significant relationship between academic self-esteem and achievement behavior. Many students experience difficulty in school not because they lack intelligence or ability, but often because they lack academic self-esteem. The source of these negative self-evaluations is often the early and consistent feedback they receive in the form of low grades. Despite their lack of self-esteem and low grades, most African-American adolescents want their parents to believe that they have the ability to achieve academically (DeSantis, Ketterlinus, & Youniss, 1990).

African-American families have always stressed the importance of education (Franklin & Moss, 1994). In fact, it was the insistence of African-American parents that their children receive educations equal to those of White children that catapulted the country into the Civil Rights era. It is difficult to entertain any perspective that blames African-American families for the supposed academic underachievement of their children. It is the family's strengths, including spirituality, role flexibility, kinship, and social organization, that have served to prepare African-American youth for their experiences in society and the school system (Littlejohn-Blake & Anderson-Darling, 1993).

Morris (1992) found that the family lives of African-American adolescents serve to shape their overall behavior and levels of academic achievement. Morris asserted that the range of economic and social factors that affect African-American families influences how their children are equipped to handle their roles in school settings. Logically, those families that better prepare their children for school will help ensure their children's future academic achievement. Similarly, Ford (1993) found that all of the African-American students participating in her study agreed either that economic and social factors strongly affect academic achievement or that their parents considered school (and participation in gifted programs) to be important. Ford also discovered that these students were optimistic about academic achievement and that they were supportive of ideologies that were achievement oriented. Similarly, Connell, Spencer, and Aber (1994) found that African-American adolescents' own experiences and perceptions of how their families support them in their school endeavors supersede family and neighborhood demographics, such as socioeconomic status (SES).

Dornbusch, Ritter, and Steinberg (1991) believed that the influence parents and families have on adolescent academic behavior is more indirect. They found that the existence of a functional community promotes competence among adolescents because functional communities support effective parenting. Dornbusch and colleagues determined that, among African-American adolescents, family status (i.e., SES) is not as reliable a predictor of school performance as is community variables (i.e., the SES of the community) or parental style. In another study, Steinberg, Mounts, Lamborn, and Dornbusch (1991) found that, although parental style (most notably, authoritative parenting) does not predict school performance as well among African Americans in comparison with other ethnic groups, African-American parents with an authoritative parenting style increase their adolescents' psychological maturity and decrease psychological distress and behavior problems.

Slaughter and Epps (1987) noted that parents serve as their children's first teachers and found that the role of the African-American mother, regardless of marital status and educational attainment, is an important variable in the academic achievement of African-American adolescents. Similarly, Bradley et al. (1993) determined that the home environment serves as a mediator in the relationship between the cognitive abilities of mothers and their children. Slaughter and Epps, however, also found that as children grow older and enter adolescence, the influence of the family lessens corresponding to the rise of the influence of the peer group. The role of the family is ultimately related to school achievement, however, because it is the family that chooses the schools that adolescents attend, that encourages and supports the students with their coursework, and so on.

Slaughter and Epps (1987) also determined that the educational environment that parents create *within* the home influences student achievement. Similarly, Johnson (1992) found that the family itself creates the appropriate milieu or climate for development and achievement in many different areas, of which academics is just one. Johnson acknowledged the omnipresence of racism and other deleterious factors in the African-American family's struggle to help their children and adolescents achieve. However, she also stated that if families are optimistic, have a sense of control, create academically related activities, and hold strong educational values and expectations, they will successfully influence the achievement of their adolescents in school.

Moore (1985, 1986, 1987) found that the ethnicity of a child's household significantly influences his or her academic performance. Moore determined that the ethnicity of the rearing environment affects African-American children's styles of responding to standardized intelligence tests and their performance on achievement tests. Moore's three consecutive studies showed a significant difference in the academic achievement levels of two groups of African-American children that favored children adopted by White families. The studies also established that the effects of ethnicity within the rearing environment appear to be mediated, at least in part, by the mother's affective (rather than analytic) problem-solving strategies.

Jackson, Johnson, and Wallace (1987) found that gifted African-American youth come from a wide range of social backgrounds, have parents with disparate levels of education, and live in households of assorted living arrangements. Jackson and her colleagues concluded that the parents of these academically talented youth held high aspirations of educational achievement for their children and passed this desire onto them. Wilson and Allen (1987) supported Jackson and her colleagues by demonstrating that African-American adolescents whose mothers had higher than average levels of education also reached comparatively high levels of educational attainment. In addition, Johnson (1992) noted that, although the family is the most important variable in the academic achievement and development of African-American adolescents, the youth's own attitudes, which are themselves influenced by the family, significantly shape academic achievement.

Although many African-American families create positive home environments that foster the academic aspirations of their youth, studies of academic expectations and achievement of African-American adolescents often focus on the adolescents' "at-risk" status and ignore the ways in which their families promote achievement. Research indicates that the current status of African Americans contributes to many of the risk and protective factors that influence the academic achievement levels of their children. Sameroff, Seifer, Baldwin, and Baldwin (1993) have suggested that African-American children are affected by cumulative indices of environmental risk, including minority status, parental occupations, maternal level of education, family size, family support, life events, parenting perspectives, level of anxiety, and mental health. Sameroff and his associates (1993) found that many of the risk factors that influence academic achievement among African Americans were independent of genetic and social factors.

Attaining educational opportunities and achieving academic goals represent a critical challenge for African Americans. Although the high school completion rate for African Americans has increased from 10% in 1940 to 73% in 1990, technological changes have required potential employees to have postsecondary educational degrees (Johnson, 1992). Educational achievement among African Americans continues to lag behind that of most other racial and ethnic groups, despite numerous examples of individual accomplishments (Dawkins, 1989). Inadequate preparation in inequitable schools and the pressure of chronic racial prejudice has trapped more than a third of African Americans in a cycle of poverty (Edelman, 1987; Mincy, 1994). Nevertheless, many African-American parents stress the need for their children to acquire college training in order to escape economic disadvantages (Hochschild, 1989; Nathan, 1989; Reid, 1982; Wilson, 1989). Similarly, many low-income African-American parents ardently believe that social and economic conditions will improve as long as their children have access to adequate schooling. However, because of limited information and unfamiliarity with career alternatives, many African-American parents may have unrealistic educational aspirations for their children, unless real change is affected within the schools that African Americans attend.

PEER INFLUENCES

Adolescence is the period in which peers exert great influence on each other's decisions about how to behave and what to do, say, think, and wear. Involvement with friends (i.e., loyal and intimate peers) and in peer groups (i.e., a set or sets of peers with whom an adolescent is loosely associated) is an integral part of development during adolescence. Savin-Williams and Berndt (1990) found that adolescents tend to talk about issues of personal importance such as sexuality and dating with friends, and to discuss issues concerning values and achievement with parents. In addition, adolescents and their friends typically have similar academic goals and levels of school achievement. There is, however, some debate about how much and what kind of influence peers have on each other's academic achievement. Entwisle (1990) noted that close friendships do not affect the academic achievement levels of students, however, peer groups do. Academic performance increases in peer groups where achievement is valued, and decreases in peer groups where achievement is not valued. Savin-Williams and Berndt (1990), however, argued that harmonious, supportive friendships are associated with better performance in school. For African Americans, the issue of peer influence is particularly salient because of lower graduation rates, fewer placements in accelerated classrooms, and lower levels of academic achievement compared to White adolescent counterparts. Although educators and social policymakers have suggested that academic performance levels among African-American students could be improved if peer relationships supported school achievement, Savin-Williams and Berndt determined that there is not enough data to support this hypothesis.

In their study of school success among African-American students, Fordham and Ogbu (1986) found that many African-American children perform poorly in school because of the burden of "acting White." These researchers contend that youths who succeed in school do so at the risk of being admonished by their African-American peers for embracing the values of White America. African Americans have defined academic advancements in school as disparate from African-American culture. The ideology espoused by adolescents, and among adults as well, is that one can lose his or her African-American identity as one becomes more entrenched in worlds that are not typically entered into by African Americans. High school youths must decide to become academically successful at the possible cost of being labeled a "sellout," or must find ways to handle success in school while not disconnecting themselves from their peers. Fordham and Ogbu described several ways that the latter choice is accomplished.

First, African-American adolescents may try to establish a persona that fits within the concept of what they believe it means to be African American. For example, some African-American youth have attempted to minimize the distance between themselves and their White peers by becoming the so-called "class clown." This strategy enables students to have a persona that is more acceptable to their peers than that of a stereotypically studious youth. African-American youth may also try to "fit in" simply by minimizing their effort in the classroom and performing below their academic potential.

Other research on peer influence has suggested that contact with white adolescents is associated with higher academic outcomes among African-American youth. Johnson (1992) found that African-American youth living in communities with high concentrations of White peers typically have higher achievement levels than youth from predominantly African-American neighborhoods. She contends that one reason for this may be that African-American children living in predominantly White environments share White cultural values that are artifacts of successful performance on tests of cognitive abilities. Hallinan and Williams (1990) examined the relationship between same and different race friendship dyads and their effects on academic aspirations and academic attainment. They found that Black students generally had better outcomes for both academic aspirations and attainment if they had a White best friend. However, when controlling for SES, Black students with a Black best friend had higher educational aspirations than Black students with White best friends.

In contrast to these findings, Goodenow and Grady (1993) hypothesized that school belonging has more influence on the success of urban adolescents than does peer influence. Their study assessed adolescent students for their expectancy of success, value of schoolwork, general achievement motivation, and effort in school. The study also assessed the influence of the student's friendship network on student motivation ("My friends think it is important to do well in school"). Most adolescents were well above the mean on measures of expectancy to succeed, value of education, and effort and persistence. However, when school belonging was measured, many students did not feel they belonged to school, or were motivated in school. Students who claimed to be more connected with the school had more academic motivation and engagement. Although Goodenow and Grady's study redirected its emphasis on motivation to achieve in school away from family and peer influences, a possible correlation seems to exist between this ideology and the ideology of peer influence. First, peer academic ideology was assessed by one item on Goodenow and Grady's measures and, therefore, may not totally encompass the realm of peer influence. In addition, school belonging was partially assessed according to how the adolescent believed he or she was perceived by school peers ("Other students in this school take my opinion seriously"). This indicates that when students felt they were valued by their peers, these perceptions played a role in connecting students with their school and with achieving success in school.

DeSantis, Ketterlinus, and Youniss (1990) conducted a study to assess the degree to which African-American students cared about the perceptions of friends and parents in different arenas. The study assessed the importance of family and peer perceptions of students' academic success vis-á-vis academic success and intelligence. The African-American students in the study cared more about being perceived as intelligent than did the White students, and both the African-American and White students cared more about parents' than friends' perception of their academic success. Other findings suggested that African-American youth from two-parent households and youth with college-educated parents cared more about being perceived as an intelligent person and a good student than youth from one-parent households and youth with non-college-educated mothers. Steinberg, Dornbusch, and Brown (1992) challenged this notion by asserting that peers exert greater influence over minority youngsters than do parents in matters of academic achievement. Steinberg and colleagues suggested that, although parents are more influential in long-term achievement, peers more directly affect daily school behaviors.

Peer influence has been deemed relevant not only to academic achievement, but also to understanding the importance of closeness in friendships among adolescents. Following Parson's framework of friendship, Hallinan and Williams (1990) asserted that friendships vary by degree of solidarity and that peer influences should be relative to the strength of the friendship. In addition, Clark (1991) suggested that the best predictor for social competence is the number of reciprocal best friends a student has, and that students whose friends are perceived as competent and achievement-oriented typically are high achievers.

The nature of peer influences on African-American adolescents is quite complex. Today's African-American youth must contend with a society that devalues them, peers that devalue each other, and an ever-increasing necessity for formal professional skills as we move farther into the computer era. Despite the low high school completion rate among African-American youth, Garibaldi (1992), in sampling a large, urban school district, found that 95% of the African-American males surveyed expected to graduate from high school. We must encourage such determination and high expectations among African-American students and support the drive that keeps them believing in their abilities. We also must help ensure that the educational system encourages the notion that academic success is not just for Whites, and that schools were created and continue to be an institution to aid in the personal advancement and enrichment of all people, regardless of race or ethnicity.

CONCLUSION: NEW RESEARCH DIRECTIONS

One focus in the literature on achievement among African-American adolescents has been on the concept of the *discriminatory job ceiling* (Taylor, Casten, Flickinger, Roberts, & Fulmore, 1994). The discriminatory job ceiling suggests that African Americans will not be able to advance as far as Whites who possess the same skills and academic background. In addition, Fordham and Ogbu (1986) found that African-American children are less inclined to succeed in school because they do not receive a fair opportunity when applying for employment or advancing within a career. Taylor and his colleagues determined that high school students who have a greater knowledge of racial discrimination are less engaged in school and place less value on academic achievement than do their counterparts. These researchers, however, also found that discrimination is unrelated to students' perceptions of their own abilities, and that a strong ethnic identity is related to school achievement and school engagement.

It is perplexing that relatively little attention has been focused on the relationship between family life and school achievement among African-American adolescents. Social and behavioral science literature has focused on the negative aspects of African-American family functioning; specifically, the purported pathological nature of African-American families (most often attributed to the high numbers of mother-only families) is highlighted, while numerous examples of adaptive functioning are notably absent.

In their 1990 review, Slaughter-Defoe, Nakagawa, Takanishi, and Johnson noted the emergence of a line of research that chose to view the African-American family and culture from a cultural and ecological perspective. That is, the study chose to examine the uniqueness of the African-American family's cultural experiences within the environments and contexts that shape its everyday life. These cultural experiences, and the contexts and environments that define them, have been delineated by Gibbs (1989) as centering around religion and church, extended family and kinship networks, flexible family roles, and education.

The research, however, on African-American youth suffers from several methodological and theoretical problems, especially when comparative research is conducted. First, academic achievement has often been equated only with the performance of African-American students on achievement and intelligence tests (Jaynes & Williams, 1989). The possible cultural incompatibility of these tests with African-American adolescents, the importance of other measurable aspects of academic achievement, and the fact that achievement tests may not accurately assess academic achievement are all reasons that comparisons based on such measures should be carefully reviewed. Second, social factors such as SES have often had an effect on the quality of education for African-American children and on their placement into lower academic tracks. Comparisons, then, that find African Americans' performance lower than that of their White peers may focus on these social factors instead of on inherent differences in academic capabilities. Third, as Slaughter-Defoe and colleagues (1990) noted in their review of the schooling and achievement of African-American and Asian-American children, African Americans are a diverse group and have often been studied in a myopic fashion. There are African-American adolescents who achieve academically; research, however, all too frequently ignores them. Finally, McLoyd (1990, 1991) asserted that there are theoretical problems inherent to the comparison of African Americans to White Americans. McLoyd believed that when comparative studies are conducted, they often highlight how African Americans do not act as opposed to how they do act (or vice versa). Because difference is viewed not in relative but instead in negative terms, these studies can lead to perceptions of African Americans as abnormal. Studying the within-group variability of African-American adolescents in relation to academic achievement might provide more insight into the diverse academic experiences of the group. It is clear that accurate assessment of the interrelationship between family, peers, and adolescent academic achievement among African Americans requires a perspective that is culturally and ecologically sensitive to the strengths and assets that exist within the African-American community.

REFERENCES

Boykin, A. W. (1979). Psychological/behavioral verve: Some theoretical explorations and empirical manifestations. In A. W. Boykin, A. J. Franklin, & J. F. Yates (Eds.), *Research directions of Black psychologists* (pp. 351–367). New York: Russell Sage.

Boykin, A. W. (1983). The academic performance of Afro-American children. In J. Spence (Ed.), *Achievement and achievement motives* (pp. 321–371). San Francisco: Freeman.

Bradley, R. H., Whiteside, L., Caldwell, B. M., Casey, P. H., Kelleher, K., Pope, S., Swanson, M., & Barrett, K. (1993). Maternal IQ: The home environment and child IQ in low-birthweight, premature children. *International Journal of Behavioral Development, 16*(1), 61–74.

Brookins, G. K. (1985). Black children's sex-role ideologies and occupational choices in families of employed mothers. In M. B. Spencer, G. K. Brookins, & W. R. Allen (Eds.), *Beginnings: The social and affective development of Black children* (pp. 257–273). Hillsdale, NJ: Lawrence Erlbaum Associates.

Brookins, G. K. (1993). Culture, ethnicity and bicultural competence: Implications for children with chronic illness and disability. *Pediatrics, 91*(5), 1056–1062.

Clark, M. L. (1991). Social identity, peer relations, and academic competence of African-American adolescents. *Education and Urban Society, 24*, 41–52.

Connell, J., Spencer, M., & Aber, J. (1994). Educational risk and resilience in African-American youth: Context, self, action, and outcomes in school. *Child Development, 65*, 493–506.

Dawkins, M. (1989). The persistence of plans for professional careers among Blacks in early adulthood. *Journal of Negro Education, 58*(2), 220–231.

DeSantis, J. P., Ketterlinus, R. D., & Youniss, J. (1990). Black adolescents' concerns that they are academically able. *Merrill-Palmer Quarterly, 36*, 287–299.

Dornbusch, S., Ritter, P., & Steinberg, L. (1991). Community influence on the relation of family statuses to adolescent school performance: Differences between African Americans and non-Hispanic Whites. *American Journal of Education, 99*(4), 543–567.

Edelman, M. W. (1987). *Families in peril: An agenda for social change.* Boston: Harvard University Press.

Entwisle, D. R. (1990). Schools and the adolescent. In S. Feldman & G. Elliott (Eds.), *At the threshold: The developing adolescent* (pp. 197–224). Cambridge, MA: Harvard University Press.

Ford, D. T. (1993). Black students' achievement orientation as a function of perceived family achievement orientation and demographic variables. *Journal of Negro Education, 62*(1), 47–66.

Fordham, S., & Ogbu, J. U. (1986). Black students' school success: Coping with the "burden of 'acting White.'" *The Urban Review, 18*, 176–206.

Franklin, J. H., & Moss, A. A. (1994) *From slavery to freedom: A history of African-Americans.* New York: McGraw-Hill, Inc.

Garibaldi, A. M. (1992). Educating and motivating African-American males to succeed. *Journal of Negro Education, 61*, 4–11.

Gibbs, J. T. (1989). Black American adolescents. In J. T. Gibbs & L. Huann (Eds.), *Children of color* (pp.179–223). San Francisco: Jossey-Bass.

Goodenow, C., & Grady, K. E. (1993). The relationship of school belonging and friends' values to academic motivation among urban adolescent students. *Journal of Experimental Education, 62*, 60–71.

Hallinan, M. T., & Williams, R. A. (1990). Students' characteristics and the peer-influence process. *Sociology of Education, 63*, 122–132.

Harrison, A. O. (1987). The Black family's socializing environment: Self-esteem and ethnic attitude among Black children. In H. P. McAdoo & J. L. McAdoo (Eds.), *Black children* (pp. 174–193). Beverly Hills, CA: Sage.

Harrison, A. O., Wilson, M. N., Pine, C. J., Chan, S. Q., & Buriel, R. (1990). Family ecologies of ethnic minority children. *Child Development, 61*, 347–362.

Hochschild, J. L. (1989). Equal opportunity and the estranged poor. *The Annals of the American Academy of Political and Social Science, 501*, 143–155.

Jackson, S., Johnson, S., & Wallace, M. (1987). Home environment, talented youth, and school achievement. *Journal of Negro Education, 56*(1), 111–121.

Jaynes, G., & Williams, R., Jr. (1989). *A common destiny: Blacks and American society.* Washington, DC: National Research Council.

Johnson, S. T. (1992). Extra-school factors in achievement, attainment, and aspiration among junior and senior high-school-age African-American youth. *Journal of Negro Education, 61,* 99–119.

Littlejohn-Blake, S., & Anderson-Darling, C. (1993). Understanding the strengths of African-American families. *Journal of Black Studies, 23*(4), 460–471.

Marshall, H. H. (1989, July). The development of self concept. *Young Children,* 44–49.

McLoyd, V. (1990). The impact of economic hardship on Black families and children: Psychological distress, parenting, and socioemotional development. *Child Development, 61*(2), 311–346.

McLoyd, V. (1991). What is the study of African-American children the study of? The conduct, population, and changing nature of research on African-American children. In R. Jones (Ed.), *Black Psychology* (3rd ed., pp. 419–440). Berkeley, CA: Cobb & Henry.

Mincy, R. B. (1994). Introduction. In R. B. Mincy (Ed), *Nurturing young Black males* (pp. 7–21). Washington, DC: Urban Institute.

Moore, E. G. J. (1985). Ethnicity as a variable in child development. In M. B. Spencer, G. K. Brookins, & W. R. Allen (Eds.), *Beginnings: The social and affective development of Black children* (pp. 101–115). Hillsdale, NJ: Lawrence Erlbaum Associates.

Moore, E. G. J. (1986). Family socialization and the IQ test performance of traditionally and transracially adopted Black children. *Developmental Psychology, 22*(3), 317–326.

Moore, E. G. J. (1987). Ethnic social milieu and Black children's intelligence test achievement. *Journal of Negro Education, 56*(1), 44–52.

Morris, D. (1992). African-American students and their families. In M. Procidano & C. Fisher (Eds.), *Contemporary families: A handbook for school professionals* (pp. 99–116). New York: Teachers College Press.

Nathan, R. P. (1989). Institutional change and the challenge of the underclass. *The Annals of the American Academy of Political and Social Science, 501,* 170–181.

Reid, J. (1982). Black America in the 1980s. *Population Bulletin, 37*(4), 1–37.

Sameroff, A. J., Seifer, R., Baldwin, A., & Baldwin, C. (1993). Stability of intelligence from preschool to adolescence: The influence of social and family risk factors. *Child Development, 64*(1), 80–97.

Savin-Williams, R. C., & Berndt, T. J. (1990). Friendship and peer relations. In S. Feldman & G. Elliott (Eds.), *At the threshold: The developing adolescent* (pp. 277–307). Cambridge, MA: Harvard University Press.

Slaughter, D., & Epps, E. (1987). The home environment and academic achievement of Black American children and youth: An overview. *Journal of Negro Education, 56*(1), 3–20.

Slaughter-Defoe, D. T., Nakagawa, K., Takanishi, R., & Johnson, D. (1990). Toward cultural/ecological perspectives on schooling and achievement in African- and Asian-American children. *Child Development, 61*(2), 363–383.

Spencer, M. B., & Markstrom-Adams, C. (1990). Identity processes among racial and ethnic minority children in America. *Child Development, 61,* 290–310.

Steinberg, L., Dornbusch, S. M., & Brown, B. B. (1992). Ethnic differences in adolescent achievement. *American Psychologist, 47,* 723–729.

Steinberg, L., Mounts, N., Lamborn, S., & Dornbush, S. (1991). Authoritative parenting and adolescent adjustment across varied ecological niches. *Journal of Research on Adolescence, 1*(1), 19–36.

Taylor, R. D., Casten, R., Flickinger, S., Roberts, D., & Fulmore, C. (1994). Explaining the school performance of African-American Adolescents. *Journal of Research on Adolescence, 4,* 21–44.

Wilson, K., & Allen, W. (1987). Explaining the educational attainment of young Black adults: Critical familial and extra-familial influences. *Journal of Negro Education, 56*(1), 64–76.

Wilson, M. N. (1989). Child development in the context of the Black extended family. *American Psychologist, 44,* 380–385.

III

*Neighborhood and Schooling
Contexts and Adolescent Adjustment*

10

Racial and Economic Segregation and Educational Outcomes: One Tale, Two Cities

William L. Yancey
Salvatore J. Saporito

For the last 30 years a wide range of social science research has debated the relative importance of racial and economic factors as determinants of family structure, crime, unemployment, and school achievement (Coleman et al., 1966; Jencks, 1972). Wilson (1987) argued that the heated controversy following the Moynihan report resulted in many social scientists withdrawing from research that examined the degree to which social and economic characteristics of the African-American population may be attributed to race culture, racial discrimination, and/or socioeconomic status (Jencks & Peterson, 1991). Very generally, public policy recommendations that have emerged from this research have been in one of two forms: the first have advocated specific remedial policies directed at the African-American community (e.g., affirmative action, racial desegregation), whereas the second have been neutral with regard to race, arguing that there are generic conditions (e.g., concentrations of urban poverty) affecting all racial and ethnic groups that must be addressed (Lawson, 1992).

With this chapter, we join this debate, describing the results of research that examined the racial and socioeconomic segregation of public schools in two very different cities: Philadelphia and Houston. We examined the following two issues: What factors explain racial and economic segregation in public schools and what is the relative importance of these two forms of segregation for the academic achievement of students?

To answer the first question, one must understand four major factors: (a) metropolitan areas, cities, municipalities, and residential communities are segregated by race/ethnicity and social class (Bartelt, 1995; Kantor & Brenzel, 1993; Massey & Denton, 1993; Orfield, 1994); (b) most public schools draw from circumscribed and proximal geographic areas; (c) children from different groups attend public and private schools at different rates; and (d) school district policies (i.e., magnet schooling and voluntary busing) designed to alleviate the effects of the first three factors attenuate racial segregation while unintentionally exacerbating economic segregation.

Understanding the relative influence of these two forms of segregation on learning is less straightforward. There are strong correlations between the percentage of students in schools who are minorities, the percentage of students who are from low-income families, and the average achievement level of schools. Because of the substantial correlations between the racial and the socioeconomic composition of schools, it is impossible to empirically isolate the effects of these two factors on achievement with cross-sectional data. It is possible to decompose the variance in achievement into that which is shared by racial and socioeconomic composition and that which may be attributed to each of these factors alone. Based on our analyses, it appears that the socioeconomic composition of schools is the more important determinant of academic success.

The present research augments a body of literature that suggests that "freedom of choice" desegregation programs—an outgrowth of a 40-year-old mandate from the Brown decision—exacerbates the economic segregation of schools (Lee, Croninger, & Smith, 1994; Moore & Davenport, 1990; Wells, 1993a, 1993b, 1993c; Witte, 1993). Economic segregation, in turn, has pernicious educational effects on poor students isolated with their peers in schools and classrooms (Crane, 1991; Fine, 1991; Kantor & Brenzel, 1993; Oakes, 1992). We, therefore, argue that these policies, which have contributed to increased rates of socioeconomic segregation, should be reconsidered and their implementation reformulated.

METHODS AND DATA SOURCES

The data used in this analysis are derived from three sources. The first is the 1990 U.S. Census Summary Tape File 3A, which summarizes the number and characteristics of persons by census tracts. For this research we used tract-level information describing the racial and ethnic composition, the percentage of students attending private schools, and the percentage of persons whose 1989 family income was below 185% of the poverty level in each tract. We use 185% of poverty, rather than the poverty level, so that the census information coincides with information available on students; to qualify for free or reduced-price lunches, a student's family income must be below 185% of poverty.

Our second source was annual reports describing school-level characteristics in each city (in Philadelphia these are known as the *Management Information Center* or *MIC* reports; in Houston, they are known as *School Profile Reports*). Our analysis focuses on 172 elementary (usually grades K–6) and 45 middle (usually grades 7–9) schools in Philadelphia, and 169 elementary (grades k–5 or 6) and 39 middle (grades 6–8) schools in Houston. We have used data describing the schools in the 1990–1991 academic years. For each school in both districts, we extracted information describing the number of students, the racial composition, the average standardized reading test score,[1] the average daily attendance rates, the pupil turnover, and the percentage of students who received free or reduced-price lunches. Information on the number of students who received transportation assistance for voluntary busing is given in Philadelphia, but not in Houston. Houston provided information on the presence of magnet school programs; this information was not given by Philadelphia. We have, somewhat arbitrarily, defined *magnet schools* in Philadelphia as those in which over 30% of the students received mass transit tokens or were bused to school.

Because we were examining the relationships between the nature of schools and the nature of the communities in which they were embedded, it was necessary to link the census information with the school information. Our premise was that the areas where students live, not necessarily the immediate neighborhood surrounding the school, comprise the communities in which a given school is embedded. Thus, it is necessary to know where the students live, to obtain information describing those areas, and to summarize that information for each school.

This task was made possible by our third source of data, Pupil Directory Files. These are databases that include all students enrolled in the public schools. Among other things, they identify the school each student attends and the census tract in which each student resides. Using a computer matching program, data describing each student's census tract were attached to each student's record. These data were then aggregated for each school by calculating the average value of the characteristic for the tracts represented in each school. Thus, if a school draws students from several different census tracts and we are attempting to characterize the rates of poverty among children between the ages of 5 and 17 years, we would multiply the poverty rates of each tract by the number of students living there. These products are then summed for the tracts represented in the school and divided by the total number of students. This creates a weighted average of the poverty rates across the neighborhoods represented in the school (Yancey, Goldstein, & Webb, 1987). After these neighborhood data were aggregated, we merged them with data describing characteristics of the school, thus producing a single data file that summarizes the characteristics of schools and the communities in which they are embedded.

---

[1]Achievement test scores are provided for each grade represented in each school. The achievement scores provided are not the same for the two districts. In Philadelphia, the average national percentile rank is given for each grade. Houston reports the "grade equivalent" test score, which is expressed in terms of the grade and month at which the median student was reading. We have taken the difference between the grade that students are in and their reading level obtained as a measure of achievement. For example, if third graders were reported reading at a 3.25 level, they were given an achievement test score of .25. In another school, if the median test score for third graders was 2.75, their achievement level was calculated at −.25. We have generated an average test score for the entire school.

BRIEF DESCRIPTIONS
OF PHILADELPHIA AND HOUSTON

Although the choice of cities to be studied was determined by the availability of necessary data, the comparison of Philadelphia and Houston provides a contrast between two very different American cities. One is in the "Rust Belt," the other in the "Sun Belt." One is an old manufacturing city currently undergoing transformation to a postindustrial economy (Adams et al., 1991). The second is a postindustrial city with an economy driven by medicine, space exploration, and the administration and distribution of oil (Shelton, 1989).

In 1990 the Philadelphia metropolitan area was larger in population (4.8 million) than Houston (3.3 million). Philadelphia experienced its highest rates of growth during the 19th and early 20th centuries. Since 1950, although the suburban population has continued to grow, the city of Philadelphia's population has declined by 25%. Houston, by contrast, experienced little growth until the 1920s, after which its growth has been exponential. The 1990 population of the city of Houston is 3.8 times larger than what it was in 1950.

The boundaries of Philadelphia have remained unchanged since 1854, whereas Houston has continued to grow by annexation of nearby areas. In 1986 Houston covered 572 square miles, more than four times Philadelphia's 136 square miles. These different histories of geographic and demographic growth have the somewhat anomalous result that, in terms of the proportion of the metropolitan area's population which is in the central city, Philadelphia is more suburbanized than Houston. Only 45% of the Philadelphia region's population lives in the central city; by contrast, 68% of the Houston metro area population lives inside the city limits. On the other hand, if one defines suburbanization not by political boundaries but by population density, one must conclude that the city of Houston is more suburban than Philadelphia. Philadelphia's population density is three times that of Houston.

The city of Philadelphia and the Philadelphia school district share common boundaries. This is not the case in Houston, where the area served by the Houston Independent School District covers about one fourth of the city of Houston, and half of the city's population.

In spite of the differences between the two metropolitan areas, there are striking similarities in the composition and character of the two school districts. In 1990 the number of school-age children was larger in Philadelphia—264,000, compared to 215,000 in the area served by the Houston Independent School District. Yet, as a consequence of the higher rates of attendance in private and parochial schools in Philadelphia (29%) than in Houston (15%) (this information is taken from Summary Tape File 3A of the 1990 Census), the number of students served by the Houston system is slightly larger (194,512) than that served by Philadelphia's public schools (190,977).

Table 10.1 summarizes the racial/ethnic and economic characteristics of the two metropolitan areas, the populations served by the two school districts, and the students attending public schools. The two metropolitan areas have

TABLE 10.1

Racial/Ethnic and Economic Characteristics of the Philadelphia and Houston
Metro Area, School District, School-Age Population, and Public School Students

		Houston			
	% White	% African American	% Latino	% Asian	% Low Income[a]
Metro area	56.5	18.2	21.1	3.7	30.6
School district	38.6	28.0	30.3	2.8	42.5
School-age population	21.9	33.0	42.4	2.7	47.5
Students 1990–1991	14.3	38.1	44.9	2.6	54.6
		Philadelphia			
	% White	% African American	% Latino	% Asian	% Low Income[a]
Metro area	75.4	18.9	3.4	2.1	21.1
School district	52.2	39.5	5.3	2.7	36.8
School-age population	40.6	47.7	8.4	3.3	42.4
Students 1990–1991	23.1	62.6	9.7	4.4	61.2

[a]Because the census does not provide specific data, there are two estimates in these tables. First the size of the White population age 5–17 is defined by subtracting African American, Latino, and Asian populations from the total. Data on race and Hispanic origin are not available by age groups. Second, data are not available describing the number of school-age persons who are below 185% of poverty. The number of persons age 5–17 whose household income falls in this category is estimated by assuming the percentage of the population between the poverty line and 185% of poverty who are age 5–17 is the same as the proportion of the population below poverty who are school age. To the degree that "low-income families" have lower fertility than those below poverty, this overestimates the number of the school-age population who are low income.

similar proportions of their populations that are African American. Houston has a substantially larger Latino population (21.1%) than Philadelphia (3.4%). The majority of Philadelphia's Latinos are Puerto Rican in origin, whereas Houston's Latino population is predominantly Mexican in origin. The proportion of low-income families is higher in Houston (30.6%) than in Philadelphia (21.1%).

These school districts share the common characteristic of providing educational services to higher proportions of minorities and the poor than actually live in their respective metropolitan areas. The percentages of students who are African American, Latino, or low income are more than twice the percentages of the regions' populations with those same respective characteristics. This is a consequence of three factors: (a) the concentration of minorities and low-income families in the central city and in the area served by these school districts, (b) differences in the age distribution between racial/ethnic and income groups, and (c) the varying rates at which students choose to attend public schools.

The centralization effects are seen when we compare the racial/ethnic and income characteristics of the metropolitan area populations with the populations served by the districts. Except for Houston's Asian population, which appears to be decentralized, the pattern is clear. There are higher proportions of minorities and low-income families, and lower proportions of Whites, living in the areas served by the school districts. It is notable that those parts of Houston not served by the Houston Independent School District had half the rate of low income and minority people than the area of Houston served by the school district.

Comparing the percentage of the population who have these characteristics with the percentage of the school-age population provides an indication of the impact of the age distributions of these groups. In both cities the proportion of the school-age population that is White is lower than the proportion of Whites in the total population. By contrast, the younger age structure of African Americans, Latinos, and those with low family income is indicated by the higher proportions of the school-age population with these characteristics.

Finally, comparing the characteristics of the school-age population with the students enrolled in these public school systems provides an indication of the impact of private school choice on the racial and ethnic characteristics of schools. The proportion of White public school students is lower than the proportion of the school-age population that is White. Conversely, the proportion of public school students who are African American, Latino, and low income is higher than the proportion of the school-age population who have these characteristics. Apparently, higher income and White students attend private schools at higher rates.

SEGREGATED CITIES AND SEGREGATED SCHOOLS

The parallels of the two cities in terms of the higher concentration of poor and minorities in the school district and in the schools is repeated when we

TABLE 10.2

Racial/Ethnic and Economic Segregation in Houston and Philadelphia:
Metro Area, School Districts, and Schools

	Houston		
	Population Across Tracts		Students Across Elementary and Middle Schools
	Metro Area	School District	
African American/ White	67	72	62
African American/ White	59	68	66
Latino/White	50	52	56
Low income/Other	38	35	48
	Philadelphia		
	Population Across Tracts		Students Across Elementary and Middle Schools
	Metro Area	School District	
African American/White	77	84	74
African American/White	67	71	78
Latino/White	64	69	70
Low income/Other	42	35	44

examine the degree to which the three major racial/ethnic groups are segregated across the metropolitan areas, the central city school districts, and in the schools. Table 10.2 presents levels of segregation, as measured by the indices of dissimilarity,[2] of population groups across census tracts comprising the metropolitan areas and school districts, and of students across middle and elementary schools.[3] The segregation of low-income families is the dissimilarity between the distributions of persons whose 1989 income was less than 185% of the poverty level and those whose income was above 185% of poverty across census tracts.

Both cities are segregated by race and ethnicity and, to a lesser degree, economic status. The major difference between the two cities is the higher levels of racial/ethnic segregation that characterize Philadelphia.[4] The difference is particularly marked in the case of segregation between Latinos and Whites. In Houston the level of segregation between Latinos and Whites is 52, whereas in Philadelphia it is 69. In both cities the highest level of segregation is found between African Americans and Whites; the lowest level, between Whites and Latinos.

Comparing the levels of racial segregation across the entire metropolitan areas to those found in the central city school districts indicates that racial segregation across the census tracts served by the school districts is higher than the segregation found across the entire metropolitan area. Thus, the areas served by these school districts not only have higher proportions of minorities but are also more highly segregated. Economic segregation across both metropolitan areas is moderately higher than in the areas served by the two central city school districts.

Given the segregation of the population across these school districts, coupled with the fact that schools generally draw students from relatively restricted geographic areas, it is expected that the level of segregation in schools will reflect the segregation of neighborhoods. Although there are strong correlations, the patterns are far from perfect. The segregation between African Americans and Latinos, and between Latinos and Whites is higher among

---

[2]The index of dissimilarity reflects the difference in the distribution of two groups across a series of nominal categories. In the case of residential segregation, it reflects the difference in the percentage distributions of two groups across census tracts. One interpretation of dissimilarity is that it reflects the proportion of either group that would have to move from census tracts which they now dominate to other tracts in order to balance the two distributions. Thus, in 1990, 82% of Whites would have to change census tracts in order to achieve racial integration. For details of calculation methods, see Taeuber and Taeuber (1965).

[3]Our measure of segregation of schools does not take into consideration levels of segregation *within* schools (Oakes, 1992). To the degree that minorities or low-income students are placed in special programs or tracts within schools, these measurements underestimate the segregation of students.

[4]An additional analysis examining residential segregation of racial/ethnic groups by poverty status indicated that the lower level of segregation of Houston's White and Hispanic populations is particularly marked among lower status Whites who are residentially integrated with Houston's Latino population.

students in schools than it is among the residential population across the school districts. Conversely, the segregation of African-American and White students across schools is lower than the segregation of the African-American and White populations across census tracts within the school districts. The segregation of students who are qualified for free or reduced-price lunches is markedly *higher* than the segregation of populations whose family income was less than 185% of the poverty level from those with higher incomes.

These anomalies, although relatively small, indicate that there are factors besides the ecological organization of cities and their neighborhoods that affect levels of segregation in schools. In spite of the expected parallels between the racial and economic characters of the cities' neighborhoods and the racial and economic characters of the schools, the two are not mirror images of one another.[5] There are at least two factors that distort the reflection. The first distortion stems from the fact that not all school-age children attend public schools. As Table 10.1 shows, minorities and students from low-income families are more likely to attend public school. To the degree that private school attendance varies across a city's neighborhoods, it affects the correlation between the character of neighborhoods and the character of schools.

The second distortion is found in the degree to which students attend schools outside their immediate neighborhoods, rather than near their homes. In order to increase the level of racial integration, both school districts have established magnet school programs in which selected schools provide special programs designed to attract pupils from throughout the school district. Participation in magnet school programs is not random, nor is it evenly distributed across neighborhoods in these cities. Students and their families must make the investment of applying to and participating in these programs, and all students who apply are not accepted (e.g., high-achieving students are more likely to be accepted). These factors result in class differences in students who do and do not attend magnet schools (Henig, 1995; Kozol, 1991; Moore & Davenport, 1990; Witte, 1993). To the degree that magnet school programs select certain types of students away from local neighborhood schools, they distort the relationship between neighborhood and school characteristics.

In order to examine the effects of students choosing to attend private or magnet schools on school segregation patterns, we have conducted a series of multiple regression analyses that relate the characteristics of school communities to the student body composition of schools. We examined four school

---

[5]The bivariate correlations between the characteristics of census tracts included in school feeder areas and the characteristics of students are presented here:

Correlations Between Characteristics of Community Areas and Schools

	% Low Income	% African American	% Latino	% White
Philadelphia	.799	.966	.980	.959
Houston	.723	.966	.932	.868

composition variables: the percentage of students from low-income families, and the percent who were African American, Latino or White. To determine the effect of choice factors on school composition, we examined several antecedents. The first are the corresponding school community characteristics (i.e., the percentage of poor students in each school and the percentage of poor children in each school's neighborhood). For each of these analyses we also included the percentage of children in the school communities who (a) attended private schools and (b) a dummy variable designating whether a school was a magnet school. The results are presented in Table 10.3.

TABLE 10.3

Results of Regression Analysis of Racial and Economic Composition
of Schools With Characteristics of School Communities

	Houston			Philadelphia		
Percent White students						
Community Character	*B*	*SE B*	*β*	*B*	*SE B*	*β*
% White	.495	.041	.618	.836	.039	.856
% Private school	.758	.147	.266	2.81	.112	.101
Magnet School	4.978	1.376	.124	2.609	1.483	.036
(Constant)	−5.739	.922		−8.276	1.205	
R Square			.802			.930
R Square 2			.840			.948
Percent low income students						
% Low income	.782	.108	.480	.835	.089	.557
% Private	−.604	.259	−.156	−.284	.127	−.140
Magnet school	−19.023	2.509	−.347	−13.519	2.372	−.260
(Constant)	39.713	7.181		39.800	5.573	
R Square			.648			.661
R Square 2			.651			.681
Percent African-American students						
% African American	1.090	.020	1.004	1.046	.028	1.013
% Private	.478	.109	.086	.212	.088	.068
Magnet school	3.159	1.433	.040	−.996	1.593	−.012
(Constant)	−4.144	1.400		1.085	2.983	
R square			.944			.934
R square 2			.945			.946
Percent Latino students						
% Latino	1.214	.033	.938	1.220	.017	.985
% Private	.456	.141	.087	.065	.026	.039
Magnet school	−5.676	1.980	−.077	−.590	.665	−.014
(Constant)	.072	1.824		−2.034	.551	
R Square			.878			.961
R square 2			.904			.962

The results obtained for the two cities are similar. They indicate that the racial and economic character of the residential areas in which a school is embedded is highly correlated with the racial and economic composition of schools. Beyond this there appear to be different models of school composition for White, low-income, and minority students. Concentrations of White students are associated with communities with high rates of private school attendance, and with schools designated as magnets. The opposite is found for low income students who are concentrated in neighborhood schools with low rates of private school attendance. The results for African American and Latino students indicate that the racial/ethnic composition of the communities acts as a powerful determinant of the racial/ethnic composition of schools. Beyond this there are weak, although significant, positive effects of private school attendance. This indicates that the percentage of African-American and Latino students is higher than expected (given the school-community population) in schools drawing from communities where private school attendance is high. In other terms, it suggests that withdrawal of Whites from the public school system results in increased minority percentages in many schools. Although magnet school programs are designed in part to achieve racial integration, the results indicate that, with the exception of African American students in Houston, minority students are underrepresented in magnet schools.

Finally, the relationships between the economic and racial composition of communities and the composition of schools are not linear.[6] The curvilinear nature of these relationships indicates that schools drawing students from communities which are economically heterogenous and are racially mixed have higher proportions of low-income, African-American, and Latino students than is expected given the communities from which they draw students. The equation for White students complements these results; White students living in racially mixed communities are less likely to attend local public schools. The proportion of White students rises sharply as one moves to school communities that are dominated by Whites. We interpret this to mean that the presence of private and magnet schools does not evenly siphon students from neighborhood schools; the abandonment of neighborhood schools is selective.

There are at least three consequences of these distortions of the relationships between the characters of communities and the characteristics of schools. First, the percentage of public school students who are minorities

---

[6]Squaring the community composition variables and including them in the equations shown in Table 10.3 significantly increases R^2 in most instances. These changes in R^2 are shown in Table 10.3 on the lines labeled "R Square 2." We have not shown the full equations, which include the square terms; multicolinearity between the community composition variable and its square results in Beta weights which exceed 1.00. Nonetheless, the coefficients found for the effects of private school attendance and magnet schools remain similar to those shown in Table 10.3.

or from low-income families is substantially higher than the percentage of the school-age population served by these school districts (see Table 10.1). This increased proportion of low-income and minority students is higher in schools that are embedded in communities with high rates of private school attendance.

Second, the regression results suggest that magnet schools have higher proportions of high-income and White students than is expected given the nature of their school communities. The degree of over- or underrepresentation of students attending magnet and neighborhood schools, by race/ethnicity and family income, is indicated in Table 10.4, which provides the distributions of students from these different groups in these two types of schools.

In Houston, although some 30% of all elementary and middle school students attend magnet schools, only 20% of low-income students and 22% of Latino students do so. Thirty-two percent of Houston's African-American students attend magnet schools, which indicates that they are slightly overrepresented. This overrepresentation is substantially smaller than the 53% of White students and 51% of those who are not low income who attend magnet schools. A similar pattern is found in Philadelphia, where some 19% of all students attend magnet schools, yet only 12% of African-American and Latino students and 14% of those with low family incomes attend, compared to 36% of White students and 36% of those whose family incomes are above 185% of poverty attend magnet schools. The effects of these magnet school programs complement the effects of students' choices to attend private schools. A two-tiered system has emerged among public schools, one which is overrepresented by White students from higher-income families, a second which is overrepresented by minorities and low-income students.

The third consequence of these processes of choice and selection across schools in these districts is their impact on the racial and economic segregation of students. As we have previously indicated, the magnet school programs in these cities were created, in part, as a means of enhancing racial integration by providing programs that attract both White and minority students from across the school districts. Evidence indicates that these

TABLE 10.4

Percentage of Students Attending Local and Magnet Schools by Race and Family: Houston and Philadelphia

	African American	Latino	White	Low Income	High Income	Total
Houston						
Local Schools	69	78	47	80	49	70
Magnet schools	32	22	53	20	51	30
Philadelphia						
Local Schools	88	88	64	86	64	81
Magnet Schools	12	12	36	14	36	19

programs have succeeded in this goal, particularly in regard to the degree of segregation between African-American and White students, which is lower in the public schools than across the school districts' neighborhoods. Moreover, they have most likely reduced the number of White students who might otherwise attend private schools.

We have seen that magnet school programs have created a two-tiered school system within public schools—one dominated by minorities and low-income students and a second overrepresented by Whites and students from high-income families. Thus, magnet schooling leads to a paradoxical result: It (slightly) reduces racial segregation across *all* schools while creating a racial and economic divide between magnet and neighborhood schools. Some of the racial and economic segregation that exists among all public schools is the result of these two tiers. In order to increase the level of racial integration across the entire district, the effectiveness of these programs must overcome the segregation that they generate. Their success in doing so is indicated by the levels of racial and economic segregation that exist among magnet schools compared to neighborhood schools. Table 10.5 presents indices of dissimilarity across neighborhood schools and across magnet schools by race and ethnicity and family income level.

The impact of these programs in both cities is similar. For every comparison, the level of racial segregation is lower among students attending magnet schools. This is particularly marked for African-American and White segregation. Segregation between Latinos and African Americans, and Latinos and Whites, is also lower in magnet schools. Students attending magnet schools are also less segregated by socioeconomic status, although the effects in Houston are minimal.[7]

One means of illustrating the impact of these programs on the economic and racial composition of schools is to measure the degree to which students are attending schools that are dominated by their own racial/ethnic or income

TABLE 10.5
Segregation of Students Attending Neighborhood and Magnet Schools:
Houston and Philadelphia

	Houston		Philadelphia	
	Neighborhood Schools	Magnet Schools	Neighborhood Schools	Magnet Schools
African American/White	72	42	80	27
African American/Latino	73	46	81	53
Latino/White	53	44	73	50
Low Income/Other	41	40	39	30

[7]The level of socioeconomic segregation among magnet schools in Houston is in part a consequence of the development of magnet school programs in several schools that have high proportions of low-income students. Thus, within the Houston magnet school system, although most magnet schools have relativley low numbers of low-income students, there are a few truly exceptional schools that provide magnet schools programs for low-income students.

TABLE 10.6

Within Group Contacts of African-American, Latino, and Low-Income Students for All
Schools, Magnet Schools, and Neighborhood Schools: Houston and Philadelphia

	Houston		
	All Schools	Magnet Schools	Neighborhood Schools
African American	66.7	51.7	73.3
Latino	69.6	49.3	75.4
Low Income	76.0	56.6	80.8
	Philadelphia		
	All Schools	Magnet Schools	Neighborhood Schools
African American	82.9	45.1	87.7
Latino	50.7	19.6	54.5
Low Income	82.3	63.0	85.4

group. Imagine asking the following question of the average African-American student: "What percentage of the students in the school that you attend are also African American"? We have done this for African-American, Latino, and low-income students, and computed the average percentage for the entire school system, for magnet schools, and for neighborhood schools.

The results, presented in Table 10.6, are similar in the two school districts. African-American students attending magnet schools attend schools that, on the average, are 52% and 45% African American. By contrast, African-American students who attend neighborhood schools attend schools that average 73% and 88% African American. Similar patterns are found for Latino students. Those who attend neighborhood schools attend schools that are dominated by Latinos. In Philadelphia, where Latino students are less than 10% of all students, the 90% of Latino students who attend neighborhood schools go to schools that are over 50% Latino. Finally, in the case of low-income students, we see that across the entire district the average low-income student attends a school that is over 75% low income. The concentrations of low-income students are smaller for the 20% who are attending magnet schools. Yet, those who attend neighborhood schools go to schools in which over 80% of their fellow students also qualified for free or reduced-price lunches.

When we compare the levels of segregation found in neighborhood schools to that in magnet schools, we are led to the conclusion that the impact of these programs on most minority and low-income students is minimal. Most attend schools that are characterized by higher proportions of students of a similar race/ethnicity. The "success" of the magnet school programs in reducing racial segregation has depended on attracting higher status students away from neighborhood schools located in relatively poor neighborhoods. The result is an increased concentration of poor students in racially and economically homogeneous schools.

RACE AND CLASS CONCENTRATIONS
AND SCHOOL SUCCESS

We now turn to an examination of the relative impact of racial and social economic concentrations on school success. Many studies have investigated the influence of racial segregation on the academic achievement of African-American students. Indeed, the 1954 Brown decision was supported by a considerable amount of evidence regarding the negative impact of segregation on African-American children. There also exists a body of research documenting the importance of concentrations of neighborhood and school poverty on the academic success of individual students (Crane, 1991; Garner and Raudenbush, 1991; Myers, 1985). Here we focus on the effects of racial and economic segregation on the success of schools (as measured by the average reading achievement level).

The effects of concentrating large numbers of students from particular racial or ethnic groups, or from low-income families, may be understood in two somewhat different ways. First, it could be argued that it reflects the cumulative effects of individual student characteristics. For example, schools with large numbers of low-income students are expected to produce lower average achievement scores because of the contribution of each individual student to the school-wide average. Alternatively, cultural, ecological, or organizational effects may be generated when students with particular characteristics are concentrated in a given school. For example, concentrations of low-income students may contribute to the creation of a negative climate among teachers (i.e., "these kids can't learn"). Magnet schools specializing in science or the arts ostensibly generate an informal culture among students that reinforces formal learning in classrooms. Ethnographers have also argued that large concentrations of low-income or minority students may generate an informal culture within the school which may erode the formal learning in classrooms (MacLeod, 1987; Ogbu, 1974, 1988; Solomon, 1992). Concentrations of students from particular economic groups may also have structural consequences on school characteristics, such as rates of student turnover and absenteeism. High rates of turnover or absenteeism make it difficult for teachers and students to follow a coherent curriculum over the school year. High turnover contributes to the social disorganization of the school and to the informal community of students.

The data that are available make it impossible to separate the cumulative effects of individual characteristics from the organizational/ecological effects of concentrations of racial groups or of poverty. To do so would require that we have information describing both individual students and their families, and information describing the compositional and organizational characteristics of schools (see Bidwell & Kasarda, 1980; Bryk & Raudenbush, 1992; and Pallas, 1994).

As a consequence of both historical and contemporary patterns of racial discrimination, coupled with the segregation of schools by race/ethnicity and socioeconomic status, there are substantial correlations between the percentage of students who are African American and/or Latino and the percentage of students who are from low-income families. These correlations are found not only in schools, but also in the neighborhoods (census tracts) comprising the school districts. We have just seen that in both Houston and Philadelphia the African-American and Latino populations are segregated both in the cities and schools. Across the census tracts and in the schools in both cities there are strong correlations between rates of poverty and the proportions of the tracts' populations that are African American or Latino. Given the strength of the correlations (.612 in Philadelphia and .757 in Houston) between the presence of minorities and concentrations of low income, it is impossible to separate the effects of these characteristics of student populations.

In addition to the racial composition of students and the percentage of students who are qualified for free or reduced-price lunches, the school profile databases include information describing some of the elements of the academic climate of the schools: the average daily attendance, the rates of student mobility into and out of each school, and the average achievement test scores. There is also information describing characteristics derived from policy decisions: school budgets; student–teacher ratios; the presence of magnet programs; and the tenure, training, and attendance rates of teachers.

Although we initially included a large number of characteristics, there were only three–in addition to racial and economic composition–that were found to have independent effects on student achievement. These were rates of student turnover or mobility, the average daily attendance, and whether a school is a magnet school.[8]

The results of the regression analyses are presented in Table 10.7, showing

TABLE 10.7

School-Level Factors Affecting Average Reading Achievement:
Philadelphia and Houston Elementary Schools

| | Standardized Regression Coefficients | |
	Philadelphia	Houston
% Low-Income Students	−.589	−.399
% Minority Students	−.137	−.279
Student Turnover	−.108	−.162
Average Daily Attendance	.172	NS
Presence of Magnet Program	.089	.107
Explained Variance R^2	.812	.652

[8]Some of the other characteristics, such as the percentage of experienced teachers, were found to be correlated with higher achievement scores, but their effects proved to be spuriously tied to the economic composition of student bodies. Apparently, experienced teachers opt to teach in schools with fewer low-income students. In Houston, the zero-order correlations indicated that low student–teacher ratios were associated with *lower* achievement scores. This correlation is also spurious—a consequence of the lower student–teacher ratios found in schools with higher proportions of low-income students.

the standardized regression coefficients for those characteristics that were significantly (beyond the .05 level) related to the average level of achievement.

The basic results are similar for both cities. Schools with higher proportions of students who qualified for free or reduced-price lunches, with higher proportions of minority students and higher rates of student turnover, had lower achievement test scores. Higher rates of attendance are associated with higher test scores in Philadelphia, although not in Houston. Finally, there are significant and positive effects of magnet school programs on test scores. These programs are effective in teaching and in attracting the better students away from neighborhood schools.

The regression results also provide a partial answer to the question of the impact of concentrations of racial/ethnic minorities and concentrations of low-income students on achievement test scores. The standardized regression coefficients are indicative of the relative importance of the variables included in the analysis. Although all of these variables are statistically significant, the Beta weights for the percentage of low-income students are larger than the Beta weights for the percentage of students who are minorities. The difference is substantial among Philadelphia schools (−.539 and −.137) and less dramatic in Houston −.399 and −.279). These results indicate that the economic characteristics of students are more important than their racial characteristics as determinants of school success. These results also indicate that the interactions between race and class are not significant.

We have already noted that in both cities, but particularly in Houston, these characteristics of schools are so highly correlated that it is impossible to measure one of these variables without the confounding effects of the second. Regression analysis provides a means of partitioning the explanatory power of two variables. We do this by computing the variance in achievement score

TABLE 10.8
Explained Variance in Average Achievement Scores
by Different Multiple Regression Analyses

Characteristics Included in Analysis	Philadelphia	Houston
% Minority Alone	.394	.545
% Low Income Alone	.769	.614
Minority and Income	.772	.622
% Low Income, % Minority, Attendance, and Mobility	.806	.645
All Variables	.812	.645
Variance Attributable to		
% Low Income	.378	.077
% Minority	.003	.009
Shared Income and Minority	.390	.536
Mobility and Attendance	.034	.022
Magnet Programs	.006	.007
Total Explained Variance	.812	.652
Unmeasured Factors	.188	.348

that is explained by each of the two variables alone, as well as the two variables simultaneously. The variance that is explained by both variables simultaneously is composed of three parts: (a) that which is attributed to racial/ethnic concentrations alone, (b) that which is attributed to low-income concentrations alone, and (c) that which is shared by both income and racial concentrations. To partition explained variance in this way, we have run a series of regression analyses in which different variables were added to the equations in a stepwise fashion. The resulting R^2s reflect the total variance that is explained by the variables included in each step. Table 10.8 presents the results of this series of analyses for the two school districts.

The first two lines provide the percentage of the variance that is explained by using the percentage of students who are minorities. These are 39% in Philadelphia and 55% in Houston. The second line indicates that, using only the percentage of students who are low income, one may explain 77% of the variance in Philadelphia and 61% in Houston. As with the Beta weights, these bivariate relationships indicate that economic concentrations are more important than are racial concentrations as determinants of school success.

The problem of shared variance is depicted on the third line, showing that the variance which is explained by the economic and racial character of students *taken together* is substantially smaller than the sum of the variances that they explain alone. To ascertain the amount of variance that may be attributed solely to concentrations of minorities or low-income students, we compute the difference between what is explained by one and two variables. For example, among Philadelphia schools the variance that may be attributed to concentrations of low-income students alone is the variance that is added by income, or, the variance explained by two variables minus the variance explained by percent minorities alone (.772 – .394 = .378). Conversely, we calculate the variance that is due to racial concentrations by subtracting the difference between what is explained by income concentration alone from the variance which is explained by both variables simultaneously, that is, .772 – .769 = .003. The amount of explained variance that is *shared* by economic and racial character of the schools is obtained by subtracting these estimates of independent variance (.003 and .378) from the total variance explained by both variables, that is, .772 – (.003 + .378) = .391. We have repeated these calculations for both Philadelphia and Houston and for each of the variables that has been included in these analyses. The results are summarized in the second half of Table 10.8.

Several conclusions may be drawn from these results. First, as indicated by the bivariate R^2, and by the variance that is explained by the racial and economic character of schools, the concentration of low-income students is the more important determinant of student achievement. The differences between the effects of these two characteristics are substantial among Philadelphia schools, yet relatively small among Houston's schools. The second, and perhaps most important, conclusion is that not only are the racial and economic character of schools correlated, but the explained variance that they share is greater than the variance which may be attributed to either alone. Indeed, in Houston the amount of explained variance which is shared between minority and low-income concentrations (53%) makes up for more than 80% of the total variance that is explained. Among Philadelphia schools, the shared variance (38%) is almost half of the total explained variance. Finally, we can see that, when they are entered into the stepwise analysis *after* low-income and racial composition, the amount of variance that may be attributed to other characteristics of schools (student mobility, attendance, and the presence of magnet programs) is substantially smaller than that which is explained by their racial and class character.[9]

SUMMARY AND CONCLUSION

The racial and economic character of student populations is the outcome of the racial and economic segregation of cities into neighborhoods of relatively homogeneous groups, the propinquity of students and schools, parental or student choice for private or public schools, and magnet school "choice" programs. In spite of the fact that this investigation has included two very different cities, the results that have been obtained regarding the impact of neighborhood segregation, parental or student choice, and the development of magnet school programs are strikingly similar.

A major difference between the schools of Philadelphia and those of Houston appears, in part, to be a result of the pattern of segregation between Latino and White populations. In Philadelphia these populations are segregated to a much greater extent than they are in Houston. The outcome of this social character of the city is that in Philadelphia there are several neighborhoods that are predominantly white and low-income ar-

---

[9]The calculations we have presented in Table 10.8 are based on the assumption that these other characteristics are independent of the racial and economic character of student populations. In fact, we know that this is an incorrect assumption. Indeed, we have seen in the first half of this chapter that magnet programs have a direct effect on both the racial and economic character of schools. That model that we used assumed that racial and socioeconomic compositions of students and school policy were exogenous (independent) variables. The character of the academic climate (measured here by rates of attendance and student mobility) is viewed as dependent on the exogeneous variables. Examination of the zero-order correlations indicated that attendance and mobility are correlated with the percentage of students qualified for free or reduced-price lunches. Lower attendance rates and higher rates of student turnover are associated with schools containing larger proportions of Latino students. This reflects the mobile character of the city's Latino population. In Houston, the opposite pattern is found—schools dominated by either Latino or African-American students have lower rates of turnover. We have conducted these analyses and partition-explained variance following each of these alternative models. That analysis indicates that a small proportion is attributable to racial character and a much larger proportion should be attributed to the economic composition of schools. Given the ambiguity and complexity of the nature of these relationships we finally resolved not to attempt to partition the variance in achievement scores that was accounted for by these characteristics to either the racial or economic composition of the schools.

eas. In Houston such neighborhoods and schools are relatively rare as a consequence of the residential integration of low-income Whites with the Latino population. The outcome is that the relationship between minority percentage and low income percentage is much stronger in Houston than in Philadelphia. Philadelphia has poor White schools, and several schools that are middle income and African American. Both of these are rare in Houston.

We have also seen that, in addition to the effects of the ecological structure of these cities and their neighborhoods, school policy has had direct effects on the patterns of racial and economic integration of the schools. Magnet school programs, characterized by voluntary busing of selected students from distant areas, have reduced the degree of racial segregation between African-American and White students in the public schools. This effect appears to be limited to students attending magnet schools.

There have been two important secondary consequences of these programs. First, they have created a two-tiered system of schools within these two public school systems. Second, they have increased the degree of economic segregation, both between magnet and neighborhood schools and among neighborhood schools. Students from higher-income families living in economically heterogeneous neighborhoods are more likely to attend magnet schools, thereby increasing the proportions of low-income students in the neighborhood schools.

Our analysis of the impact of racial and economic concentrations of students and other characteristics of schools indicates that the most important determinant of academic success is the proportion of students who are from low-income families. The failure of such schools is the result of a series of characteristics such as the withdrawal of resources, diminished teacher commitment, and alienated families and communities. These schools are also characterized by higher rates of student turnover, lower attendance, and higher rates of disorder. A prescription for school failure must include concentrating minority populations in poverty. That has occurred in both of these cities and particularly in their neighborhood schools.

Over the last decades following the 1954 Brown decision, a substantial amount of educational resources have been invested in efforts to reduce levels of racial segregation in schools. There has been a corresponding amount of social science research and debate generated around the necessity and outcome of these efforts. Our research has focused on two very different school districts that have established similar and successful programs to reduce racial segregation. These programs have had the unintended consequence of increasing concentrations of low-income students in neighborhood schools.

One of the important lessons that should be derived from this analysis is that policy interventions that focus on relatively narrow outcomes are likely to have consequences that are not anticipated. School systems are systemic; change in one element is likely to reverberate throughout the system. Policy development must be broadly, not narrowly, conceived and implemented. The second major conclusion that must be drawn from this analysis is that (at least in these two cities) if the choice must be made between reducing racial segregation or economic segregation, the latter is more important for academic achievement. The agenda for change in public schools must include efforts to reduce the concentrations of low-income students. Finally, a note regarding magnet schools. They are clearly successful, either as a consequence of the nature of the programs that they provide or of the students they attract, or both. The problems that they generate are systemic and selective, not internal. We see them as important models for urban schools if they are inclusive and widespread rather than exclusive and concentrated in a relatively few (often better off) neighborhoods.

REFERENCES

Adams, C., Bartelt, D., Elesh, D., Goldstein, I., Kleniewski, N., & Yancey, W. (1991). *Philadelphia*: *Neighborhoods, division and conflict in a postindustrial city*. Philadelphia: Temple University Press.

Bartelt, D. (1995). The macroecology of educational outcomes. In L. C. Rigsby, M. C. Reynolds, & M. C. Wang (Eds.), *School–community connections: Exploring issues for research and practice* (pp. 159–192). San Francisco: Jossey-Bass.

Bidwell, C., & Kasarda, J. D. (1980). Conceptualizing and measuring the effects of school and schooling. *American Journal of Education, 88*(4), 401–430.

Brown v. Board of Education of Topeka. (1954). 347 U.S. 483–493.

Bryk, A., & Raudenbush, S. (1992). *Hierarchical linear models: Applications and data analysis methods*. Newbury Park, CA: Sage.

Census of Population and Housing, 1990: Summary Tape File 3A. Prepared by the Bureau of the Census, Washington, DC.

Coleman, J. S., Campbell, E. Q., Hobson, C. J., MacPartland, J., Weinfeld, F. D., & York, R. L. (1966). *Equality of educational opportunity*. Washington, DC: U.S. Government Printing Office.

Crane, J. (1991). Effects of neighborhoods on dropping out of school and teenage childbearing. In C. Jencks & P. E. Peterson (Eds.), *The urban underclass* (pp. 299–320). Washington, DC: Brookings Institute.

Fine, M. (1991). *Framing dropouts: Notes on the politics of an urban high school*. Albany, NY: State University of New York Press.

Garner, C., & Raudenbush, S. (1991, October). Neighborhood effects on educational attainment: A multilevel analysis. *Sociology of Education, 64*, 251–262.

Henig, J. R. (1995). Race and choice in Montgomery County, Maryland magnet schools. *Teachers College Record, 96*(4), 729–734.

HISD District and School Profiles 1990–1991. 1991. Houston Independent School District, Houston, Texas.

Jencks, C. (1972). *Inequality, a reassessment of the effect of family and schooling in America*. New York: Basic Books.

Jencks, C., & Peterson, P. E. (1991). *The urban underclass*. Washington, DC: Brookings Institute.

Kantor, H., & Brenzel, B. (1993). Urban education and the "truly disadvantaged": The historical roots of the contemporary crisis, 1945–1990. In M. Katz (Ed.), *The underclass debate: Views from history* (pp. 366–402). Princeton, NJ: Princeton University Press.

Kozol, J. (1991). *Savage inequalities: Children in America's schools*. New York: Crown.

Lawson, B. E. (Ed.). (1992). *The underclass question.* Philadelphia: Temple University Press.

Lee, V., Croninger, R. G., & Smith, J. B. (1994). Parental choice of schools and social stratification in education: The paradox of Detroit. *Educational Evaluation and Policy Analysis, 16*(4), 434–457.

MacLeod, J. (1987). *Ain't no making it: Leveled aspirations in a low-income neighborhood.* Boulder, CO: Westview.

Massey, D. S., & Denton, N. A. (1993). *American apartheid: Segregation and the making of the underclass.* Cambridge, MA: Harvard University Press.

Moore, D., & Davenport, S. (1990). School choice, the new improved sorting machine. In W. L. Boyd & H. J. Walberg (Eds.), *Choice: Educational potential and problems* (pp. 135–178). Berkeley, CA: McCutchan.

Myers, D. E. (1985). *The relationship between school poverty concentration and students' reading and math achievement and learning.* Washington, DC: Decision Resources Corporation.

Oakes, J. (1992, May). Can tracking research inform practice? Technical, normative and political considerations. *Educational Researcher, 21*(4), 12–21.

Ogbu, J. (1974). *The next generation: An ethnography of education in an urban neighborhood.* New York: Academic Press.

Ogbu, J. (1988). Class stratification, racial stratification and schooling. In L. Weis (Ed.), *Class, race and gender in education* (pp. 163–182). Albany, NY: State University of New York Press.

Orfield, G. (1994). The growth of segregation in American schools: Changing patterns of segregation and poverty since 1968. *Equity and Excellence in Education, 27*(1), 5–8.

Pallas, A. M. (1994). Schooling in the course of human lives: The social context of education and the transition to adulthood in industrial society. *Review of Educational Research, 63*(4), 409–447.

Pupil Directory Files. 1991. Prepared by Office of Research and Evaluation, School District of Philidelphia. Philidelphia, PA.

Shelton, B. A. (1989). *Houston, growth and decline in a sunbelt boomtown.* Philadelphia: Temple University Press.

Solomon, P. (1992). *Forging a separatist culture.* Albany: State University of New York Press.

Superintendent's Management Information Center, School District of Philidelphia. (1990–1991). Office of Research and Evaluation, School District of Philadelphia, Philadelphia, PA.

Taeuber, K. L., & Taeuber, A. F. (1965). *Negroes in cities: Residential segregation and neighborhood change.* Chicago, IL: Aldine-Atherton.

Wells, A. S. (1993a). *Parents' resistance to racially mixed schools and classrooms: Developing a normative theory of "rational" action.* Paper presented at the American Sociological Association Meetings, Miami, FL.

Wells, A. S. (1993b). The sociology of school choice: Why some win and others lose in the educational marketplace. In E. Rasell & R. Rothstein (Eds.). *School choice: Examining the evidence* (pp. 12–62). Washington, DC: Economic Policy Institute.

Wells, A. S. (1993c). *Time to choose: America at the crossroads of school choice policy.* New York: Hill & Wang.

Wilson, W. J. (1987). *The truly disadvantaged.* Chicago: University of Chicago Press.

Witte, J. (1993). The Milwaukee parental choice program. In E. Rasell & R. Rothstein (Eds.), *School choice: Examining the evidence* (pp. 176–212). Washington, DC: Economic Policy Institute.

Yancey, W. L., Goldstein, I., & Webb, D. (1987). *The ecology of health and educational outcomes.* Philadelphia: Temple University, Institute for Public Policy Studies.

11

Developmental Considerations of Gender-Linked Attributes During Adolescence[1]

Dena Phillips Swanson
Margaret Beale Spencer

Identity formation is one of the most prominent developmental tasks associated with adolescence (Erikson, 1968; Havighurst, 1973). Evolving through this process requires an integration of information from one's past, present, and anticipated future ability to achieve desired goals given diverse social demands, constraints, and opportunities. It involves personal reflection and observation of oneself in relation to others. Interactions with the outside world increase, allowing further integration of cognitive skills, social skills (i.e., behavior), and emotions. Erikson emphasized the role of social and cultural factors on development. By adolescence, minority youth are well aware of the values of the majority culture and its standards of performance, achievement, and beauty. Therefore, adapting to the developmental demands also requires balancing aspects of the self with the social environment (Compas, 1987; Kagan, 1983). For McCandless and Evans (1973), this process further involves an integration of "selves or identifications" with perceptions of future development. As such, synthesizing prior experiences with future expectations represents a critical aspect of identity formation.

In examining an individual's perception of intra- and interpersonal experiences, a person–process–context perspective (Bronfenbrenner, 1979, 1989; Spencer, 1995) "is critical since it affords a method for capturing the adolescent's ability to understand the shared-in-common and mutually endorsed societal expectations and expressed categories gen-

[1]The research reported was supported by funds awarded to the second author from several sources: The Spencer, Ford, and W. T. Grant Foundations, the Commonwealth Fund, and the Social Science Research Council. In addition, supplemental funding was provided by the Annenberg Foundation.

erally shared within a culture (for example, sex role stereotypes and biases)" (Spencer, 1995, p. 49). Gender, like ethnicity, has been routinely supported as an important factor in development. It has been addressed with respect to physical and physiological issues (Wingard, 1987); certain idiosyncrasies such as changes in achievement patterns for girls entering adolescence (Hare & Castenell, 1985); its relationship to parental characteristics, behaviors, and beliefs (Allen, 1985; Clark, 1983; Spencer, 1990); and various temporal patterns (e.g., years of schooling achieved, employment attained) (Gibbs, 1988).

Literature incorporating adolescent identity processes addresses links to outcomes such as achievement, delinquency, career choices, and teen pregnancy. Studies have linked sex role orientation to developmental concerns such as identity achievement status (Streitmatter, 1993) and adolescent relationships (see Maccoby, 1990). It has also been associated with problematic outcomes during adolescence (e.g., delinquency and teen parenting; Hagan, Simpson, & Gillis, 1987; Merrick, 1995). The "dysfunctional family" and negative peer relations have historically provided an interpretational frame for negative outcomes particularly noticeable during adolescence. However, a close examination of the literature reveals that minority adolescents exhibiting problematic behaviors (e.g., aggressive acts, early engagement in sexual activity) are also more likely to be among those with the fewest economic resources and inadequate educational opportunities. An understanding of identity processes is critical for interpreting unfavorable (i.e., adverse) as well as favorable life-course experiences. Contributing factors include educational aspirations, expectations for the future, level of ego development, parental and "other kin" support, and cognitive maturity.

What continues to elude understanding is the extent to which family interactions and prior educational experiences impact the development of personality attributes during adolescence. Much of the available research on the development of gender orientation focuses on the preschool and early childhood periods, and on sexual orientation during adolescence. Better understanding is needed of factors that impact minority youths' identity development and parental characteristics (Spencer, 1983, 1990) that are specifically linked to minority experiences in a majority culture. Within this chapter, developmental processes are addressed that are linked to issues of minority status among African-American adolescents. The major purpose of the study is to investigate factors contributing to gender-linked (i.e., personality) attributes among African-American youth. In responding to these issues, the impact of family experiences (given psychosocial maturation during adolescence) and educational experiences on personality attributes is examined. A theoretical framework for interpreting these constructs is presented, followed by a discussion of parental and school influences, respectively.

THEORETICAL CONSIDERATIONS AND INFLUENCES
ON GENDER-LINKED ATTRIBUTES

Theoretical Perspective

The context in which adolescents develop has important implications for psychological functioning (Bronfenbrenner, 1979; Garbarino, 1982). Ecological factors such as cultural stereotypes, family composition, school experiences, and peer relations perform a major role in the time, vigor, and content of sex differentiation. Spencer (1995) introduced a conceptual framework that is concerned with risk, vulnerability, and resiliency of urban youth growing up in high-risk environments. This framework, referred to as an identity-focused and cultural ecological (ICE) framework, illustrates the association of context variables with developmental processes. The perspective theorizes that developmental and self-appraisal processes, especially for visible minority group members, are linked to experiences of risk associated with socially sustained stereotypes. These risks impact experiences of stress, coping methods employed, adaptive identity processes (particularly relevant during adolescence) and patterned outcomes (Spencer, 1995). Within Spencer's ICE perspective, phenomenological processes (how individual's "make meaning" of their experiences shared by the group) provide an additional interpretational frame that is as crucial to the explanation of patterned outcomes as the actual experience. To illustrate, Cunningham (1994) examined African-American adolescent males' perceptions of their environment. He found that adolescents adopt coping strategies based on how safe they perceive their environment to be. Perceiving an adequate fit between self and the context significantly influenced negative coping responses (i.e., higher machismo attitudes), which were exaggerated by negative environmental experiences (i.e., the presence of gangs). Spencer, Cunningham, and Swanson (1995) proposed that these attitudes, initially serving as coping responses that are linked to contextual experiences, influence how these youth come to identify themselves as males as they approach adulthood.

The ICE approach provides a basis "for capturing the individual's intersubjectivity . . . [which] is especially relevant given the unique status of adolescent thought processes, which allow a degree of recursive thinking unavailable at earlier periods in development" (Spencer, 1995, p. 49). Furthermore, the ICE perspective is useful in explaining how development-related stressors (e.g., negotiating greater independence) can be mediated by family dynamics and environmental stimuli. Parental supervision of adolescents living in "hostile environments" may conflict with adolescent expectations for increased independence and may, instead, be perceived as family hassles from the youths' perspective. However, such monitoring activities may be necessary in high-risk environments. Thus, particularly for underrepresented and minimally researched groups, the ICE perspective affords significant utility for examining relationships between self and context in groups.

There are unavoidable and interactive aspects of development related to cognitive, emotional, social, and biological processes that occur and become transformed in multiple ecologies; the transition is sensitive to experiences in the past and the present (Spencer, 1995). Most importantly, however, the resolution of these issues undergirds the quality of adolescents' later adult life, such that the self-appraisal processes for specific groups may be associated with unique strategies for addressing developmental concerns. For example, in assessing parental responses to neighborhood police presence, parents of African-American adolescent boys viewed their presence negatively, while parents of African-American girls were more positive about police presence. This suggests, on the other hand, the parental perception of police as being a source of hassles for parents of males and communicate a source of protection as seen by parents of females.

Although the African-American community is inundated with assumptions concerning the experiences of its youths, too few studies are available that specifically examine or link sex role socialization within a developmental framework (see Cunningham, 1993, 1994, and Spencer et al., 1995 for assessments related to males). As suggested by Bandura (1978), self-system development is reciprocally determined from self/other appraisal processes. Accordingly, being either a male or female requires unavoidable appraisals that consider "the self" in the context of sex roles. Historically, a well-adjusted male was expected to be independent and assertive while females were expected to be sensitive and nurturant. Within the self/other appraisal processes, then, females are expected to consider various views concerning femininity. Males, on the other hand, ordinarily consider instrumentality, given unavoidable sex role stereotypes about the anticipated provider role assumed by men. For example, the role of "house husband," although existent, has not gained currency to the extent that it is viewed as generally desirable and valued by males.

Ladner's (1972) research on sex role development suggests that positive characteristics of adulthood, including strength and independence, are less sex-role differentiated among poor African-American adolescents than among their Anglo, middle class counterparts. Multiple gender roles have been a reality for African-American women for generations. Their identity has been defined in terms of roles in addition to those of mother and wife, in contrast to white middle-class American women for whom dual roles are a more recent phenomenon. Black women expect to maintain paying positions as adults which influences their motivation toward educational and occupational attainments (see Hyde, 1991).

Traditional masculinity in many Western societies includes engaging in certain behaviors that are not socially sanctioned, but nevertheless validate masculinity. That is, male adolescents perceive themselves masculine, and believe that others will also perceive them as masculine, if they engage in risk taking behavior that may include premarital sex, alcohol and drugs, and participating in delinquent activities.

In a recent study of the gender role orientation of problem behaviors among high school males, Pleck, Sonenstein, & Ku (1994) found that problem behaviors in adolescent males were associated with their attitudes toward masculinity. Adolescent males who reported traditional beliefs about masculinity (e.g., "A young man should be tough, even if he's not big," "It is essential for a guy to get respect from others," and "Men are always ready for sex") also were more likely to have school difficulties, engage in alcohol and drug use, participate in delinquent activities, and be sexually active.

Family Effects

Although negotiating the desire for greater autonomy and experiencing an increase in parental conflict, numerous studies have also confirmed the importance of the parent–child relationship on forming positive relationships, a confident sense of identity, and successful separation and autonomous functioning (Steinberg, 1987, 1988). The development of independence from parents is a critical psychosocial task adolescents must complete in becoming autonomous, self-sufficient, productive, and competent adults. Negotiating roles and boundaries as challenges to autonomy are characteristic of adolescent behavior. Adolescence, as a transitional period, is also characterized by conflicting behaviors that may oscillate between immature, child-like behavior and mature, adult-like behavior. Parental relationships provide feedback and expectations congruent with increased maturation (i.e., more responsibility) whereas peer relationships provide feedback more consistent with physical development. The expectation of greater autonomy provides the potential for parent–child conflicts when behavior is inconsistent with parental expectations.

Parents have historically been recognized as providing different socialization experiences during early childhood for males and females. Considerable emphasis, for example, has been given to the effect of father absence and female-headed homes on identity. Males are encouraged to be physical and allowed more independence, while females are more likely to receive assistance rather than encouragement toward independent mastery. Fathers have been found to encourage more sex-appropriate activities in their children, and both parents tend to be more attentive and controlling toward same-sex children. It is the effects of the latter finding that suggest that males and females may present differential outcomes to father absence versus mother absence (Ruble, 1988). It has been suggested, for example, that males who are reared in female-headed homes without a positive male figure lack identification with a male role model and, therefore, overexaggerate a sense of maleness by being excessively aggressive, assertive, and often antisocial (see Cunningham, 1993; Ketterlinus & Lamb, 1994).

In a sample of African-American and White older female adolescents, Harris, Gold, and Henderson (1991) examined the influence of father absence on gender role orientation and achievement. Given prior findings indicating that fathers played an important role in forming more traditional traits in their daughters, they expected females without fathers during their development to exhibit greater masculine-linked attributes and have higher achievement motives. Although not supported for the overall sample, they found that for their African-American sample, there were significantly higher achievement needs and higher masculinity and androgynous attributes.

School Effects

Educational experiences provide opportunities for addressing developmental tasks. Specifically, schools provide an environment that is critical to the psychosocial development of adolescents. Students' academic experiences can either support or undermine normative developmental processes. Individuals develop and adapt through interactions that occur within particular environmental settings (Bronfenbrenner, 1989; Kellam, Branch, Agrawal, & Ensminger, 1975). Positive school experiences are, therefore, necessary to ensure healthy identity development and a sense of competence. For African-American students, competence and identity formation also reflect gender-related expectations. Minority status represents an aspect of the self that provides a framework for defining parameters for life course choices and opportunities, while gender expectations further delineate the available opportunities. The extent to which African-American adolescents experience competence in academic endeavors is critical because these experiences form a foundation for establishing a more productive and fulfilled future in a society that offers African Americans limited support. For example, Scott-Jones (1991) found that adolescent females were more likely to postpone sexual behaviors if they were academically invested.

During this developmental period, preparation for a career is largely established through school experiences. Theoretically, schools are a microcosm of the larger society. Many African-American males still fall far behind their cohorts in educational attainment and basic literacy skills (Reed, 1988). They have frequently been retained an average of 1.5 years before reaching ninth grade. This level of retention seriously impedes school-related performance and affects future job marketability, which is directly linked to concerns of adult male instrumentality (Bowman, 1989).

Erikson (1968) suggested that experiences prior to adolescence appear influential for attitude formation. Consequently, personality attributes become more salient as youth get older and accrue more life experiences. For example, adolescent males who exhibit less socially appropriate male traits or devalue female traits have higher machismo attitudes that increase with age. As previously discussed, such attitudes are influenced by contextual experiences and are expressed in diverse ways as male youths form a personal identity. It is important to note that cognitive awareness of gender biases is unavoidable and become heightened in the experiences of adolescents (Spencer et al., 1995).

Rose and Montemayor (1994) examined relationships among gender, gender role orientation, and perceived self-competencies for students in sixth through twelfth grades. They found that adolescents with both positive masculine and feminine attributes (i.e., androgynous) as well as those that expressed masculine attributes had high perceived academic and peer competencies. Androgyny predicted global self-worth for males and females, while masculinity predicted it for females only. Femininity predicted perceived academic competence for males. They found no grade differences among the predictor variables.

The psychosocial implications of academic competence are not only a pivotal resource for healthy, positive identity development during adolescence, but also for navigating the difficult transition to gainful employment in adulthood. Few studies address the developmental precursors of gender-linked identity processes, particularly among African-American adolescents. This study addresses these processes for early and middle adolescents by examining the effects of developmental issues relevant during this period (e.g., family interactions).

METHODOLOGY

Subjects

The research used in the following analyses is from a longitudinal study that addressed the developmental effects of persistent poverty among African-American youth. Students from across four middle schools in a large, southeastern urban city completed a brief self-report survey. From this sample, 394 adolescent males and 168 females attending either sixth, seventh, or eighth grade were randomly selected for continued project participation. As part of their participation, each adolescent completed several scales over three sessions, in small groups, and attended a one-on-one interview at their respective schools. Due to the high retention rate for students of the school district, the participants' ages in the initial year (Year 1) of data collection ranged from 11–15 years. Data for the current analyses were collected during the 1989–1990 (Year 1) and the 1991–1992 (Year 3) academic years. During Year 1, students were in either the sixth ($N = 254$), seventh ($N = 164$), or eighth ($N = 174$) grade. In the third year they were primarily in the eighth ($N = 192$), ninth ($N = 239$), or tenth ($N = 95$) grade.

Procedure

Each student completed the individual measures as part of either a battery of group-administered surveys or an individual interview during the 1989–1990 academic year. The Self-Efficacy Measure, Personality Attribute Questionnaire (PAQ), and Perceived Family Conflict were each group-administered by grade during the Year 1 winter and spring quarters. The PAQ was administered again in the spring of Year 3. A parent or guardian of each student provided demographic data and parental child-linked hassles in an individual parental interview during the spring term of Year 1. The interview consisted of two parts: a survey incorporating several measures of psychosocial processes, and an open-ended interview providing more in-depth knowledge of parental expectations and perceptions of their youth's development. All measures were read to respondents to control for varying levels of reading ability. National Percentile Ranks (NPR) from the Iowa Test of Basic Skills (ITBS) were obtained from school-based data at the end of the academic year.

The majority of the small-group testers were the same race as the participants. All testers were well-trained graduate, undergraduate, or older adult interviewers who were hired specifically as adolescent interviewers. All of the in-home parental interviewers were same-race examiners. The in-home interviewers were local mental health professionals who had earned at least one degree in mental health. For the 1st year, approximately 80% of the youth had parents that completed the in-home interview.

Instruments/Data Sources

Background Measures.   Parental education and occupation were coded and standardized as a composite score. Higher scores indicate higher social status. Female headship was measured as a dichotomous variable where there was neither a husband nor live-in boyfriend in the home (two thirds of the sample lived in a female- headed home). Grade in school reflected a student's actual grade in Year 1 (sixth, seventh, or eighth) and was included to address potential developmental effects.

Perceived Context Variables

Parental child-linked hassles were assessed using eight items from the Year 1 parental protocol. Parents responded to (a) how frequently and (b) how irritating they perceived issues such as "reminding child to take on adult responsibilities," "struggles over how long they can stay out," and "children wanting rights to make their own decision." The scale reflects challenges to parental expectations for more responsible behaviors from their maturing children. A high score on these summed items indicates a higher frequency of child related hassles for the parents (Chronbach's alpha = .82).

Adolescent perceived family conflict is comprised of four items resulting from a factored composite of child perceived context variables included in the Year 1 measures where students were asked (a) how frequently and (b) how irritating (i.e., how much of a hassle) they perceived arguments or fights with parents and siblings to be. A high summary score indicates a higher level of perceived family conflict (Chronbach's alpha = .71).

The Hare self-esteem measure was originally constructed to assess adolescents' home, school, peer, and global self-esteem. The measure correlated highly (.83) with two established self-esteem scales (the Coopersmith and Rosenberg general self-esteem scales) during its original construction. The school and peer subscales correlated .75 with the comparable Coopersmith subscale. The Hare measure also has empirically supported construct validity (see Shoemaker, 1980). In the current analyses, the school and peer subscales are used as indicators of self-efficacy in each context. In essence, the items reflect the adolescent's assessment of "goodness of fit" in the person–context interactions. Reliability for the current sample is .65 for peer self-esteem and .69 for school self-esteem.

Standardized test scores from the Iowa Test of Basic Skills (ITBS) comprised the student-based data needed for assessing academic performance. The ITBS was administered throughout the school district during Year 1, including all the current sample participants. It is part of a state criteria for annually assessing students' academic achievement and is widely used in planning students' academic curriculum (e.g., remedial or advanced courses).

The national percentile ranks (NPR) from the mathematics and language total score assessments are used. These ranks provide information concerning how well a student performed compared to other students nationally to whom the measure was administered during the same period of time. Assessments for the math total NPR include math concepts, problems, and computation. Language NPR assessments include spelling, capitalization, punctuation, usage, and expression.

The Personality Attributes Questionnaire (PAQ) is a measure of personality (e.g., sex role) attributes. Consisting of several subscales, it is a self-reported instrument that assesses limited types of abstract personality traits that stereotypically have been shown to be gender-differentiating (Spence, Helmrech, & Stapp, 1975). A short version of the PAQ was used for the Year 1 data comprising three scales. An extended version was used for the Year 3 data, from which four subscales are used in the current study. The masculine positive (MAS+), feminine positive (FEM+), and the masculine/feminine (MasFem) are a part of both data points with masculine negative (MAS-) being added at the second data collection. The MAS+ is described as containing socially desirable expressive traits more characteristic of males than females, although socially appropriate for either (e.g., independent, assertive). Feminine positive (FEM+) is stereotypically more characteristic of females than males, although socially desirable for both (e.g., altruistic). The MasFem contains items for which socially desirable expressive traits are different for the two sexes. In content, the MasFem scale contains items (e.g., cries easily and aggressive) that are acceptable for one gender but not the other. MAS– (Year 3 only) is described by the original authors as reflecting expressive traits more characteristic of males than females, but socially undesirable for both.

RESULTS AND ANALYSES

Setwise regressions were conducted in predicting gender-linked attributes during middle school (Year 1) and early high school (Year 3) years. Independent variables were grouped into three categories: personal and demographic, perceived context, and academic achievement. Demographic variables are social status (e.g., parental education and occupation), female headship, and the adolescent's grade in school. Context variables include parental reports of child-linked hassles and adolescent perceptions of family conflict. School and peer self-esteem are also incorporated as reflecting self/other appraisal processes within specific contexts. Achievement variables are language and math NPRs.

Correlational Findings for Gender-Linked Attributes in Year 1 and Year 3

Table 11.1 findings indicate that in Year 1, MAS+ attributes are related to family conflict and MAS– attributes in Year 3. Adolescent perceptions of family conflict are associated with fewer socially acceptable masculine attributes in Year 1 and negative masculine attributes in Year 3. Positive correlates exist with peer self-esteem, school self-esteem, and achievement scales, as well as with MAS+ and FEM+ in Year 3. In essence, positive self-efficacy and academic experiences are related to future positive gender-linked attributes.

FEM+ attributes in Year 1 are also related to peer self-esteem, school self-esteem, achievement scales, MAS+Year 3, FEM+Year 3, while negatively related to MAS–Year 3. MasFem attributes correlate with peer self-esteem, MAS+Year 3, and FEM+Year 3. Masculine positive and feminine positive attributes in Year 3 also show negative correlates with parental reports of child-linked hassles and a positive correlate with parental status.

MasFem3 (Year 3) attributes are also related to parental status. Identifying with the more positive attributes associated with each gender during middle adolescence is related to parental social status. Year 3 MAS shows expected inverse relations with school self-esteem, peer self-esteem,

TABLE 11.1
Intercorrelations of Variables in the Study

Variable	Marital Status	Female Headship	Parent Hassles	Adolescent Hassles	Peer Esteem	School Esteem	Language NPR	Math NPR	PAQ-Mas (pos.) Yr1	PAQ-Fem (pos.) Yr1	PAQ-MF (pos.) Yr1	PAQ-Mas (pos.) Yr3	PAQ-Fem (pos.) Yr3	PAQ-MF (pos.) Yr3	PAQ-Mas (neg.) Yr3
Grade	.08	.01	.02	-.03	.06	.05	-.02	-.04	-.04	-.02	.06	.04	.09*	.02	-.04
Social Status		-.08	-.16***	0.0	.17***	.12*	.28***	.35***	.10*	.14	.04	.26***	.22***	.11	-.17**
Female Headship			.05	-.04	.01	.03	-.02	0.0	-.04	-.03	-.03	.02	.01	.03	-.01
Parent Hassles				.05	-.05	-.04	-.15**	-.15**	-.06	-.11*	-.01	-.14**	-.16**	-.08	-.07
Family Conflict					-.20**	-.16***	.03	-.07	-.11*	-.02*	-.04	-.09	-.06	-.05	-.06
Peer Esteem						.34***	.15**	.20***	.29***	.13**	.19***	.21**	.13***	.08***	-.10*
School Esteem							.25***	.21***	.28***	.25***	.04	.27***	.22**	.02	-.13**
Language NPR								.59***	.24***	.16***	.02	.32***	.29***	.05	-.30***
Math NPR									.19***	.10*	.02	.25***	.19***	.06	-.16**
PAQ-Mas (pos) Yr1										.64***	.11**	.34***	.19***	.08*	-.21***
PAQ-Fem (pos) Yr1											-.14***	.14**	.21***	-.08	-.21***
PAQ-MF (pos) Yr1												.18***	0.0	.30***	.02
PAQ-Mas (pos) Yr3													.68***	.13**	-.36***
PAQ-Fem (pos) Yr3														-.13**	-.43***
PAQ-MF (pos) Yr3															.12*

Note. *p < .05, **p < .01, and ***p < .0001.

191

achievement scales, and parental status. Negative perspectives of self in context (i.e., area-specific self-esteem) and academic experiences are related to more negative gender-linked attributes. Unexpected, however, is a positive correlation with MasFem, suggesting that less well defined gender attributes during early adolescence are associated with MAS– attributes later. Older adolescents showed a positive relation with FEM+Year 3 as seen in the grade in school correlates. Female-headed household showed no significant correlates.

The results of *t*-test analyses as shown in Table 11.2 reflect significant gender differences in the majority of the listed variables. Males' mean scores were significantly different from those of females on school self-esteem, FEM+, FEM+Year 3, and Language and Math NPR. Females' mean scores differed significantly from those of males in parental reports of child-linked hassles, MasFem, MasFem Year 3, and MAS– Year 3.

Based on these results, and to identify developmental influences on gender-linked attributes, the following regression analyses are conducted separately by gender.

Setwise Regression Findings

Variable groups (i.e., demographic, contextual, and achievement) were individually added to each regression model based on the strength of the *F* statistic. Each group had to meet an *F* statistic significant to at least $p < .09$ to enter and remain in the model. Any variable group not meeting that criterion on entry into the model was dropped from the analyses. In addition, a group could also be dropped if it failed to maintain statistical significance after other groups were added. The final step represents the

TABLE 11.2
Descriptive Statistics and *t*-Tests Coefficients for Subscales by Gender

Variables	Male (N = 364)		Female (N = 161)		
	Mean	SD	Mean	SD	t
Child-linked hassles	16.08	5.33	14.86	4.71	2.25*
Family conflict	7.89	3.46	8.23	3.90	−.96
Peer self-esteem	2.86	.42	2.89	.43	−.79
School self-esteem	2.83	.40	2.93	.44	−2.43*
Masculine Positive Yr1	29.91	6.04	29.70	5.72	.37
Feminine Positive Yr1	28.78	6.36	30.78	6.36	−3.41***
Masculine/Feminine Yr1	24.93	4.21	22.95	4.37	5.00***
Masculine Positive Yr3	29.44	5.96	30.10	5.96	−1.06
Feminine Positive Yr3	28.24	5.67	31.34	6.51	−4.96***
Masculine/Feminine Yr3	25.68	3.60	23.90	4.23	4.22***
Masculine Negative Yr3	21.93	4.36	20.91	4.71	2.18***
Language NPR Yr1	39.90	26.40	56.38	25.34	−6.26***
Math NPR Yr1	42.64	26.41	50.39	29.83	−2.79**

Note. *$p < .05$, **$p < .01$, and ***$p < .001$.

TABLE 11.3

Setwise Regression Analysis of Context and Achievement
on Year 01 Personality Attributes for Males

Dependent Variables	Predictor Variables				
	Step[a]	Cumulative R^2	Variables in Equation	Beta[b]	F
Masculine Positive Yr1	Context	.12	Peer SE	3.05**	7.86***
School SE			School SE	3.01**	
	Achievement Context	.16	Language NPR	.05*	7.50***
			Peer SE	2.96**	
			School SE	2.57*	
Feminine Positive Yr1	Context	.10	Family Conflict	.23*	6.47***
			School SE	4.19***	
Masculine Feminine Yr1	Context	.04	Peer SE	1.82*	2.53*

Note. * $p < .05$, ** $p < .01$, and *** $p < .001$.

strongest predictors, within the model, for the gender-linked attributes
(e.g., dependent variable). The total N used in analyses may fluctuate
slightly due to occasional cases with missing variables.

Predictors of Year 1 Gender-Linked Attributes for Males.   As indicated in Table 11.3, context variables entered the model for MAS+ accounting
for 12% of the variance, with peer and school self-esteem being significant
variable contributors. However, when achievement is added to the model,
language NPR also contributes to the model's overall significance $F(6,229) =$
$7.50, p < .01$, now accounting for 16% of the variance. This suggests a strong
school-based influence along with peer self-esteem in predicting MAS+.

Family conflict and school self-esteem are contextual variables predicting FEM+ for males with school self-esteem ($p < .001$) appearing as a more
statistically powerful predictor. Peer self-esteem was the single most significant contributor of MasFem ($p < .05$). Neither demographic nor achievement variable groups contributed to the models for FEM+ or MasFem.

Predictors of Year 1 Gender-Linked Attributes for Females.   T a b l e
11.4 indicates that for females, school self-esteem is the single most significant
context-related predictor for MAS+, $F(4,100)=2.91, p < .05$, accounting for 10%
of the variance. A more positive sense of school competence suggests more
positive masculine attributes. Demographic and achievement groups were
not significant predictors of MAS+. Group predictors for FEM+ and MasFem
are not significant, nor do they reach trend ($p < .09$) level.

Predictors of Year 3 Gender-Linked Attributes for Males.   Findings
listed in Tables 11.5 and 11.6 reflect the use of Year 1 variables to predict

TABLE 11.4
Setwise Regression Analysis of Context and Achievement
on Year 01 Personality Attributes for Females

Dependent Variables	Step[a]	Predictor Variables Cumulative R^2	Variables in Equation	Beta[b]	F
Masculine Positive Yr1	Context	.10	School SE	2.57*	2.91*
Feminine Positive Yr1	—	—	—	—	—
Masculine Feminine Yr1	—	—	—	—	—

Note. *p < .05. [a]Steps are reported based on those groups that were included in the model by meeting significance of p < .09 (groups not reported did not meet this criteria and were automatically dropped from the analysis). Groups entered the model based on the largest F statistic. [b]All beta values reported in this table were those obtained for significant groups as they entered the model.

TABLE 11.5
Setwise Regression Analysis of Context and Achievement
on Year 03 Personality Attributes for Males

Dependent Variables	Step[a]	Predictor Variables Cumulative R^2	Variables in Equation	Beta[b]	F
Masculine Positive Yr3	Achievement	.15	Language NPR	.06**	17.35***
			Math NRP	.04**	
	Demographic	.18	Social Status	.87*	8.50***
	Achievement		Language NPR	.06**	
			Math NRP	.04*	
Feminine Positive Yr3	Achievement	.07	Language NPR	.04*	7.11**
	Context	.11	School SE	2.73*	4.14***
Masculine Feminine Yr3	Demographic	.08	Social Status	.74***	6.16***
Masculine Negative Yr3	Achievement	.05	Language NPR	−.03*	4.91**

Note. *p < .05, **p < .01, and ***p < .001. [a]Steps are reported based on those groups that were included in the model by meeting significance of p < .09 (groups not reported did not meet this criteria and were automatically dropped from the analysis). Groups entered the model based on the largest F statistic. [b]All beta values reported in this table were those obtained for significant groups as they entered the model.

TABLE 11.6
Setwise Regression Analysis of Context and Achievement
on Year 03 Personality Attributes for Females

Dependent Variables	Step[a]	Predictor Variables Cumulative R^2	Variables in Equation	Beta[b]	F
Masculine Positive Yr3	Context	.20	Child-linked hassles	−.26*	
			School SE	3.73*	5.04**
Feminine Positive Yr3	Achievement	.08	Language NPR	.07[t]	3.38*
Masculine Feminine Yr3	—	—	—	—	—
Masculine Negative Yr3	Achievement	.11	Language NPR	−.06*	5.01**
	Demographic	.18	Grade	−1.29*	3.46**
	Achievement		Language NPR	−.05[t]	

Note. *p < .05, **p < .01, and ***p < .001. [a]Steps are reported based on those groups that were included in the model by meeting significance of p < .09 (groups not reported did not meet this criteria and were automatically dropped from the analysis). Groups entered the model based on the largest F statistic. [b]All beta values reported in this table were those obtained for significant groups as they entered the model.

gender-linked attributes at Year 3. Table 11.5 shows the findings for males. Achievement entered the model as having the strongest predictive group value for MAS+Year 3. However, when demographic variables were added, parental status is seen as an additional contributor ($p < .05$) while language NPR and math NPR ($p < .01$ and $p < .05$, respectively) maintain their beta weight significance in the overall model. The three variables (status, language NPR, and math NPR) together contribute to the noted 18% of the variance, $F(5,191) = 8.50$, $p < .001$. Peer and school self-esteem, which were predicted of MAS+ (Year 1), as seen in Table 11.3, are not significant predictors in this model for Year 3.

Achievement is noted as contributing to the model for FEM+Year 3 with language NPR as the sole predictive variable. However, when context is added into the model, achievement is no longer significant and school self-esteem becomes the single most significant predictor of FEM+year 3 for males, $F(6,192) = 4.14$, $p < .001$, accounting for 11% of the variance.

The demographic variable, parental status, accounts for the significance noted in the model of MasFem Year 3, $F(3,194) = 6.16$, $p < .01$, suggesting that for older adolescent males, more androgynous attributes are linked to parents' education and occupational status—more so than factors related to peer self-esteem as seen in predicting MasFem for males in Year 1. MAS-Year 3 is predicted by lower language NPRs, indicating less socially desirable attributes being linked to language performance. Note that demographic and context variables do not contribute to this model, even though there were several strong correlates.

Predictors of Year 3 Gender-Linked Attributes for Females.

Mas+ Year 3 for females, as seen in Table 11.6, is predicted by fewer parental child-linked hassles and school self-esteem, $F(4,80) = 5.04$, $p < .01$. Demographic and achievement groups were not significant.

Achievement is seen as a significant group predictor for FEM+Year 3 ($p < .05$), although language NPR contributes to this model at the trend level ($p < .09$). Neither demographic nor context groups were significant predictors of FEM+ Year 3. There were also no significant group predictors of MasFem Year 3 for females.

Achievement enters the model for MAS– Year 3, accounting for 11% of the variance, with lower language NPR being the sole significant variable. When demographics were added, grade in school became a significant contributing variable, with lower language NPR scores remaining in the model at a trend level, but together accounting for 18% of the variance $F(5,79) = 3.46$, $p < .01$.

DISCUSSION

Perceptions of context, achievement experiences, and demographic factors were used to assess developmental trends in gender-linked attributes for minority youth. During both investigation years (i.e., Years 1 and 3), positive male attributes were expressed by females with positive school self-esteem. The introduction of fewer reported child-linked hassles during the later year suggests the positive, more assertive and independent attributes established during early adolescence were consistent with parental expectations of maturity. Although there were no predictors for females regarding positive feminine attributes in the initial year, or in either year for masculine/feminine attributes, language performance emerged as a consistent predictor in the later year. This finding was relevant for both positive feminine and negative masculine attributes. Poor language ability also predicted the expression of negative masculine attributes for adolescent males in Year 3. It appears, therefore, that although language serves as a powerful indicator of general academic performance, it also impacts school relationships and associated expectations (i.e., teacher interactions) of students' academic potential and behavioral expectations. Younger females in Year 1 (i.e., sixth grade) with poor language abilities later expressed more negative masculine attributes. These females would be potential candidates for behaviors related to early pregnancy or gang affiliation because their behavior is less academically engaging and, in general, they have fewer positive educational experiences than their more academically focused, task-oriented female counterparts.

Language performance, academic competence, and peer self-esteem intuitively predicted positive masculine attributes for males in Year 1. These constructs foster experiences that encourage the development of stereotypic male-oriented attributes: autonomy, assertiveness, and self-assurance. Adolescent perception of family conflict, however, was a counterintuitive predictor of positive feminine attributes among younger males. The type of conflict or interpretations of the reasons for conflict potentially influence attributes such as heightened sensitivity. This variable did not remain a significant predictor for males, however, suggesting perhaps age sensitivity, unique experiences of the participants, or desensitization.

Also of interest is the absence of peer self-esteem as either a positive or negative predictor of gender-linked attributes for males in Year 3, although prevalent in Year 1. Parental social status displaced peer self-esteem as a partial predictor of positive masculine and masculine/feminine attributes, highlighting the supportive influence of parental values and expectations.

Math performance is seen as a predictive variable of positive masculine attributes for males during Year 3, but not as a predictor for females. Math is a subject that has historically been male oriented and dominated. Although females overall exceed males academically throughout their educational experiences, the attributes fostered by successful education are more characteristic of a masculine orientation. In addition, there are a myriad of differential predictors for males' and females' gender-linked attributes, but being reared in a female-dominated home was not a relevant predictor for either.

These data serve to underscore the significance of positive academic experiences and competencies for producing positive and preventing negative outcomes. They also reflect the need to more actively assist adolescent females in translating their positive academic experiences into positive life-course attributes. It is assumed that because females do not exhibit behavioral problems to the same extent or magnitude as males that they are experiencing a successful transition into adulthood, barring such social problems as pregnancy or drug abuse. Although faring better than males more generally, there remains the need for more active assistance to females in translating positive attributes during the transition into broader life-course opportunities.

The findings from this study disturbingly suggest that as long as females feel positive about their school experiences and are demonstrating responsible behavior at home, they possess the attributes necessary for pursuing life goals. What, in essence, they appear to possess is the ability to recognize the limits of social expectations and to not waver too far from them, which may stifle their motivation to pursue later independent-based life options. The extent to which this trend continues or is later disrupted, and the impact it has on future goal orientation, is an area requiring further investigation. In addition, this study also underscores the necessity of examining differential gender patterns related to developmental tasks.

REFERENCES

Allen, W. R. (1985). Race, income and family dynamics: A study of adolescent male socialization processes and outcomes. In M. B. Spencer, W. R. Allen, & G. K. Brookins (Eds.), *Beginnings: The social and affective development of Black children* (pp. 273–292). Hillsdale, NJ: Lawrence Erlbaum Associates.

Bandura, A. (1978). The self system in reciprocal determinism. *American Psychology, 33*(4), 344–358.

Bowman, P. (1989). Research perspectives on Black men: Role strain and adaptation across the adult life cycle. In R. L. Jones (Ed.), *Black adult development and aging* (pp. 117–150). Berkeley, CA: Cobb & Henry.

Bronfenbrenner, U. (1979). *The ecology of human development.* Cambridge, MA: Harvard University Press.

Bronfenbrenner, U. (1989). Ecological systems theory. In R. Vasta (Ed.), *Annals of child development* (pp. 187–248). Greenwich, CT: JAI Press.

Clark, R. (1983). *Family life and school achievement: Why poor Black children succeed and fail.* Chicago, IL: University of Chicago Press.

Compas, B. E. (1987). Coping with stress during childhood and adolescence. *Psychological Bulletin, 101*(3), 393–403.

Cunningham, M. (1993). Sex role influences on African Americans: A literature review. *Journal of African American Male Studies, 1,* 30–37.

Cunningham, M. (1994). *Expressions of manhood: Predictors of educational achievement and African-American adolescent males.* Unpublished doctoral dissertation, Emory University, Atlanta, GA.

Erikson, E. (1968). *Identity, youth and crisis.* New York: Norton.

Garbarino, J. (1982). *Children and families in the social environment.* New York: Aldine-Atherton.

Gibbs, J. R. (1988). *Young, Black, and male in America: An endangered species.* Dover, MA: Auburn House.

Hagan, J., Simpson, J., & Gillis, A. R. (1987). Class in the household: A power-control theory of gender and delinquency. *American Journal of Sociology, 92*(4), 788–816.

Hare, B. R., & Castenell, L. A., Jr. (1985) No place to run, no place to hide: Comparitive status and future prospects of black boys. In M. B. Spencer, G. K. Brookins, & W. R. Allen (Eds.), *Beginnings: The social and affective development of Black children* (pp. 201–214). Hillsdale, NJ: Lawrence Erlbaum Associates.

Harris, S. M., Gold, S. R., & Henderson, B. B. (1991). Relationships between achievement and affiliation needs and sex-role orientation of college women whose fathers were absent from home. *Perceptual and Motor Skills, 72*(3, Pt. 2), 1307–1315.

Havighurst, R. J. (1973). History of developmental psychology: Socialization and personality development through the lifespan. In P. B. Baltes & K. W. Schaie (Eds.), *Life-span developmental psychology* (pp. 4–24). New York: Academic Press.

Hyde, J. S. (1991). *Half the human experience: The psychology of women* (4th ed). Lexington, MA: Heath.

Kagan, J. (1983). Stress and coping in early development. In N. Garmezy & M. Rutter (Eds.), *Stress, coping and development in children* (pp. 191–216). New York: McGraw-Hill.

Kellam, S. G., Branch, J. D., Agrawal, K. C., & Ensminger, M. E. (1975). *Mental health and going to school: The Woodlawn program of assessment, early intervention, and evaluation.* Chicago, IL: University of Chicago Press.

Ketterlinus, R., & Lamb, M. E. (1994). *Adolescent problem behaviors.* Hillsdale, NJ: Lawrence Erlbaum Associates.

Ladner, J. A. (1972). *Tomorrow's tomorrow: The Black woman.* New York: Doubleday.

Maccoby, E. E. (1990). Gender and relationships: A developmental account. *American Psychologist, 45*(4), 513–520.

McCandless, B. R., & Evans, F. D. (1973). *Children and youth: Psychosocial development.* Detroit, MI: Dryden.

Merrick, E. N. (1995). Adolescent childbearing as career "choice": Perspective from an ecological context. *Journal of Counseling & Development, 73*(3), 288–295.

Pleck, J. H., Sonenstein, F. L., & Ku, L. C. (1994). Problem behaviors and masculine ideology in adolescent males. In R. Ketterlinus & M. E. Lamb (Eds.), *Adolescent problem behaviors* (pp. 165–186). Hillsdale, NJ: Lawrence Erlbaum Associates.

Reed, J. (1988). Education and achievement of young Black males. In J. T. Gibbs (Ed.), *Young, Black, and male in America: An endangered species* (pp. 37–95). Dover, MA: Auburn House.

Rose, A. J., & Montemayor, R. (1994). The relationship between gender role orientation and perceived self-competency in male and female adolescents. *Sex Roles, 31*(9–10), 579–595.

Ruble, D. N. (1988). Sex-role development. In M. H. Bornstein & M. E. Lamb (Eds.), *Developmental psychology: An advanced textbook* (2nd ed., pp. 411–459). Hillsdale, NJ: Lawrence Erlbaum Associates.

Scott-Jones, D. (1991). Adolescent childbearing: Risks and resilience. *Education and Urban Society, 24*(1), 53–64.

Shoemaker, A. L. (1980). Construct validity of area specific self-esteem: The Hare self-esteem scale. *Educational and Psychological Measurement, 40*(2), 495–501.

Spence, J. T., Helmreich, R., & Stapp, J. (1975). Ratings of self and peers on sex role attributes and their relation to self-esteem and conceptions of masculinity and femininity. *Journal of Personal and Social Psychology, 32*, 29–39.

Spencer, M. B. (1983). Children's cultural values and parental child-rearing strategies. *Developmental Review, 3*(4), 351–370.

Spencer, M. B. (1990). Parental values transmission. In J. B. Stewart & H. Cheatham (Eds.), *Interdisciplinary perspectives on Black families* (pp. 111–130). New Brunswick, NJ: Transactions Press.

Spencer, M. B. (1995). Old issues and new theorizing about African American youth: A phenomenological variant of ecological systems theory. In R. L. Taylor (Ed.), *Black youth: Perspectives on their status in the United States* (pp. 37–70). Westport, CT: Praeger.

Spencer, M. B., Cunningham, M., & Swanson, D. P. (1995). Identity as coping: Adolescent African-American males's adaptive responses to high-risk environments. In H. W. Harris, H. C. Blue, & E. H. Griffith (Eds.), *Racial and ethnic identity: Psychological development and creative expression* (pp. 31–52). New York: Routledge.

Steinberg, L. D. (1987). Impact of puberty on family relations: Effects of pubertal status and pubertal timing. *Developmental Psychology, 23*(3), 451–460.

Steinberg, L. D. (1988). Reciprocal relation between parent–child distance and pubertal maturation. *Developmental Psychology, 24*(1), 122–128.

Streitmatter, J. (1993). Gender differences in identity development: An examination of longitudinal data. *Adolescence, 28*(109), 55–66.

Wingard, D. L. (1987). Sex differentials in health and mortality. *Women and Health, 12,* 103–145.

12

Determinants of Student Educational Expectations and Achievement: Race/Ethnicity and Gender Differences

Leo C. Rigsby
Judith C. Stull
Nancy Morse-Kelley

This chapter addresses the question of whether the academic experiences of adolescents from different racial/ethnic and gender groups differentially affect the schooling outcomes and performances of these groups in U.S. schools. The authors' approach is comprised of two stages. First, we determine whether a single explanatory model is sufficient to assess distinct racial/ethnic and gender groups; we then consider the similarities and differences among the academic experiences—particularly expectations for success and access to specific school programs and resources—of these groups.

The primary model for analyzing inequalities in educational outcomes is the status attainment model, which was developed in large part by sociologists at the University of Wisconsin in the 1960s (Sewell & Hauser, 1980). The model was constructed and enhanced using data from predominantly White male subsamples (Alexander & Eckland, 1974; Alexander, Eckland, & Griffin, 1975; Duncan, Haller, & Portes, 1968; Haller & Portes, 1973; Sewell, Haller, & Strauss, 1957; Sewell & Shah, 1967, 1968a, 1968b). In fact, Sewell and Hauser (1980) reported that the Wisconsin data included less than 2% non-Whites. Many of the initial publications based on this data focused on White males because of researchers' original concern with low aspiration and achievement levels among farm-reared, Wisconsin boys. Sewell and Hauser have suggested that continued emphasis on a White, male population may be due to the homogeneous focus in these early articles by Wisconsin scholars.

In the middle 1970s, other scholars sought to extend the Wisconsin model to include women and racial/ethnic minority populations, in particular, African Americans. A number of these scholars reported that the basic Wisconsin model better explained educational expectations and attainments for White males than for women or minority males. Using data sets that did not include the full range of race/ethnicity or gender types, researchers found the model explained less variance and exhibited complex statistical interactions (Alexander & Eckland, 1974 [females]; Hout & Morgan, 1975 [African Americans and females]; Kerckhoff & Campbell, 1977 [African-American males]; Porter, 1974 [African Americans]; Portes & Wilson, 1976 [African Americans]; Treiman & Terrell, 1975 [African Americans and females]). Even the major analyses of the High School and Beyond data (Alexander & Pallas, 1985; Coleman & Hoffer, 1987; Coleman, Hoffer, & Kilgore, 1982; Hoffer, Greeley, & Coleman, 1985; Jencks, 1985; Willms, 1985) shed little light on the effects of race/ethnicity and gender on schooling outcomes as race/ethnicity and gender were not treated as variables that warranted further exploration because of their intrinsic value, but were viewed as phenomena to be eliminated through statistical control.

Other researchers began to address the relative lack of success in applying the Wisconsin model to the different patterns of schooling outcomes of non-White and/or nonmale students. This literature, mostly ethnographic in approach, focused explicitly on schooling outcomes among women and minorities, and on the complex interactions between the schooling processes and family background and cultural processes of African Americans and other minority groups (Grant, 1984; Ogbu, 1981, 1986, 1987; Ogbu & Matute-Bianchi, 1986; Peshkin, 1991; Schofield, 1989; Weis, 1990).

Only recently have researchers begun to combine insights from the ethnographic tradition with the methodological rigor of the status attainment tradition. Though the populations they utilized were limited, Lawrence Steinberg, Sanford Dornbusch, and Bradford Brown, along with their numerous collaborators, have made major contributions to this effort (Dornbusch, Ritter, & Steinberg, 1991; Dornbusch, Steinberg, & Ritter, 1990; Lamborn, Mounts, Steinberg, & Dornbusch, 1991; Steinberg, 1986; Steinberg, Brown, Cider, Kaczmarek, & Lazzaru, 1988; Steinberg, Dornbusch, & Brown, 1992; Steinberg, Lamborn, Dornbusch, & Darling, 1992). These researchers have enacted data sets that allow the study of student–peer and student–family processes in a small number of ethnically diverse schools. Their research has explored the effects of differences among ethnic/racial groups in (a) parent perceptions of the value of student success in the classroom, (b) conflicts between parent and peer pressures relating to school performance, and (c) the relationships between parenting practices and adolescent educational achievement. The research findings of Steinberg and his colleagues support Mickelson's (1984, 1990) argument that the expectation–achievement paradox for African-American children (high educational expectations despite low school achievement) can be accounted for by the discrepancy between abstract values (i.e., the commonly-held belief that people can get ahead by hard work and education) and concrete values (i.e., the personal belief that someone like myself cannot get ahead by hard work and education).

The present research combines and enhances the ethnographic and status attainment traditions, broadening their dual focus to include diverse racial/ethnic and gender groups so that direct intergroup comparisons can be made.

THEORETICAL BACKGROUND

This chapter builds on several relevant known facts: that family and peer interaction processes, differential access to school programs and resources, the development of skills and the acquisition of knowledge, and the accumulation of success/failure experiences in school all affect the educational outcomes of adolescent students. It is reasonable to believe that some of these processes may operate differently among diverse analytic categories.

The authors have anticipated the criticism that scientific procedure often prefers the most parsimonious model for analyses of this sort. Clearly this was the mind-set that led researchers to apply the status attainment model of the 1960s to other data sets and samples, and to interpret results that show some differences as largely convergent with the dominant model (see Featherman & Hauser, 1976a, 1976b; Treiman & Terrell, 1975). There is a delicate balance, however, between emphasizing differences and emphasizing similarities in the analysis of social phenomena; generalization often glosses over the former while focusing solely on the latter.

Although there has been a recent emphasis on race and gender differences in postmodern and cultural-identity projects, a major challenge for women and racial/ethnic minorities—to question the fundamentally reductionist character of the dominant research model—still remains. For a variety of reasons, that model has de-emphasized structural processes affecting aspirations and achievement (i.e., differential socialization and expectations, differential access to education and work, and differential evaluation processes in educational and work settings) that critics believe are important to understanding schooling and work experience. The pressure to recognize and validate the different experiences of women and minorities has, as its logical extreme, the stance that every case or instance is unique and that there can be no generalization. Some balance, therefore, is needed between over-generalization and extreme specificity.

Several explanations have been posited to account for differences among the educational expectations and achievement of varying racial/ethnic and gender groups. Differential levels of family poverty most directly apply to racial/ethnic minorities. Studies have shown that higher levels of poverty among African Americans can account for some of the achievement differences relative to Whites. Variations in school district expenditures can also have this effect because the wealthier districts can offer greater technology and a richer menu of advanced-level courses.

At the school level, Yancey and Saporito (1995) found that elementary schools with high levels of poverty and racial isolation and high student turnover rates have much lower levels of average achievement than could be accounted for by the linear additive effects of these conditions. Such cumulative processes may work on the individual level as well. If several factors affect educational achievement and educational development, then one or two negatives could be offset or balanced by one or two positives. On the other hand, a preponderance of negatives may create an interactive composite that is difficult, if not impossible, to overcome or counteract.

Parenting practices that support educational achievement have also been shown to reflect expectation–outcome differences among varying race/ethnicity and gender groups. Yao (1985) argued that the highly structured family life of Asian Americans accounts for their high achievement rates. Steinberg and his associates showed that the parenting practices that are the most effective in supporting school performances evidence racial/ethnic differences. Parenting practices that result in high achievement among White, middle-class students (e.g., see Dornbusch et al., 1991; Steinberg et al., 1992) are different from those that are successful among African-American students (for example, see Taylor, 1994; Taylor & Roberts, 1996).

Taken together, these explanations argue that educational achievement and development among female and minority adolescents may be representative of the skills and knowledge each student brings to his or her developmental context. There is continuity in educational achievement because there is continuity in the structures and processes that affect it. This implies that if race and gender structure the educational experiences of adolescents, these variables must be incorporated into the framework that explains their educational development and achievement.

METHODS

This chapter uses data from the National Educational Longitudinal Survey of 1988 (NELS:88) to explore race/ethnic and gender similarities and differences in patterns of student educational expectation and achievement patterns using two-stage least square regression analysis to compensate for the posited simultaneous relationship between the two variables.

NELS:88 is the third of a series of national longitudinal studies of adolescent educational development conducted under the aegis of the U.S. Department of Education. The NELS:88 study began in 1988, with a national sample of 24,599 eighth-grade students drawn from public, religious, and private (nonreligious) schools. Students have been contacted every 2 years and will continue to be contacted until they enter the labor force. The present research focuses on those students who participated in both the 1988 (base year) and 1990 (first follow-up) surveys. Because of their very small numbers, Native Americans were excluded, as were students who dropped out of school. Interestingly, students who dropped out of school by the end of tenth grade were evenly distributed across the eight analysis groups. To account for sampling effects, all data were weighted according to National Center for Education Statistics (NCES) specifications (i.e., using the panel weight divided by the mean of that weight).

The traditional strategy of representing the effects of race/ethnicity and gender on student expectations and achievement by including dummy variables in the equations was initially tested, but was found to be insufficient to capture the issues of concern in this chapter. Instead, students were separated according to their race/ethnicity and gender into eight groups (male and female Asians, Latinos, African Americans, and Whites) and separate analyses were conducted for each group.

Variables

The study's dependent variables included student scores on the standardized test of mathematics achievement given in 1990, and student educational expectations in 1990. The mathematics test was chosen in order to lessen the effect of a non-English speaking, non-American background among the student population. The test was timed and was comprised of 40 questions which assessed various levels of mathematical skills and knowledge. Three different forms of this test were given in the first follow-up, with a more difficult form given to those scoring in the highest quartile on the base year test and a less difficult form given to those who scored in the lowest quartile. The middle two quartile scorers received the "regular" form. The NCES-provided IRT scores were used to ensure that the comparisons drawn among all students were equivalent. These scores represent the dependent variable in the first regression analysis (see Table 12.2, later in this chapter). The students' educational expectations, which were ranked according to the number of years of educational experience associated with each category (i.e., high school graduate = 12 years; college graduate = 16 years, and so forth) represent the dependent variable in the second analysis. The questions on which measures were based are described in greater detail in Appendix A.

Family Influence Measures.   NCES created a measure of family socioeconomic status (SES) from student questionnaire data on parent education and occupation, family income, and possessions. Probably the most consistent finding in the literature of the sociology of education has been the positive relationship between SES and educational achievement.

In addition to SES, parental support has generally been shown to be important to the well-being of adolescents, with "proper support" promoting educational achievement. "Proper support" may vary from group to group, depending on the maturity and self-monitoring capacity of the adolescent. For some students, the most consistent support system seems to be general monitoring (some rules and high performance expectations) that excludes direct intervention in homework and tight behavioral control. The latter were found to be inconsistent with the development of adolescent responsibility and self-monitoring (Steinberg et al., 1988). On the other hand, Taylor (1994) and Brown, Mounts, Lamborn, & Steinberg (1993) argued that appropriate parenting practices also vary within the family's social context. Neighborhoods with high levels of drug use and/or teen violence may elicit greater parent monitoring and control. In less threatening environments, tight control and detailed intervention seem to indicate that school performance and/or behavior are already problematic. That is, to some extent the schooling and social behaviors of children and adolescents mandate a combination of support and control from parents. Parents optimally support, but do not control, where children are developing within the typical bounds of acceptable behavior. They often intervene after the fact, when social behavior or educational achievement fall outside the typical bounds of acceptability.

The weighted scale "Parental Involvement" was constructed from data regarding ways in which parents were involved in their child's high school. Going to a school event (e.g., a baseball game or school play) was given the least weight, and volunteering in school the highest. A positive correlation was expected between the level of parent involvement and student educational achievement and expectations.

The dummy variable "Mom Expects College" was used to determine what level of education the target student believed his or her mother expected him or her to attain. Using the number of years of education either parent expected did not prove significant, but this variable, which focused specifically on maternal expectation, did. As Smith (1989) found, fathers' expectations do not factor significantly into student expectations or achievement. A positive relationship was anticipated between student expectations and achievement and maternal expectations.

Peer Pressure Measures.   Since the early 1960s, when Coleman's (1961) *The Adolescent Society* was published, researchers have been studying the effects of peer group processes on the schooling commitments and performances of adolescents. A number of studies have reported on the contextual effects of peers—that is, relationships between middle class peers (Coleman et al., 1966; Sewell & Armer, 1968). However, few have documented the kinds of direct interpersonal influences from peers that many parents seem to fear or aspire to for their children (Epstein & Karweit, 1983). Nevertheless, there is substantial intuitive appeal to the notion that peers affect and reinforce both positive and negative schooling behaviors

(Rigsby & McDill, 1972). The present study explored a number of different measures of peer influences and found that only one had any systematic effect on educational achievement.

The scale "Nonacademic Peer Pressure" was constructed from student reports on the social priorities of their friends (the importance of athletics, dating, attending parties, and so forth). This variable measured peer support for nonacademic activities and Coleman's logic suggested a negative effect.

Influences of Other Adults. The counted scale "Number of Others Who Expect College" was modeled after a component of the Wisconsin studies that documented the importance of adult influence on student expectation and achievement. Students were asked to choose from a pool of seven significant adults (parents, favorite teachers, coaches) to determine who, in the student's opinion, wanted him or her to attend college.

Students' Values Relating to Future Success and School Commitment. The sociology of education has long argued that personal values and ambition play a key role in developing the commitment and self-discipline necessary to achieve academic success among adolescents who, entering an age where they have some degree of autonomy, can treat school as either a serious obligation or a distraction to be avoided. Although not wishing to be reductionist about educational achievement, the authors of this chapter have included several measures of students' personal commitments and values, which may stem from home and school experiences and peer interactions.

The scale "Want Good Life" was used to measure students' optimism about their future economic and social successes. A positive relationship between this measurement and student educational performances was anticipated.

The scale "Belong in HS" measured the degree to which students felt they belonged in high school and was used as a measure of school engagement. A positive correlation was expected.

"Locus of Control" was constructed by NCES from items in the student survey and measured the extent to which each student felt in control of his or her life. A positive relationship was expected.

Students' School-Related Behaviors. Specific behaviors and habits relating to school work were also important determinants of school performances. "Number Hours of Homework/Week" measured the average number of reported hours that students spent per week on their homework. Time spent on homework was expected to be positively related to academic achievement.

School-Related Opportunities and Attitudes.   "In Public School" was a dummy variable that indicated whether the student attended a public school at the time of the follow-up survey. Most of the students in the study (74.9%) were in public schools in 1990. Based on previous research (Coleman et al., 1982), public school enrollment was expected to lower educational achievement.

"In Vocational HS Program and In Academic HS Program" were used as dummy variables for, respectively, students enrolled in vocational programs and in academic programs in high school. Membership in the general high school program, the largest category, was excluded and comparisons were made to that group. Enrollment in either of the named programs was expected to enhance student performance relative to the general program—the nonspecific residual category. The effect was expected to be more pronounced for those in the academic programs.

"Teachers Are Okay" measured students' assessments of the quality and caring of teachers in the high school. This measure was expected to be positively related to educational achievement.

Another factor that was expected to add to the model for mathematics achievement was an indicator of whether students were in the "fast track" for mathematics (prealgebra in seventh grade, algebra in eighth grade, geometry in ninth grade, and algebra II in tenth grade). A dummy variable, "8th-Grade Advanced Math," was included and was based on questions in the student questionnaire asking whether students were in advanced math courses in eighth grade. This variable was expected to be positively related to mathematics achievement.

ANALYSIS

Different Resources: Means.   Table 12.1 delineates the means and standard deviations (for interval variables) and proportions (for dummy variables) for the varying student groups and reveals significant differences in student resources and access to education between males, females, and minority students. A simple *F* test (the results of which are not given in the table) of the means and proportions in Table 12.1 shows that, for each measure, the means differed significantly across the eight groups. The 10th-grade math scores evidenced the greatest range of differences. Asian students had the highest mean scores and African-American students the lowest. Indeed, on average, Asian students scored 12.6 points higher than their African-American counterparts, a difference greater than in the 8th-grade mathematics tests (9.5 point difference), but less than in the 12th-grade exams (18.05). The patterns were similar for both males and females.

Despite these test score differences, there was only a 1-year difference in educational expectations ("Expected Years' Education"). One might ask on what do students base their expectations if not academic achievement? The

TABLE 12.1
Means/Proportions and Standard Deviations of Included Variables

| | Male | | | | | | | | Female | | | | | | | |
| | Asian | | Latino | | Af American | | White | | Asian | | Latina | | Af American | | White | |
Variable	Mean	St Dev	Mean	St Dev	Mean	St Dev	Mean	St Dev	Mean	St Dev	Mean	St Dev	Mean	St Dev	Mean	St Dev
Parental involvement	4.14	3.7	3.95	3.7	4.42	3.9	5.08	3.7	3.81	3.5	3.83	3.4	4.58	3.7	5.02	3.5
SES	.22	.9	-.46	.8	-.38	.8	.19	.7	.26	.9	-.54	.8	-.41	.8	.15	.8
Mom expects college*	.89		.86		.84		.87		.91		.84		.87		.88	
Nonacademic peer pressure	12.38	2.4	12.33	2.6	12.17	2.7	12.14	2.5	12.85	2.0	12.17	2.4	12.16	2.3	12.27	2.3
# of others expect college	4.19	2.4	3.38	2.5	3.49	2.4	3.59	2.6	4.26	2.1	3.46	2.3	3.71	2.2	3.71	2.3
Belong in HS	4.35	1.8	3.82	2.1	3.84	2.1	4.25	1.8	4.53	1.6	4.12	1.8	4.11	1.8	4.44	1.6
Want good life	34.14	3.4	32.68	4.2	32.73	3.8	32.76	3.7	33.21	3.1	32.39	3.9	32.82	3.8	32.87	3.4
Locus of control	.00	.6	-.01	.6	-.01	.6	.03	.6	.01	.6	-.03	.6	.00	.7	.07	.6
Hours homework/wk	9.22	7.6	6.53	6.0	5.41	5.1	7.55	6.5	10.50	7.2	7.03	5.7	6.26	5.5	8.71	6.7
Teachers are okay	4.73	1.5	4.52	1.6	4.43	1.6	4.40	1.7	4.86	1.4	4.63	1.6	4.51	1.5	4.51	1.6
In academic HS program*	.45		.27		.26		.36		.49		.27		.31		.39	
In vocational HS program*	.09		.14		.20		.11		.07		.12		.16		.07	
In public school*	.85		.93		.92		.84		.85		.93		.90		.85	
Eighth grade advanced math*	.43		.19		.19		.28		.44		.21		.22		.28	
Tenth grade math score	42.4	12.9	32.5	11.2	29.8	10.3	39.0	12.2	42.7	10.7	31.4	10.5	29.9	11.1	38.7	11.2
Expected years education	16.52	2.4	15.10	2.4	15.26	2.3	15.46	2.3	16.91	2.3	15.43	2.6	15.90	2.7	15.86	2.3

*Proportion

discussion of the study's two-stage regression analysis later in the chapter will help answer this question, and will also address the lack of a one-to-one relationship between educational expectations and performance on the mathematics test.

Although the differences among groups in means and proportions were subtle, some patterns warranted closer attention. Greater differences appeared among the racial/ethnic minority groups rather than across gender categories. On the average, Asian and White students appeared to be similar in patterns of means, while the patterns of means for Latino and African-American students were similar. For some variables—optimism/desire for future material goods ("Want Good Life"), loci of control, positive attitudes toward teachers ("Teachers Are Okay"), and mothers' expectations for college ("Mom Expects College")—the groups had virtually the same means or proportions. In other respects, the groups were highly dissimilar. Indeed, as one might expect, students of Latino or African-American descent were generally more disadvantaged than Asian or White students in terms of personal, family, and school resources. That is, Asian and White students reported higher family SES, positive personal values (e.g., school engagement as measured by the "Belong in HS" scale), and more hours devoted to homework ("Number Hours Homework/Week"). Additionally, students of Asian or White backgrounds were more likely than Latino or African-American students to be enrolled in selective, mobility-oriented curricular options. Asian and White students tended to be involved in advanced academic programs ("In Academic HS Program"), enrolled in advanced math classes ("8th-Grade Advanced Math"), and/or attending private schools ("In Public School"). African-American students, on the other hand, were more likely to be enrolled in vocational programs ("In Vocational HS Program"). In addition, Asian and White sophomore students had higher standardized test score averages ("10th-Grade Math Score") than sophomores of Latino or African-American descent.

Using the same data to make gender comparisons, female students scored higher than male students in encouragement to attend college ("Number Others Expect College"), school engagement ("Belong in HS"), hours spent doing homework ("Number Hours Homework/Week"), qualitative assessment of teachers ("Teachers Are Okay"), and nonenrollment in the vocational track ("In Vocational HS Program"). Female students had lower average mathematics test scores as sophomores than boys ("10th-Grade Math Score"), but generally had higher average educational aspirations ("Expected Years' Education").

It is important to note a number of race/ethnicity and gender interaction patterns. Regarding the resources and experiences previously discussed, Latino and African-American males were often in an unusually disadvantaged position relative to other groups and were less engaged in school ("Belong in HS"), had lower expectations for future success ("Expected

Years' Education"), and spent less each day on homework assignments ("Number Hours Homework/Week"). Thus, certain personal support systems important to the positive educational development of adolescent students were lower for Latino and African-American males than for other groups.

To summarize, the analytic groups delimited for this analysis exhibited important differences in family supports, personal values and behaviors, schooling experiences, and schooling outcomes. Some of these differences were patterned systematically along race and gender lines, while others represented interactions of a more complex nature. Some questions, however, remain. Although conditions of risk, access to schooling experiences, and family supports were different for these analytic groups, were the models different as well? And were the determinants' educational aspirations and outcomes different also? The circumstances that structure different schooling processes are addressed in the regression analyses presented in Tables 12.2 and 12.3.

Different Educational Processes. The model underlying the analyses presented in Tables 12.2 and 12.3 builds on the status attainment tradition, which, in a sense, represents a baseline model of student educational achievement and expectations. It posits that adolescents want to do as well as they can in school, that they want to attain the highest level of education they can to maximize their potential earning power and occupational success, and that their families will support such efforts as much as they are able. The model also assumes that personal academic values and commitments, parental and peer schooling support, positive school experiences, extent of work expended, and the existing store of school skills and knowledge account for successful performances.

Why conduct two-stage least squares regression analyses? In the past, studies on educational achievement and expectations among students have tended to explain the relationship between expectations and achievement in two ways: achievement as a function of expectations, as in the case of the Wisconsin model, or expectations and aspirations as a function of achievement patterns and other, related variables. One difficulty with these oppositional approaches is that a simultaneous relationship is likely to develop between the two variables. The authors believe that test scores shape aspirations, with high levels of achievement leading to greater student expectations, and that aspirations, in turn, affect test scores. Students with high aspirations take learning and academic tasks more seriously, and are more likely to have higher scores. Hout and Morgan (1975) and Summers and Wolfe (1977), among others, emphasized the mutual relationship between student aspirations and expectations in their research.

If such a simultaneous relationship between these two variables does indeed exist, the regression coefficients produced in an ordinary least

TABLE 12.2
Two-Stage Least Squares Regression Coefficients for the Effects of Family, Peer, and Student Behaviors and Attitudes on Sophomore Mathematics Test

Variable	Male				Female			
	Asian	Latino	Af American	White	Asian	Latina	Af American	White
Parental involvement	-.3204*	-.1681*	-.1883	-.0238	-.3664*	-.0520	-.1758	-.0372
SES	2.9020*	2.1413*	2.2952*	2.3938*	3.7089*	2.0774*	2.4682*	2.9732
Nonacademic peer pressure	.5427*	.2781	.0477	.4963*	.2115	.1697	.0424	.2165*
Belong in HS	-.2110	.1350	.3139	-.0265	.6427	.1.24	-.0872	.0717
Locus of Control	1.0215	1.4255*	2.6974*	1.0548*	1.0621	1.4659*	2.1802*	1.0073*
# hours homework/wk	.1994*	.1564*	.1056	.1797	.3817	.2351	.3111*	.2051
Teachers are okay	.5734	.0402	-.0442	.5931*	.5675	.1971	.7244*	.2913*
In academic HS program**	3.6909*	4.3631*	3.1266*	2.7705	3.0572*	4.9049	3.6842*	2.5204*
In vocational HS program**	-2.0256	-.1114	-2.0725*	-2.3677*	-6.7784*	-1.6150	-2.0929*	-2.3296*
Eighth grade advanced math**	6.2499*	4.3990*	6.7439*	5.8168*	6.2536*	5.3621*	6.5598*	6.3185*
Expected years education (predicted)	1.5980*	1.4556*	1.1556	1.4193*	-.3960	.9452*	.8654	1.3733*
Constant	2.7242	5.0755	9.5461	3.8293	34.0238	10.5951	10.1147	7.6073
R Square	.4904	.3142	.3268	.3696	.4090	.3568	.4194	.4251

Note. * $p < .01$ and ** dummy variable.

TABLE 12.3
Two-Stage Least Squares Regression Coefficients for the Effects of Family, Peer, and Student Behaviors and Attitudes on Educational Expectations in Sophomore Year

Variable	Male				Female			
	Asian	Latino	Af American	White	Asian	Latina	Af American	White
Parental involvement	.0109	.0112	.0036	.0135*	.0296	.0224	.0393	.0251*
SES	.1192	.2027	.3774*	.4835*	.5603*	.4329*	.3585*	.4209*
Mom expects college*	-.0911	-.0268	.3644	.5539*	.1458	.2834	.6130*	.5789*
Nonacademic peer pressure	-.0696	.0163	-.0167	-.0093	-.0127	.0416	.0486	.0265*
# others expect college	.1065	.1851*	.1867*	.1293*	.1112*	.2772*	.1950*	.1133*
Belong in HS	.0473	.0380	.0094	.0525*	.0986	.0400	.0527	.0724*
Want good life	.1482*	.1689*	.1093*	.1206*	.1588*	.1260*	.1514*	.1456*
Locus of control	.3201	-.0592	.3664	-.1475*	.0582	.3173*	.0763	.2274
In academic HS program**	.1028	.4123	.1988	.3044*	.2547	.0366	-.2412	.3941*
In vocational HS program**	.3637	-.1238	.1805	-.0214	-.3658	-.0786	-.2624	-.2121
Tenth grade math test score (predicted)	.1224*	.0965*	.0552	.0806*	.0687*	.0858*	.0949*	.0609*
Constant	6.6089	5.4841	9.4777	6.9934	7.4854	6.9784	6.1355	6.7890
R Square	.3694	.3968	.3021	.4509	.3467	.3647	.3216	.4000

Note. * p < .01.

squares regression analysis would be biased and inconsistent. One way to address this problem is by doing a two-stage least squares regression analysis. This approach yields estimators that are consistent, but still biased—that is, estimators whose bias diminishes as N gets larger. In a two-stage least squares analysis, two regressions are estimated, but only the second is analyzed. In the data presented in Table 12.2, all the independent variables are included in the first stage and the educational expectations serve as the dependent variable. A new variable is created which, in our example, is represented by the predicted educational expectations, and these predicted scores are then entered in the second stage as an explanatory variable. This procedure eliminates the posited simultaneous relationship between the two variables, educational expectations and test scores (Gujarati, 1988).

It should be noted that three variables were dropped from the analysis. The base year (8th-grade) reading and math test scores were initially included as measures of academic performance, but were later dropped because they were too highly correlated with the 10th-grade results. This is not unexpected given the way the Educational Testing Service constructed the variables. Grades from the base year also were excluded because they had not been standardized for lack of consistency between schools. In addition, the analysis was not concerned with whether students attended public or private schools, because this variable never proved significant for any of the groups in either of the analyses.

Mathematics Achievement.   In Table 12.2, academic achievement as measured by students' 10th-grade mathematics test scores ("10th-Grade Math Test Score") represents the dependent variable. Different data in this table suggest that the authors' strategy of examining explanations of achievement and educational aspirations separately for each analysis group is fruitful. Differences in the R squares indicate that the underlying model works differently for different groups; that is, the adequacy of the common model to account for achievement and aspirations varies across the groups. This conclusion is further bolstered by considering the differences in the direction and magnitude of the regression coefficients. Also, the lack of patterns consistent for ethnic and gender groups gives no support for a simplistic, biologically deterministic model.

If statistical significance is ignored and only the sign and rough magnitude of the coefficients are examined, common elements that explain educational achievement among minority and female students emerge. In the present study, effects of family SES, enrollment in an academic high school program (vs. a general program), enrollment in advanced mathematics in eighth grade, number of hours spent on homework per week, and having a sense of controlling one's destiny all contributed positively to student achievement. Enrollment in a vocational program (vs. a general program) and parental involvement contributed negatively to student achievement for all groups. Though the results for parental involvement are not what was originally predicted, this is not unusual given the ambiguities in relevant literature. As previously noted in the discussion of family influence measures, there is a tension at the high school level between granting sufficient autonomy for routine growth and development and providing sufficient monitoring to assure safety and security. The effects of parental involvement here are net of family background, educational expectations, and so forth. It is reasonable to account for the negative effects of parental involvement by suggesting that this residual effect net of the other variables is the result of poor performance eliciting greater parental involvement rather than parental involvement affecting performance negatively. Of course, to the extent that greater parental monitoring creates conflict between adolescents and their parents, a negative effect may result.

For all groups, enrollment in (and having access to) advanced math curricula in eighth grade and participation in academic programs in high school were very important predictors of high performance on the mathematics test. Among African-American adolescents, participation in advanced mathematics in the eighth grade was the most important predictor of performance on the mathematics test. The unstandardized coefficient is significant for this group, because this variable has the largest Beta value for African-American males. This is not surprising because eighth-grade placement determines student access to advanced mathematics curricula in high school. This result is particularly significant in light of the widely documented fact (Oakes, 1985) that minority/poor children are more likely to be assigned to lower academic tracks or special education tracks than middle class or White children. If African-American adolescents do not have the same access to advanced mathematics classes (controlling for past performance) as other students, their mathematics achievement is inevitably and significantly dampened. For African-American males and females and for Asian females in the study, the relationship between educational achievement (test scores) and educational expectations was not statistically significant.

Turning back to Table 12.2, there are three elements that support the argument for separate group analyses. First, the fit of the model (R square) varies across the groups; this is a common finding. Second, variations in the relative magnitudes of Beta coefficients (given in Table 12.4) occur across groups, indicating that different explanatory variables have different degrees of importance for different groups. Third, regressions carried out with the entire NELS:88 sample that ignore individual groups discount the variations in sign and magnitude of coefficients from the group analyses. In addition, these regressions confound differences in the distributions of the independent variables across groups with variations in these variables within groups.

TABLE 12.4
Beta Coefficients From Two-Stage Least Squares Regressions for the Effects of Family, Peer, and Student Behaviors and Attitudes on Sophomore Mathematics Test

Variable	Male				Female			
	Asian	Latino	Af American	White	Asian	Latina	Af American	White
Parental involvement	-.0961*	-.0552	-.0656	-.0069	-.1180*	-.0165	-.0562	-.0115
SES	.1998*	.1475*	.1645*	.1432	.2984	.1472	.1686*	.1973*
Nonacademic peer pressure	.1069*	.0640	.0114	.0997*	.0389	.0377	.0085	.0527*
Belong in HS	-.0263	.0207	.0498	-.0034	.0826	.0142	-.0116	.0089
Locus of control	.0483	.0852*	.1601*	.0535*	.0581	.0882*	.1273*	.0539*
# hrs homework/wk	.1225*	.0822*	.0487	.0937*	.2442*	.1263*	.1549*	.1207
Teachers are okay	.0705	.0056	-.0063	.0799*	.0711	.0284	.0980	.0419*
In academic HS program*	.1510*	.1735*	.1285*	.1086*	.1400*	.2051*	.1523	.1090*
In vocational HS program*	-.0459	-.0033	-.0753	-.0587*	-.1578*	-.0500	-.0670	-.0525*
Eighth grade advanced math*	.2532*	.1516*	.2428*	.2188*	.2844*	.2067*	.2439*	.2508
Expected years of eduction predicted	.3164*	.3107*	.2378	.2773*	-.0843	.2294	.2027	.2855*
R Square	.4904	.3143	.3264	.3956	.4090	.3568	.4194	.4251

Note. * p < .01.

Table 12.4 indicates where Betas for the equations reported in Table 12.2 are given. For five groups, excluding African-American students and Asian girls, the strongest predictor of mathematics performance was the variable "Expected Years of Education." The strongest predictor of mathematics achievement among African-American students, as previously noted, was participation in advanced mathematics in the eighth grade. The "Locus of Control" variable was a strong predictor for test performance among Latino students and African-American students and is one of the top five highest Betas in the equations contained in Table 12.4. Because many Latino and African-American students are subject to negative stereotyping, ethnic discrimination, and negative peer influences, it is likely that each of these groups needs an especially strong sense of personal efficacy to succeed in school.

Taken together, these patterns point to the relevance of the aspirations–achievement paradox (Mickelson, 1990). Being a "good" student (signified by relatively high scores on the mathematics test) affects educational expectations for some of these groups, but not all. It should be emphasized that differences in social class cannot explain the different effects of educational expectations across groups, because SES was included in the equation and was significant for each group.

SES was the most important predictor of test performance for Asian girls although educational expectations were the most important predictor for Asian boys. These two results suggest that in Asian families, where cultural and economic resources are limited, sons receive preferential treatment in access to education. Where resources are plentiful, daughters receive support as well. Among Asian boys and girls, parental involvement had a significantly negative effect on mathematics performance. These are the only cases in which parental involvement had a significant effect.

A final point is in order regarding the estimation of different models for the different groups: these models were compared with results from a pooled regression in which groups were ignored (these data are not shown). The order of importance of variables was necessarily different from the diverse individual equations. SES was the most important predictor (largest Beta) in the pooled equation and predicted educational expectations dropped to third place. In the individual group equations, the educational expectations variable was either the most important or second most important predictor of educational achievement in seven of the eight groups. Other analyses revealed that SES varied more among these groups than any other variable. About 10% of the variation in SES and slightly more than 2% of the variation in predicted educational expectations were between groups. Clearly, some of this difference between groups is reflected in (confounded with) the larger effects of SES in the pooled equation.

Educational Expectations

Table 12.3 provides data illustrating the variable "Expected Years of Education" as a function of personal and social influences. Here again there is evidence relevant to the issue raised at the beginning of the chapter, namely whether a single model is sufficient for understanding schooling performances. Ignoring statistical significance and attending to sign and gross magnitude, common elements of a model emerge. As Table 12.3 shows, family social class, nonparental adults encouraging the student to go to college ("Number Others Expect College"), predicted mathematics performance, and optimism for future material gains ("Want Good Life") were all positively correlated with educational aspirations in the study. Enrollment in a vocational high school program was predominantly negatively related. These effects make sense in terms of social learning and socialization theories. Uniformly, the most important predictor (highest Beta) for all groups was predicted mathematics performance (see Table 12.5).

Once again, there seem to be some notable differences between the groups. Among minority males, social integration in the high school ("Belong in HS") either added little or was negatively correlated to educational expectations, while for White boys and girls, this correlation was positive, but low. For Whites and African-American males, the effects of the variable "Locus of Control" were positive and significant. For White students, enrollment in the academic program had strong positive effects, but these effects were less important (and nonsignificant) for other groups. For Whites and African Americans, maternal encouragement to attend college ("Mom Expects College") had a positive and significant effect on student achievement, but was not positive for Asian and Latino boys and was not significant for Asian and Latino girls.

Again, these results support the argument that analyses of adolescents' schooling performances ought to be done separately for gender and ethnic/racial groups. Although the pattern of Betas for the pooled regression does not show changes in the order of importance of variables, it does mask the differences across groups previously discussed.

CONCLUSION

The most important results of this study show the overriding importance of student access to advanced mathematics curricula beginning in the eighth grade. The skeptic may suggest that results merely reflect a sympathetic effort by school staff to prevent young people who may not perform well in advanced mathematics classes from the frustration of failure, and to steer them toward "more appropriate" curricular choices. The problem with such a strategy is that it closes doors to learning opportunities that cannot easily be reopened. Evidence suggests that decisions to grant or

TABLE 12.5

Beta Coefficients From Two-Stage Least Squares Regressions for the Effects of Family, Peer, and Student Behaviors and Attitudes on Educational Expectations in Sophomore Year

Variable	Male				Female			
	Asian	Latino	Af American	White	Asian	Latina	Af American	White
Parental involvement	.0615	.0172	.0061	.0286*	.0442	.0294	.0538	.0373*
SES	.0420	.0651	.1304*	.1531*	.2110*	.1260*	.1049*	.1342*
Mom expects college*	-.0117	-.0038	.0591	.0791*	.0177	.0401	.0775*	.0805*
Nonacademic peer pressure	-.0695	.0175	-.0192	-.0098	-.0110	.0378	.0420	.0257
# others expect college	.0977*	.1849*	.1908*	.1411*	.0987*	.2328*	.1578*	.1113*
Belong in HS	.0299	.0275	-.0073*	.0358*	.0599	.0229	.0305	.0434*
Want good life	.2021	.2961*	.1839*	.1875*	.2146*	.1864*	.2074*	.2072*
Locus of control	.0769	-.0166	.1046*	.0397*	.0150	.0783	.0192	.0584*
In academic HS program*	-.0212	.0769	.0393	.0631*	.0551	.0063	-.0427	.0820*
In vocational HS program*	.0424	-.0172	-.0316	.0028	-.0406	-.0098	-.0358	-.0229
Tenth grade math test score (predicted)	.6185*	.4569*	.2648	.4276	.3217*	.3513*	.4048*	.2939*
R Square	.3694	.3970	.3021	.4509	.3467	.3646	.3216	.4000

Note. * p < .01.

219

limit access to advanced mathematics curricula are often made to reflect the convenience of scheduling by school staff or to preserve elite classes for the most cooperative and well-behaved students (Useem 1990a, 1990b). If our society is serious about the need to preserve educational opportunities for all children in order to ensure their success in an increasingly high-tech society, we have to encourage them to take advantage of the most challenging classes and academic opportunities.

The present study has yielded two significant findings. First, the eight-group analysis proved a fruitful effort. Although there were some male–female and race/ethnicity differences, important new patterns emerged when both gender and race/ethnicity were simultaneously taken into consideration. The schooling performances of African Americans, especially males, were least well explained, a finding that was consistent with earlier literature (Hout & Morgan, 1975; Mickelson, 1990). The factors that were not common to all groups should ultimately be explicated and explored further.

The second significant finding was that the student educational expectations and achievement embodied in the status attainment model were best applied to Asian males and White students. Mickelson's paradox of expectation–achievement, then, holds true not only for African-American males, but also for Asian students and African-American females.

This study, then, raises a challenging question: What is the proper balance between generalization and specificity in assessing school performance? One answer to this question is that the academic experience of every person is unique. This is much too extreme a stance because it ignores the salient influences of common group phenomena. However, although life circumstances structure recognizable commonalities of experience within cultural groups, the authors believe that a "single-model" answer is no longer viable. The challenge for future research, then, is to answer the question posed at the beginning of this chapter: What balance can we strike between the differences and similarities in educational achievement among various minority groups? What standards shall we use to determine the analytic categories for quantitative analysis? Reliance on strict statistical procedures and on strict notions of parsimony have led us to a position that privileges a "single model" over a "multiple model." Consequently, for a long time, differences among populations that may be very important for educational policy have been ignored or minimized. Though there are no clear answers to this dilemma, the present study strongly suggests that answers that would have been given only a few years ago are less satisfactory in the face of new challenges from the forces of diversity.

REFERENCES

Alexander, K. L., & Eckland, B. K. (1974). Gender differences in the educational attainment process. *American Sociological Review, 39*, 668–682.

Alexander, K. L., Eckland, B. K., & Griffin, L. (1975). The Wisconsin model of socioeconomic achievement: A replication. *American Journal of Sociology, 81*, 324–334.

Alexander, K. L., & Pallas, A. (1985). School sector and cognitive performance: When is a little a little? *Sociology of Education, 58*, 115–128.

Brown, B., Mounts, N., Lamborn, S. D., & Steinberg, L. (1993). Parenting practices and peer group affiliation in adolescence. *Child Development, 64*, 467–482.

Coleman, J. S. (1961). *The adolescent society.* New York: Free Press.

Coleman, J. S., Campbell, E. Q., Hobson, C. J., McPartland, J., Mood, A. M., Weinfeld, F. D., & York, R. L. (1966). *Equality of educational opportunity.* Washington, DC: U.S. Government Printing Office.

Coleman, J. S., & Hoffer, T. (1987). *Public and private high schools: The impact of communities.* New York: Basic Books.

Coleman, J. S., Hoffer, T., & Kilgore, S. (1982). *High school achievement: Public, Catholic, and private schools compared.* New York: Basic Books.

Dornbusch, S. M., Ritter, P. L., & Steinberg, L. (1991). Community influences on the relation of family statuses to adolescent school performance: An attempt to understand a difference between African Americans and non-Hispanic Whites. *American Journal of Education, 99*, 543–567.

Dornbusch, S. M., Steinberg, L., & Ritter, P. L. (1990, March). *Ethnic differences in beliefs about the value of school success: An empirical assessment of Ogbu's hypothesis.* Paper presented at the biennial meetings of the Society for Research on Adolescence, Atlanta, GA.

Duncan, O. D., Haller, A. O., & Portes, A. (1968). Peer influences on aspirations: A reinterpretation. *American Journal of Sociology, 74*, 119–137.

Epstein, J. L., & Karweit, N. (1983). *Friends in school.* New York: Academic Press.

Featherman, D. L., & Hauser, R. M. (1976a). Changes in the socioeconomic stratification of the races. *American Journal of Sociology, 82*, 621–51.

Featherman, D. L., & Hauser, R. M. (1976b). Gender inequalities and socioeconomic achievement in the United States, 1962–1973. *American Sociological Review, 41*, 462–83.

Grant, L. (1984). Black females' "place" in desegregated classrooms. *Sociology of Education, 57*, 98–111.

Gujarati, D. (1988). *Basic econometrics.* New York: McGraw-Hill.

Haller, A. O., & Portes, A. (1973). Status attainment processes. *Sociology of Education, 46*, 51–91.

Hoffer, T., Greeley, A. M., & Coleman, J. S. (1985). Achievement growth in public and Catholic schools. *Sociology of Education, 58*, 74–97.

Hout, M., & Morgan, W. R. (1975). Race and gender variations in the causes of the expected attainments of high school seniors. *American Journal of Sociology, 81*, 364–394.

Jencks, C. (1985). How much do high school students learn? *Sociology of Education, 58*, 128–135.

Kerckhoff, A. C., & Campbell, R. T. (1977). Black–White differences in the educational attainment process. *Sociology of Education, 50*, 15–27.

Lamborn, S. D., Mounts, N. S., Steinberg, L., & Dornbusch, S. M. (1991). Patterns of competence and adjustment among adolescents from authoritative, authoritarian, indulgent, and neglectful families. *Child Development, 62*, 1049–1065.

Mickelson, R. A. (1984). *Race, class, and gender differences in adolescents' academic achievement, attitudes, and behavior.* Unpublished doctoral dissertation, Los Angeles: University of California.

Mickelson, R. A. (1990). The attitude–achievement paradox among Black adolescents. *Sociology of Education, 63*, 44–61.

Oakes, J. (1985). *Keeping track: How schools structure inequality.* New Haven, CT: Yale University Press.

Ogbu, J. U. (1981). Origins of human competence: A cultural-ecological perspective. *Child Development, 52*, 413–429.

Ogbu, J. U. (1986). The consequences of the American caste system. In U. Neisser (Ed.), *The school achievement of minority children: New perspectives* (pp. 19–56). Hillsdale, NJ: Lawrence Erlbaum Associates.

Ogbu, J. U. (1987). Variability in minority school performance: A problem in search of an explanation. *Anthropology & Education Quarterly, 18,* 312–334.

Ogbu, J. U., & Matute-Bianchi, M. E. (1986). Understanding sociocultural factors: Knowledge, identity, and school adjustment. In California State Department of Education (Ed.), *Beyond language: Sociocultural factors in schooling, language, and minority students* (pp. 71–143). Sacramento, CA: Bilingual Education Office, California State Department of Education, Evaluation, Dissemination, and Assessment Center.

Peshkin, A. (1991). *The color of strangers, the color of friends.* Chicago: The University of Chicago Press.

Porter, J. (1974). Race, socialization, and mobility in educational and early occupational attainment. *American Sociological Review, 39,* 303–316.

Portes, A., & Wilson, K. L. (1976). Black–White differences in educational attainment. *American Sociological Review, 41,* 414–431.

Rigsby, L. C., & McDill, E. L. (1972). Adolescent peer influence processes: Conceptualization and measurement. *Social Science Research, 1,* 305–321.

Schofield, J. W. (1989). *Black and White in school: Trust, tension, or tolerance?* New York: Teachers College Press.

Sewell, W. H., & Armer, J. M. (1968). Neighborhood context and college plans. *American Sociological Review, 31,* 159–168.

Sewell, W. H., Haller, A. O., & Strauss, M. A. (1957). Social status and educational and occupational aspiration. *American Sociological Review, 22,* 67–73.

Sewell, W. H., & Hauser, R. M. (1980). The Wisconsin longitudinal study of social and psychological factors in aspirations and achievement. *Research in Sociology of Education and Socialization, 1,* 59–99.

Sewell, W. H., & Shah, V. P. (1967). Socioeconomic status, intelligence, and the attainment of higher education. *Sociology of Education, 40,* 1–23.

Sewell, W. H., & Shah, V. P. (1968a). Parents' education and children's educational aspirations and achievements. *American Sociological Review, 33,* 191–209.

Sewell, W. H., & Shah, V. P. (1968b). Social class, parental encouragement, and educational aspirations. *American Sociological Review, 33,* 559–572.

Smith, T. (1989). Mother–father differences in parental effects on school grades and educational goals. *Sociological Inquiry, 59,* 88–98.

Steinberg, L. (1986). Latchkey children and susceptibility to peer pressure: An ecological analysis. *Developmental Psychology, 22,* 1–7.

Steinberg, L., Brown, B. B., Cider, M., Kaczmarek, N., & Cary, L.. (1988). *Noninstructional influence on high school student achievement.* Madison, WI: National Center on Effective Secondary Schools.

Steinberg, L., Dornbusch, S. M., & Brown, B. B. (1992). Ethnic differences in adolescent achievement: An ecological perspective. *American Psychologist, 47,* 723–729.

Steinberg, L., Lamborn, S. D., Dornbusch, S. M., & Darling, N. (1992). Impact of parenting practices on adolescent achievement: Authoritative parenting, school involvement, and encouragement to succeed. *Child Development, 63,* 1266–1281.

Summers, A. A., & Wolfe, B. L. (1977). Do schools make a difference? *The American Economic Review, 67,* 639–652.

Taylor, R. D. (1994). Risk and resilience: Contextual influences on the development of African-American adolescents. In M. C. Wang & E. W. Gordon (Eds.), *Educational resilience in inner-city America: Challenges and prospects* (pp. 119–130). Hillsdale, NJ: Lawrence Erlbaum Associates.

Taylor, R. D., & Roberts, D. (1996). Kinship support and maternal and adolescent well-being in economically disadvantaged African-American families. *Child Development, 66(6),* 1585–1597.

Treiman, D., & Terrell, K. (1975). Gender and the process of status attainment: A comparison of working women and men. *American Sociological Review, 40,* 174–200.

Weis, L. (1990). *Working class without work: High school students in a deindustrialized economy.* New York: Routledge.

Willms, J. D. (1985). Catholic school effects on academic achievement: New evidence from the High School and Beyond follow-up study. *Sociology of Education, 58,* 98–114.

Useem, E. L. (1990a, April). *Getting on the fast track in mathematics: School organizational influences on math track assignment.* Paper presented at the annual meeting of the American Educational Research Association, Boston, MA.

Useem, E. L. (1990b). Student selection into course sequences in mathematics: The impact of parental involvement and school policies. *Journal of Research on Adolescence, 1,* 231–250.

Yancey, W. L., & Saporito, S. J. (1995). Ecological embeddedness of educational processes and outcomes. In L. C. Rigsby, M. C. Reynolds, & M. C. Wang (Eds.), *School-community connections: Exploring issues for research and practice* (pp. 193–227). San Francisco: Jossey-Bass.

Yao, E. (1985). A comparison of family characteristics of Asian-American and Anglo-American high achievers. *International Journal of Comparative Sociology, 26,* 198–208.

APPENDIX A*

Dependent Variables:

- Educational expectations in tenth grade
- R's educational aspirations measured in years (range: 11–20)
- Mathematics test scores in tenth grade

Independent Variables:

- Belong in HS (Do feel you belong in HS?)
  —Why R goes to school scale range: 0–6; alpha: .76)
  —Locus of control (Range: –2.79–1.460)
- Socioeconomic Status
  —Socioeconomic status scale (Range: –2.790–2.954)
- Nonacademic Peer Pressure
  —Friends support nonacademic activities; peer social integration
  (Range: 0–15 [strong negative support]; alpha: .55)
- Want good life
- Well-rounded success indicator, future looks good, number of items of
  good life R wants (Range: 12–36; alpha: .84)
- High School Programs (0 = no, 1 = yes)
  —In academic HS program (36.2% yes)
  —In vocational HS program (10.2% yes)
  —In general HS program (53.6% yes)
- Number of Hours Homework per Week
  —Number of homework done in and out of school per week (Range:
  0–34)
- Mom expects college (0 = no, 1 = yes; 87.2% yes)
- Number of others expect college
- Number of nonparental adults encouraging R to go to college (Range:
  0–7)
- Teachers are okay
  —Number of ways R thinks teachers are okay (Range: 0–6; alpha: .70)
- Parental involvement
  —Number of ways parents are involved in school; parent attends
  meetings, speaks to teacher, goes to school events, volunteers at school
  (Range: 0–10; alpha: .69)
- In public school (0 = no, 1 = yes; 86.1% yes)

---

*Scales are constructed so that high numbers indicate acceptance of whatever the scale is measuring; "0" indicates rejection of whatever the scale is measuring.

Epilogue

Ronald D. Taylor
Margaret C. Wang

In what is now regarded by many as a seminal article, Vonnie McLoyd (1990) noted that the prevalence of research on ethnic minority children and families has shifted with changes in the nation's economic and political climate. Historically, interest has mostly been crisis oriented. A group largely ignored in developmental literature in times past, ethnic minority families, particularly African Americans, became the focus of much concern beginning in the early 1960s as domestic poverty was thrust into the forefront of the nation's attention. A resurgence of interest occurred during the 1980s, due in large part to the alarming decline of ethnic minority families on indicators of quality of life. As the status of these families as a priority for research was subject to change, so too was the focus of the research itself.

During the 1960s, research was largely guided by the assumption that minority families were pathological—mired in poverty because of problematic patterns of behavior (Massey & Denton, 1993). As a result, research on minority families during this period was done at the expense of collecting data on the normative functioning of children and families, ignoring for the most part the resilience of families facing economic and social disadvantages (Wang & Gordon, 1994).

In more recent years, calls for increased research on ethnic minority children and families have been based on the recognition that (a) minority children represent a growing segment of the U.S. population, a segment whose development and functioning will likely have ramifications for the social well-being and global competitiveness of the country (Taylor, Casten, Flickinger, Roberts, & Fulmore, 1994; Yancey & Saporito, 1995; see also Rigsby, Stull, & Morse-Kelly, chap. 12, this volume); and (b) research and theoretical models based upon European-American children and families may not be readily applicable to ethnic minority families (Chao, 1994; Steinberg, Mounts, Lamborn, & Dornbusch, 1991; see also Mason, Cauce, & Gonzales, chap. 6, this volume).

Several key issues have emerged from the work discussed in this volume. First, theoretical models aimed at understanding family relations and adolescents' adjustment and competence must be integrative and based on ecological constructs that incorporate multiple contexts. As Bronfenbrenner (1979; 1986) has argued, actions, policies, or relationships that exist in one context (for example, school or neighborhood) are likely to affect the nature of behaviors in others (for example, peer or family). There is a substantial research base that links local school policies regarding tracking and/or school district policies on the enrollment criteria of magnet schools to school achievement, families' economic decisions, and peer group environments (Wang & Kovach, 1995; Yancey & Saporito, 1995). Similarly, the characteristics of families' neighborhoods and communities affect parents' child-rearing practices which, in turn, are linked to adolescents' functioning (Taylor & Roberts, 1995).

Second, the work of the contributing authors clearly indicates the need for an emphasis on within-group processes and functioning—there is substantial variation within ethnic minority populations that must be integrated into the framing of research questions and the analyzation and interpretation of findings. Research on majority populations has traditionally noted variation in behavior ranging from school achievement and achievement-related attitudes to sexual activity, to problem behavior. It is reasonable to expect that, for instance, middle class African-American youngsters and their families will function differently than their poorer African-American counterparts. The research presented in this volume indicates that multiple models from varied theoretical disciplines are needed to delineate causal influences and to explain functioning in many important areas of development of subgroups within same populations.

Third, normative research on minority children and families is critical to intervention and prevention efforts. Knowledge of intragroup variation in minority groups helps identify factors which may buffer some children and families from stressful experiences that may be catastrophic for others. In addition to its usefulness in addressing social problems experienced by minority adolescents and families, research focusing on the normative development of children and adolescents from minority backgrounds will contribute specifically to furthering our understanding of culturally distinctive patterns of behavior. For example, research has shown that parenting styles differ across ethnic groups, with fewer minority than European-American parents displaying the authoritative styles of parenting that have been positively linked to adolescents' school achievement (Steinberg et al., 1991). Interestingly, however, though Asian-American parents are less likely to display authoritative parenting styles than their European counterparts, Asian-American youngsters outperform European-American teens in school. Research focusing on how parenting styles and practices of ethnic minority parents vary as a function of the cultural traditions of a particular group is essential to addressing practical implications for improving family services and informing public policy.

Furthermore, there is a clear need to distinguish behaviors linked to families' cultures from those which exist as adaptations to families' living conditions. There is a tendency in much of the extant literature on ethnic minority families to assume that adaptations made as individuals adjust to their living conditions and circumstances are components of the individuals' culture (Wilson, Cook, & Arrington, chap. 9, this volume). Clearly, to advance our understanding of ethnic minority families, the overlapping and independent effects of culture and families' social ecologies must be assessed.

Finally, although more research and newer, more culturally sensitive models are needed to further the study of all ethnic minority children families, there is a critical lack of research-based information on Latino, Asian-American, and Native-American families and their adolescents. Among these groups, data on parenting practices and styles, peer relations, neighborhood effects, and parent-school linkages, among myriad others, are particularly scant. The number of chapters in this book devoted to these three groups is a reflection of this shortage; given the growing diversity of the U.S. population, this lack is particularly problematic and merits much attention by researchers, service providers, and policymakers.

REFERENCES

Bronfenbrenner, U. (1979). *The ecology of human development: Experiments by nature and design.* Cambridge, MA: Harvard University Press.

Bronfenbrenner, U. (1986). Ecology of the family as a context for human development: Research perspectives. *Developmental Psychology, 22,* 723–742.

Chao, R. K. (1994). Beyond parental control and authoritarian parenting style: Understanding Chinese parenting through the cultural notion of training. *Child Development, 65.*

Massey, D. S., & Denton, N . A. (1993). *American apartheid: Segregation and the making of the underclass.* Cambridge: Harvard University Press.

McLoyd, V. C. (1990). The impact of economic hardship on black families and children: Psychological distress, parenting, and socioemotional development. *Child Development, 61,* 311–346.

Steinberg, L., Mounts, N. S., Lamborn, S. D., & Dornbusch, S. M. (1991). Authoritative parenting and adolescent adjustment across varied ecological niches. *Journal of Research On Adolescence, 14,* 19–36.

Taylor, R. D., Casten, R., Flickinger, S., Roberts, D., & Fulmore, C. D. (1994). Explaining the school performance of African-American adolescents. *Journal of Research On Adolescence, 4,* 21–44.

Taylor, R. D., & Roberts, D. (1995). Kinship support and maternal and adolescent well-being in economically disadvantaged African-American families. *Child Development, 66(6),* 1585–1597.

Wang, M. C., & Gordon, E. W. (Eds.). (1994). *Educational resilience in inner-city America: Challenges and prospects.* Hillsdale, NJ: Lawrence Erlbaum Associates.

Wang, M. C., & Kovach, J. A. (1995). *Bridging the achievement gap in urban schools: Reducing educational segregation and advancing resilience-promoting strategies* (CEIC Publication Series No. 95-9). Philadelphia: National Center on Education in the Inner Cities.

Yancey, W. L., & Saporito, S. J . (1995). Ecological embeddedness of educational processes and outcomes. In L. C. Rigsby, M. C. Reynolds, & M. C. Wang (Eds.). *School–community connections: Exploring issues for research and practice* (pp. 193–227). San Francisco: Jossey-Bass.

Author Index

Subject Index